U.S. TELEVISION NEWS AND COLD WAR PROPAGANDA, 1947–1960

Television news and the Cold War grew simultaneously in the years following World War II, and their history is deeply intertwined. In order to guarantee sufficient resolve in the American public for a long-term arms buildup, defense and security officials turned to the television networks. In need of access to official film and newsmakers to build themselves into serious news organizations, and anxious to prove their loyalty in the age of blacklisting, the network news divisions acted as unofficial state propagandists. They aired programs that were produced, scripted, and approved by the White House and the Departments of State and Defense as news and public affairs programs. Ironically, these programs defined freedom as the absence of government control.

Based on extensive primary research, this book provides evidence of thoroughgoing collaboration between U.S. television networks and government during the early years of the medium, and it reveals how the Cold War was effectively "sold" to the American public.

Nancy E. Bernhard is Associate Editor of *The Long Term View,* a public policy journal published by the Massachusetts School of Law.

CAMBRIDGE STUDIES IN THE HISTORY OF MASS COMMUNICATION

This series includes books that examine the communications processes and systems within social, cultural, and political contexts. Inclusive of empirical, effects-based research, works in this series proceed from the basis that the histories of various media are an important means to understanding their role and function in society. The history of a medium – its pattern of introduction, diffusion, acceptance, and effects – varies in each society, interacting with, and in turn, shaping its culture. Moreover, each society reacts differently to the introduction of a medium, and regulatory policies are shaped by both political and cultural forces. The detailed study of various communications forms and their complex message systems are now understood to be the key to unraveling the evolution of modern society and its culture.

Other Books in the Series

U.S. TELEVISION NEWS AND COLD WAR PROPAGANDA, 1947–1960

NANCY E. BERNHARD

CAMBRIDGE
UNIVERSITY PRESS

PUBLISHED BY THE PRESS SYNDICATE OF THE UNIVERSITY OF CAMBRIDGE
The Pitt Building, Trumpington Street, Cambridge, United Kingdom

CAMBRIDGE UNIVERSITY PRESS
The Edinburgh Building, Cambridge CB2 2RU, UK
40 West 20th Street, New York NY 10011–4211, USA
477 Williamstown Road, Port Melbourne, VIC 3207, Australia
Ruiz de Alarcón 13, 28014 Madrid, Spain
Dock House, The Waterfront, Cape Town 8001, South Africa

http://www.cambridge.org

First published 1999
First paperback edition 2003

Typeface Sabon 10/13 pt.   System QuarkXPress™   [CS]

A catalogue record for this book is available from the British Library

Library of Congress Cataloguing-in-Publication Data
Bernhard, Nancy E. 1962–
    U.S. television news and Cold War propaganda, 1947–1960 / Nancy E.
Bernhard.
    p.   cm. – (Cambridge studies in history of mass
communications)
    Includes bibliographical references and index.
    ISBN 0 521 59415 4 hardback
    1. Television broadcasting of news – United States. 2. World
politics – 1945– 3. Public opinion – United States. 4. Cold War.
I. Title. II. Series.
PN4888.T4B47 1999
070.1′95 – dc21   98–24721
CIP

ISBN 0 521 59415 4 hardback
ISBN 0 521 54324 X paperback

Transferred to digital printing 2003

To my parents,
Harry and Ruthe Bernhard

The task of a public officer seeking to explain and gain support for a major policy is not that of the writer of a doctoral thesis. Qualification must give way to simplicity of statement, nicety and nuance to bluntness, almost brutality, in carrying home a point. It is better to carry the hearer or reader into the quadrant of one's thought than merely to make a noise or to mislead him utterly. . . . If we made our points clearer than truth, we did not differ from most other educators and could hardly do otherwise.

Dean Acheson, 1969 (recalling 1949)

How can you know history? You can only imagine it. Anchored though you may be in fact and document, to write a history is to write a novel with checkpoints. . . . A "definitive" history is only one in which someone has succeeded not in recreating the past but in casting it according to his own lights, in *defining* it. Even the most vivid portrayal must be full of sorrow, for it illuminates the darkness of memory with mere flashes and sparks, and what the past begs for is not a few bright pictures but complete reconstitution. Short of that, you can only follow the golden threads, and they are always magnificently tangled.

Mark Helprin, 1995

CONTENTS

ILLUSTRATIONS AND TABLES

Illustrations

Tables

ACKNOWLEDGMENTS

This book began in 1987 while I was a graduate student, during one of many long conversations with Edward S. Herman. I cannot think of a better tutor on the power and interests of media institutions. I was also very lucky to have Michael Zuckerman as a dissertation reader.

Bruce Kuklick served as my thesis advisor. From Bruce I learned to steer clear of methodological fads and lazy habits of mind. He made it plain that I should be able to articulate my place in twentieth-century intellectual life, and that expectation has been a taxing and marvelous gift.

Many scholars generously gave their time to read portions of the manuscript. I would like to thank Bob McChesney, Chris Simpson, Michael Curtin, Jim Baughman, Walter Hixson, Scott Lucas, John McGreevy, Lawrence Velvel, and Robert Beisner. Archivists Kathy Nicastro at the National Archives, Dennis Bilger at the Truman Library, David Haight at the Eisenhower Library, and the staff of the film division of the Library of Congress answered many silly and obscure questions, and guided me to documents and films that shed their fascinating light on the past. I received financial support from the Eisenhower World Affairs Council, the Joan Shorenstein Barone Center for Press and Politics at Harvard's Kennedy School of Government, the Henry Luce Foundation, and the Center for Values and Public Life at Harvard Divinity School.

Despite pockets of goodwill and resources, academic downsizing during the last decade has eroded the spirit of many young scholars. You have to love the work, and you need friends. This book truly would not have been possible without the humor, brilliance, and commiseration of John Noakes, John Gennari, and Pat Kelly. Brett Gary has been my exemplary instructor in communications scholarship, the joys of Flathead Lake, and bullheaded persistence. My next book won't have any footnotes.

I also wish to thank the friends and family that sustained me while this book took shape. Diana Gordon, Kate Shaw, Ellen Atenazio, and the mothers and children of a remarkable play group took exemplary care of me and my children. The extended Margolin clan provided love and support. Michael Bernhard and Paula Golombek know what it's like, and they know how to laugh. My parents, Ruthe and Harry Bernhard, provided sound advice, supplementary scholarship funds, and love of learning.

In the same month that I started researching this book, I fell in love with the man I later married. The book goes to press just after the birth of our second child. To David, and to Eliza and Jacob, go my heart.

ABBREVIATIONS

AP	Associated Press
ASNE	American Society of Newspaper Editors
BAC	Broadcasters Advisory Council
CIA	Central Intelligence Agency
CONELRAD	Control of Electromagnetic Radiation
DOD	Department of Defense
DOS	Department of State
ECA	Economic Cooperation Agency
FCC	Federal Communications Commission
IBD	International Broadcasting Division
IBF	International Broadcasting Foundation
INS	International News Service
MSA	Mutual Security Agency
NAB	National Association of Broadcasters
OC	Office of Censorship
OIC	Office of International Information and Cultural Affairs
OII	Office of International Information
OPI	Office of Public Information
OSS	Office of Strategic Services
OWI	Office of War Information
PA	Office of Public Affairs
PRWG	Public Relations Working Group
RFE	Radio Free Europe
UP	United Press
USAIC	United States Advisory Commission on Information
USIA	United States Information Agency
VOA	Voice of America

THE MARKETPLACE OF IDEAS: SELLING THE COLD WAR CONSENSUS

Network television news was born at the dawn of the Cold War. These two behemoths have shaped American political life during the second half of the twentieth century, and their history is deeply intertwined.

Television news portrayed the communist threat to the American way of life through the lens of consumer capitalism. In the first five years of regular network news reporting, Americans saw or heard about the Marshall Plan, the Berlin Airlift, the Communist revolution in China, the explosion of the first Soviet atomic bomb, the conviction of Alger Hiss, the Korean War, and the Senate hearings on subversion conducted by Joseph McCarthy from their Farnsworth, RCA, or DuMont television sets. They learned about the fearsome new nuclear age from a medium that, between news reports, sold them toothpaste, automobiles, cigarettes, refrigerators, laundry detergent, beer, and aluminum siding. Images of annihilation were bound up with teasers for consumption.

But underlying this simple proximity of images, the institutional interests of the broadcasting networks exerted basic and powerful influence on television's portrayal of events. The networks were corporations whose purpose was to generate revenue for their shareholders. Capitalism, with its complex and sometimes contradictory impulses, set limits on the range of debate about political issues, selected the voices that would have legitimacy in national debates, and established standards for news reporting that fundamentally shaped the way Americans came to understand the world struggle.

Television became an emblem of, as well as a conduit for, the West's position in the Cold War. In its battle against communism, the U.S. prized the freedom of information – in thinking, speaking, writing, publishing, and broadcasting – as a fundamental value to be protected from totalitarian lies. Most Americans believed that the corporate owned and commercially sponsored television industry represented the freest, best, and only alternative to state-controlled information. The pitfalls of trading political information in a carnivalesque marketplace paled in comparison with the specter of Soviet-style enforced ideology.

Despite this faith in the superiority of a market society, the global military threat posed by communism seemed to so endanger freedom that many cold warriors did not trust that democracy would prevail in a free marketplace of ideas. The agencies comprising the national security state[1] established offices, bureaus, and services to control the flow of information both abroad and at home, to ensure that it would serve the cause of anticommunism. As so often happens in war, even in just war, truth was the first casualty.

This book tells the story of a partnership between government information officers and network news producers to report and sell the Cold War to the American public. It chronicles dozens of news and public affairs series produced in collaboration between the inexperienced federal information bureaus and the fledgling network news divisions. Much of the news about the early Cold War on television was scripted, if not produced, by the defense establishment. These programs defined American freedom as the absence of government control.

While individuals on both sides of the public–private divide held firm Cold War convictions and saw their work as the fulfillment of a patriotic duty, each set of institutions principally followed its own self-interested logic in producing these programs. Government information agencies sought to control the information reaching the public, and the networks needed extensive help from the government to produce their early news programs. As the 1950s progressed, this neat dovetailing diminished, and while government officers continued to advise the news operations, they relinquished the official role of co-producer. Yet the stunning and outright collaboration practiced between 1948 and 1954 in producing news and public affairs programs shaped the institutional relationships between the defense establishment and the television industry for decades, and it disseminated a picture of East–West relations steeped in consumer-oriented anticommunism.

Voluntarism was the hallmark of television's contribution to the Cold War mobilization. From President Truman and the network chairmen through the clerks and technicians charged with the daily release of government information and its broadcast through the air, these men believed in the freedom guaranteed by private ownership of communications facilities. Yet they worked together to use those channels principally for the distribution of official information, to indoctrinate the American public to support U.S. Cold War policy. It was war, and all information became military information. Public service programming, required of stations for the use of the public frequencies, became the distribution channel for federal propaganda.

The scope of this domestic U.S. effort pales in comparison with the aggressive anticommunist propaganda campaigns that the United States waged abroad, and with the thoroughgoing ideological control exerted within the Soviet Union. Even in its infancy, television provided endless information and opinion, much of it conscientiously produced, some of it admirable. Yet the story told here shows how the very routines of objective journalism supposed to guarantee freedom of information fit the needs of the national security state and embraced the specific and virulent anticommunism of the early Cold War. The belief that the American system of broadcasting was a valuable stake and a crucial weapon in the Cold War quickly transposed into the assumption that the system was actually and fully free, a belief it became nearly impossible to challenge.

The American devotion to freedom of thought limited the extent of domestic propaganda, but it also shaped the propaganda itself. The networks tailored the programs made with official guidance to look spontaneous and voluntary, and the government avoided direct association with any one network or any individual broadcaster. In effect, propaganda had to be competitive. Most officially produced shows gained the typical audience for news, and government involvement remained invisible, or at least uncontroversial. Between 1948 and 1954, what amounts to a joint public–private propaganda operation distributed defense and security information to the American public through the commercial broadcast system, and no one objected, or even seems to have noticed. As television matured, information officials grew more sophisticated at embedding Cold War messages into more popular entertainment programs, and avoided the apparent, if unremarked, impropriety of official control of news programming.

Ironically, television's commercialism suggested to homegrown ideologues that the medium was ripe for traitorous infiltration. Its frivolity, and the sheer number of artists required to fill a network schedule, suggested a dangerous softness. Anticommunist blacklisters policed the broadcasting industry to prevent secret brainwashing of the viewing public by agents of the Soviet Union. The networks, due to their dependence on skittish corporate sponsors, dutifully fired suspected leftists and required loyalty oaths from their employees. Despite these fearful accommodations, the networks retained their claims to be vigilant protectors of freedom. It was axiomatic that private control of information surpassed state control in protecting liberty, and that belief eclipsed the broadcasting industry's vulnerability to commercial blackmail or other forms of corporate bias, including their tendency to support uncritically the defense and security establishment.

This is a story about deliberate attempts to construct what historians call the "Cold War consensus." The people involved wrestled with the hard question of how to ensure public support in a democracy for sustaining a long-term, worldwide mobilization. Sometimes they admitted that their practices mimicked totalitarian methods, only dressed up for a public invested in freedom of information. Most of the time, they professed a fierce belief that their government and private American institutions comprised the greatest counterpoint to Soviet power, and they defended their practices as necessary to democracy's survival. When they lied, they worried that exposure might harm them and their institutions, but they also believed sincerely that their lies served the ultimate interests of freedom. Such problematic exposure never came, in part because Americans overwhelmingly shared their belief in the righteousness of American institutions, and in part because they worked hard to disguise their programs. They fought to guarantee proper thought and sufficient resolve in the American public to wage Cold War.

Institutional Logics

How did these collaborations begin, why did they end, and why are they important? Government information officials saw many advantages in recruiting private media companies to sell the Cold War. The Congress and the American public would not tolerate direct government propaganda. Information officials saw programs of their own design go on the air, and through voluntary network public service, they exerted virtually all the control over content that they wanted. They avoided the political imbroglios over state control of information that had plagued the information services during World War II (described in Chapter One), and they garnered evidence for the Cold War propaganda claim that Americans supported their government's security policies freely, without totalitarian coercion. This system saved the government a great deal of money and testified to claims of business's superior efficiency.

The answer to the question of why the networks participated is more complicated. The television medium matured rapidly, both in its reach and in its polish. Between 1949 and 1959, Americans bought six or seven million sets each year, until eighty-six percent of homes had one. The number of stations on the air jumped from 69 to 609, with more than ninety percent affiliated with a major network. The networks posted their first profits in 1951 and cleared almost $90 million by 1959.[2] But that future was by no means clear in 1948. Well into the 1950s, the news divisions had small budgets and lost more money than they made. Coverage of even the most climactic political crises always had to be (and still are) weighed in terms of profitability. Government-produced and co-produced programs filled their schedules cheaply and easily.

A second financial factor was the harsh political climate of the Second Red Scare. Network sponsors shied away from programs with independent editorial voices, particularly those that counseled restraint in erecting a security state. Government-produced programs were politically safe. If they rarely attracted direct sponsorship, they cost nothing and did not alienate sponsors from the network.

Why, then, did the networks co-produce so many programs with the Department of State, the agency most fiercely attacked by McCarthy and others for harboring secret communists? In part this collaboration reflected the close personal ties between public and private information professionals. Broadcasters knew their counterparts at the Department of State to be patriotic Americans; many were World War II veterans from the same units of the Office of War Information or the Army Signal Corps. Executives and correspondents privately (and very rarely, publicly) dismissed the accusations of mass disloyalty. State department officials invited close scrutiny from such basically friendly reporters as a way of disproving charges against the department. And getting the inside story about official government activity actually enhanced broadcasters' standing in the mainstream journalism community.

In addition, broadcasters judged the long-term goodwill of high-ranking officials and continued access to exclusive government information to be more important to the news divisions' success and to corporate stability than placating red-baiters in the Congress. By demonstrating respect for the executive branch, and by stressing their faith in the harsh light of publicity to uncover any real wrongdoing, network brass overrode any reticence about working with temporarily suspect agencies.

Why did these collaborations end? By the mid-1950s, the networks no longer had an acute need for cheap news programs. They could afford to produce or buy better quality programming to satisfy the growing and more demanding television audience. The news divisions produced their own programs with continued government help and approval, and they garnered the same public service return for their efforts, but these programs were no longer labeled as having been produced by or with the assistance of a federal agency. Production values improved, and problematic institutional ties grew harder to see.

The question of why these programs were important can be answered in several ways. Government information officials foresaw that television would be increasingly important to citizenship, and from the outset of the Cold War, they used television principally to sell policy. The Cold War was the most important news story of the decade, and the government was overwhelmingly the networks' most important, and often sole, source for breaking news. The routines of television news gathering were shaped and embedded in this mutual dependency. The most crucial terms for the relationship between television news and the federal defense and security establishment were set when these institutions worked in close collaboration, yet this story has never been told before.

The story is also important to counter a general misperception about the relationship between the government and the media. Most Americans construe their news media as aggressively oppositional and never see the extent to which the government controls the release of information, sells its version of events, and receives media cooperation in promoting its agenda. In the 1980s, for instance, the federal government spent a billion dollars a year on public relations programs.[3] Officials tightly controlled the release of information, did so in extremely calculated ways ("spin"), insisted on the use of manageable journalistic pools in combat areas, and continually used television as a diplomatic and military tool. Far more than dissent, support of government programs by the news media was the basic pattern in the Cold War era, if not since. Although the orientation to profit drives a limited oppositionalism in news programming, the networks rarely pursue stories against their fundamental interest in corporate and social stability.[4]

And perhaps this history is most important because in the early Cold War interlude in communications history, we can see how a particular world view, representing particular interests and sometimes extreme interpretations of world events, was naturalized as objective, true, and free. Truth, as always, took on the particular cast and hue of its era. In the interest of democracy, we must continue to historicize and contextualize the truth claims of both the government and the news media.

Excavating Culture

My purpose here is not to prove, or even to explore, a theoretical model of culture. I wish to describe a particular culture and to explode two assumptions deeply embedded in the political culture of the Cold War in the United States. These two assumptions – that the U.S. government valued a free marketplace of ideas, and that the commercial marketplace guaranteed free debate – are astonishingly resilient and, at the height of the Second Red Scare, had a quality of irrefutability. This logic held that because communists followed a preset ideological line, they were incapable of objectivity. Therefore to be objective, one could not be a communist. And because neutrality was untenable in the bipolar world, to be objective, one had to be anticommunist, which was to say, capitalist.

It does not diminish the horror of totalitarianism to say that the market-based system in the United States has not served freedom and democracy perfectly. Indeed, inasmuch as private broadcasters gave the airwaves over to state designs, they duplicated totalitarian practices.

The "marketplace of ideas" that the United States so fervently defended in the Cold War has many meanings. Proponents of free speech in the American legal tradition have used the phrase when defending the right to subversive speech. They argue that all ideas, no matter how foreign or radical, should be subject to open debate and that sound ideas will survive the fray. In this usage, the market refers not to an arena for commercial transactions but to a forum for rational argumentation and critique. Throughout most of Western history, the state has posed the principal threat to this right. The poet John Milton expressed the perennial belief that truth always triumphs over tyranny this way: "and though all the windes of doctrin were let loose to play upon the earth, so Truth be in the field, we do injuriously by licensing and prohibiting to misdoubt her strength. Let her and Falsehood grapple; who ever knew Truth put to the wors, in a free and open encounter."[5]

In twentieth-century American culture, this notion has fused with a more literal understanding of the marketplace. Rather than intellectual rigor, the mechanism for sifting ideas is the invisible hand of commercial exchange. If an idea has value (this equation goes), it will sell. Proponents of free enterprise assume that the marketplace acts with the same fine discrimination as protracted argumentation, and that the best ideas, often defined as the most useful as opposed to truest, will prevail after a competitive contest. They often imply that this sifter is more democratic than the elitist pursuit of rational debate. Financial rewards as well as intellectual satisfaction flow to the winner, and what could be more American than that?

Throughout the twentieth century, critics of this notion have warned that a substitution of commerce for intellectual discipline would undermine the American political system. The advent of mass media, by placing vast distances between political writers and their audiences, and by requiring large amounts of capital to distribute political information, seemed to impair the deliberative processes of democracy. In 1947, a distinguished panel of public intellectuals called the Commission on Freedom of the Press, funded principally by Time-Life founder Henry Luce, issued a report on the future of "A Free and Responsible Press." It pointed clearly to the conflict between the moral responsibility of the press to protect unpopular or even dangerous speech and the financial pressures facing mass media corporations to censor such speech.[6] Luce, understandably, rejected these conclusions and, predictably, tried to suppress the publication of the report. He did publish it as a supplement to his *Fortune* magazine, but he hardly needed to worry. The grave concerns of Robert Hutchins, Zechariah Chaffee, Reinhold Niebuhr, and their eminent colleagues on the commission barely remained afloat in the vast ocean of enthusiasm for the rewards of consumer capitalism that swept over the nation in the decade after World War II.

The Cold War cemented the rhetorical triumph of the marketplace as the best guarantor of liberty in human relations and freedom in the exchange of ideas. Yet a deep irony remains at the heart of this triumph. Commercial broadcasters volunteered to do the ideological work of the national security state at home, and the rhetoric of the market shielded this collaboration from public scrutiny. The broadcasting industry acted as a shill for the state and set to work selling the Cold War to the American public. In a country that defined freedom as the presence of markets and the absence of government control, this requires some explanation, and that explanation begins in the dilemmas of a total fight for democracy.

Whether this effort to sell the Cold War succeeded is another question, and one that lies beyond the scope of this book. Hard-line anticommunist views unquestionably pervaded the country, but gauging the precise effects of a government information program designed to garner public support for a particular policy or even to promote a general climate of opinion is just not possible. One problem lies with the sources that chart public opinion. Not only are surveys notoriously selective, but Christopher Simpson has powerfully demonstrated how between 1945 and 1960 the emerging discipline of mass communications research, particularly the prominent centers for public opinion research and the *Public Opinion Quarterly*, were shaped by the direct influence of CIA, state department, and military psychological warfare programs. Perhaps because they knew this, public information officials in the state department deeply distrusted the mechanisms for measuring public opinion as unscientific.[7]

Another difficulty lies in separating the effects of one cultural source from another. How can we separate the effects of the dozens of news and public affairs programs co-produced by government agencies from those of many others produced independently by the networks, or the effects of news and public affairs programs from those of entertainment programs with Cold War plots and themes, or the effects of television news from those of films, radio, newspapers, or magazines? We cannot.

The trickiest and most interesting question in gauging the effects of these programs is how to identify preexisting public sentiment, or how to recognize genuine consent. Anticommunism certainly suffused American culture and policy well before 1947. Most Americans shared an ideological repugnance toward the Soviet experiment before and while the United States was allied with the USSR to defeat the Nazis. There was good reason for democrats to fear Joseph Stalin and to loathe the diplomatic and geopolitical outcomes to World War II in Eastern Europe. Yet we can also mark several junctures where U.S. information agencies exaggerated Soviet military aims and capabilities, usually to wrest appropriations for containment programs through a cost-conscious, isolationist Congress. We shall examine several of these junctures, notably around the passage of the Truman Doctrine and Marshall Plan and at the time of NSC-68 and the beginning of the war in Korea. Raising the Soviet threat rarely failed to close the ranks and get the funding, but the "peddlers of crisis" often forgot that it was their own rhetoric. Any means became justifiable. U.S. Cold War propaganda, comically and tragically, became a self-fulfilling prophecy.[8]

I leave aside the question of effects to focus on institutions, and more specifically, to explore the dynamics of information production. A body of scholarship has emerged in the last few years that, taken together, shows an aggregate effort by consumer-oriented corporations to promote a particular brand of Americanism that must be reckoned with in any discussion of the postwar consensus.[9] Individual corporations, trade associations, and business advocacy groups all engaged in energetic campaigns to promote a world view, as well as particular policies, tied to their own prosperity.

The rhetoric of these campaigns successfully tied corporate self-interest to notions of the broader public interest, just as the marketplace-of-ideas metaphor conflated commercial competition with intellectual debate. The most emblematic statement of this view, though one consistently misquoted, is Charles Wilson's statement before the Senate Armed Services Committee considering his nomination as secretary of defense in 1953, "What was good for our country was good for General Motors, and vice versa."[10] Beyond this equation of corporations with the nation was the notion that corporations were more efficient and politically better than government. Acting voluntarily, free enterprise could accomplish social ends quickly and easily, without the taint of totalitarian coercion.

The sources drawn on here are intoxicatingly explicit in showing how the corporate producers of culture cultivated their own legitimacy. For this reason, I sympathize with those who stress the power of institutions in recent scholarly debates about cultural hegemony. Because the subjects were themselves concerned with selling their own credibility as well as their policies, many ingredients in the hegemony recipe can be found here. I certainly do not, as this position is often misrepresented, deny the power of audiences to resist mass-produced meaning. Indeed, this book documents as many failures as successes in the attempt to mold public opinion about specific issues, or even to gain an audience for the attempt. But it seems to me that the concept of cultural hegemony, used as a descriptive tool rather than a scientific model, aids our understanding of certain moments in history, as well as certain kinds of questions about culture.[11]

When consensus is strong, dominant institutions exert tremendous power to delineate legitimate lines of debate and exclude others. The political climate during the early Cold War, especially concerning questions of foreign policy, is perhaps the foremost example of that kind of time in U.S. history. The concept of hegemony may be a less appropriate tool when describing times more ridden by dissent or when describing entertainment genres rather than "actuality" forms like news. In the story told here, a network oligopoly worked collaboratively with the federal government to sway viewers into supporting national security policies. Furthermore, powerful political players in this era successfully defined opposition to these policies as sedition. That would certainly seem to qualify as hegemonic.

We have to ask how much of the postwar consensus is a manufactured product. This was a seductive world view full of shining goods, moral righteousness, and military power, with the full arsenal of public relations, advertising, and broadcasting behind it. Audiences still had the power to resist and still found different orientations to the world in their churches, unions, neighborhoods, and elsewhere, which may or may not have offset more concentrated forms of culture. They also truly believed. But the mass-produced enjoinders to embrace a consumer Cold War world view were more deliberate and consistent than we have previously seen documented. The producers of this onslaught believed in the American genius for salesmanship, and they felt themselves to be at war.

Even when these campaigns failed to garner support for particular policies or even to gain a significant national audience, they still reached tens of thousands of Americans on a daily basis and introduced a set of slogans and catchwords that suffused the culture. Robert Griffith writes about the Advertising Council's contemporaneous attempts to sell consumer capitalism through public service advertising. If this effort was ham-handed, he concludes, "it was nevertheless repetitious, pervasive and unchallenged, surrounding Americans in all walks of life with an omnipresent if distorted reflection of their society, and thus helping shape, to a degree no less real for being difficult to measure, the political culture of postwar America."[12]

Such imprecise (yet still important) conclusions drove one "crusty" political historian to call intellectual history the art of "nailing jelly to the wall."[13] But if we can never get a sure fix on the currents of culture, I propose to look hard at producers as embodiments of culture, to do a sort of intellectual ethnography of those who claimed expertise in manipulating it.

Information professionals on both sides of the public–private divide articulated their views on propaganda, truth, the propriety of public versus private control of information, the nature of public opinion, and the nature of the Cold War as they went about their business. They thought long and hard about the proper role of propaganda in a democracy and, at mid-century, faced a difficult dilemma when answering this question. They believed that propaganda undermined American democracy but that it was a necessary instrument of modern warfare. Some, like poet and World War II information policy maker Archibald MacLeish, maintained that the United States should never compromise freedom at home or abroad out of fear. Others, epitomized by psychological warrior and *Fortune* publisher C. D. Jackson, asserted that democracy could not afford such faith in a hostile world. Prominent historians have inscribed this conflict as a variant of ahistorical dualisms between morality and interests, or between idealism and realism.[14] We can more usefully chart the progress of these views in postwar political culture. The anticommunism that intensified through the late 1940s in the United States gave renewed and lasting sanction to the use of selected or distorted information, both abroad and at home. Identifying this trend does not tell us whether Americans changed their opinions as a result, but it is crucial to know that the public was not trusted with straightforward information.

I try to respect these information professionals and their embodiment of a particular moment in U.S. history, but I am not their apologist. Their methods for gaining public support were often arrogant and self-righteous. They habitually moralized and deliberately oversimplified the contest between East and West. I disagree with some of the policies they promoted and deplore some of the methods they used. But I also envy the certainty with which they defended their nation as the guardian of world freedom and have sometimes admired their insight, skill, or restraint.

I don't know if the overall costs of the Cold War were worth the gain. Researching this book has taught me how very difficult it was to gauge the real threat to freedom and when sacrifices in its name went too far. It remains entirely in the eye of the beholder whether the ends justified the means in these Cold War information programs and, indeed, how the domestic costs of the Cold War balanced against the drive to contain communism everywhere, or whether the United States had any alternatives. For me, the central question raised by this slice of history boils down to the age-old tradeoff between security and freedom. If all means are justified in a fight for freedom, when do we cease defending it and become its saboteurs?

Overview

The first two chapters provide a historical framework for the collaborations between the networks and the government described in later chapters.

Chapter One outlines government–industry wrangles over control of information during and just after World War II, just before the spread of commercial television broadcasting. Myriad factions in Congress, the state department, and the broadcasting industry differed over who should control the distribution of official information. Whereas proponents of private control seemed triumphant in 1945, by 1948, the first skirmishes in the Cold War convinced all but the most dogmatic defenders of free enterprise that only the government had the oversight necessary to control information campaigns that would vanquish world communism. Commercial programming, although popular, could not take account of increasingly complex and crucial policy needs. Officials began to coordinate domestic information as well as overseas propaganda, and they found willing allies at the television networks. Conservative opponents of government information in both Congress and industry saw clearly what hypocrisy the permanent establishment of government information programs represented for a country at war to protect freedom of information.

Chapter Two looks at how the advent of television news fit into these plans. It asks how programs tailored by the federal government passed as independently produced news that fulfilled the networks' legal obligation to provide public service. Long-term cultural constellations defining capitalism, professionalism, and technology explain how these propaganda operations satisfied public expectations for free and objective news. As a commercial medium, television shared in the celebration of capitalism itself. Yet to gain credibility as news organizations, the network news divisions had to be shielded from obvious commercial pressures. A professional code of objectivity, as well as the promise of the medium to deliver government directly into America's living rooms, provided adequate assurance that the public would be protected from inappropriate influences.

Chapters Three through Six chronicle early Cold War propaganda on television. The Truman State Department's public information officers faced a dual public relations challenge: to sell expensive containment policies to a hostile Congress and to reclaim public trust in the Truman administration as competent and loyal. Their efforts were clumsy, and they failed to rehabilitate the image of the Truman state department, but they succeeded at selling the militarization of containment through systematic scare campaigns. As the Cold War progressed, they gradually abandoned their aim to present "full and fair" information, and they borrowed persuasive and manipulative techniques from advertising and psychological warfare.

Chapters Four and Five detail a massive public relations effort directed by the White House during the Korean War. Chapter Four tells the story of the Broadcasters Advisory Council (BAC), a voluntary industry-wide group formed under the auspices of the National Association of Broadcasters. The BAC consulted with cabinet officials on securing broadcasting facilities from enemy attack, the imposition of censorship in the combat theater, and the maintenance of morale. By working closely with the

White House and thereby averting the formation of an official wartime information agency, the BAC solidified industry voluntarism as the preferred method for distributing war information.

Chapter Five chronicles the unique television program, *Battle Report – Washington,* that ran for more than two years on NBC. Hosted and produced by President Truman's assistant, Dr. John Steelman, the program showcased the government's war effort in order to raise confidence and boost allegiance. NBC provided air time, and the White House provided the guests and the scripts. Conflicts arose over whether such an official venue could receive corporate sponsorship and over whether the program was a partisan Democratic effort. Steelman encouraged the sale of commercials because "ours is a commercial society." NBC finally abandoned the program a few months before the 1952 election to avoid irritating Republicans further.

Chapter Six profiles television programs made by the Department of Defense (DOD). The radio-TV branch in the Pentagon's Office of Public Information was responsible for some of the most widely seen public affairs programming in television history. Throughout the 1950s, the Pentagon continually adapted its own operations to television's growing popularity and sophistication. In the late 1940s, it produced dreary public affairs programs, such as *The Armed Forces Hour,* but by the mid-1950s put its resources into rousing documentaries like *Victory at Sea* and *Air Power.* Late in the decade, it authorized dramas such as *Navy Log* and *The West Point Story.* DOD's cooperation was increasingly obscured in the movement toward entertainment forms.

How did professional journalists square this history of close collaboration with their professional ideology of objectivity? Chapter Seven surveys previous work on objectivity in the early Cold War and finds it inadequate to explain broadcasters' performance. Far from being a timeless set of professional principles, this code changes according to prevailing political orthodoxy. In this period, objectivity was predicated on anticommunism, as evident in the quote from NBC's *Meet the Press* founder and producer, Lawrence Spivak, that "ideologically I never really took a position . . . and of course we carried on the most vigorous anticommunist campaign from the beginning."[15] Journalists' oppositional stance took the form of a vigorous policing of the government's efforts to rid the nation and the world of communism. The chapter situates this variant of journalistic objectivity in mid-century intellectual history, particularly the embrace of a tough-minded realism determined to avoid appeasement at all costs.

The concluding chapter examines the question of whether we should construe the work of a class of professionals involved in the deliberate construction of culture as a conspiracy. It examines this fine line in light of evidence for systematic network assistance to the Central Intelligence Agency. What are the basic tradeoffs between the requirements of truth and those of national security? In acting as a conduit for official information, the private television networks performed one essential public service but, imprisoned by Cold War orthodoxy, neglected their additional responsibility to provide context for government pronouncements. Because network television did not operate under formal government control in an era when such control reeked of appalling totalitarianism, it was embraced as free. Perhaps the most lasting legacy of the simultaneous growth of television news and the Cold War is the habitual confusion of the prerogatives of capitalism with the processes of democracy.

CHAPTER ONE

MARKET FAILURE: BUSINESS, THE STATE, AND INFORMATION FROM WORLD WAR II TO COLD WAR

The belief that truth always triumphs over falsehood died a fitful death in the West's mid-century struggles against totalitarianism. Despite the onslaught of fascist propaganda during World War II, the men who initially led the U.S. wartime information agencies clung to a "strategy of truth," claiming it would vanquish Axis lies. They promised that the U.S. government would control information just enough to ensure security. Private communications companies – newspapers, magazines, radio stations, motion picture studios – would censor themselves in an unprecedented voluntary effort. But those who championed truth lost control of U.S. information policy to more "nervous liberals," who believed that the dangers posed by fascism required more systematic control and coloring of information.[1]

The Cold War fully and finally eclipsed adherence to truth, even among the most dogged idealists. U.S. information officers saw the dangerous lies promulgated by the Soviet propaganda machine among U.S. allies, and they worried about how to bolster American resolve, so crucial to the defeat of world communism. They began to flood the marketplace of ideas with an ambitious propaganda program abroad and a more limited one at home. What started as a tentative choice between the lesser of two evils soon turned into systematic propaganda, and its creators knew this effort smacked of the enemy's totalitarianism. Whereas overseas propaganda could be sold to Congress and the public as "psychological warfare" against an implacable foe, domestic propaganda had to appear spontaneous and voluntary. They knew they could not fully manage domestic information about the Cold War, but they found important allies in the nascent network television news divisions.

This chapter recounts a succession of public and private agencies that distributed information vital to U.S. security during and just after World War II, as well as the gradual abandonment of private control of information in favor of information management by the state. Paradoxically, the Cold War, which the United States waged in the name of freedom and capitalism, rendered free enterprise inadequate for the distribution of information. Private corporations simply could not sufficiently coordinate their output with the requirements of national security policy. Overseas, the democratic glories of commercial programming, its accessibility and popularity, translated into embarrassing political liabilities in the struggle for world prestige and dominance.

Conservative business leaders saw clearly what hypocrisy the permanent establishment of government information programs represented for a country at war to protect freedom of information. These opponents of government information failed to win their point, and myriad propaganda agencies were established. But the conservatives' rhetoric about free enterprise promoting a genuine marketplace of ideas remained central to Cold War propaganda, and their indignation over the betrayal of capitalism was quickly drowned out by the propagandists' claims to objectivity. The "nervous liberals" who staffed the official information bureaus understood that for propaganda to work in a capitalist democracy, it had to look like independently produced news.

The Failure of Truth

The men who developed the government's information agencies during World War II believed their work was a necessary evil, demanding slight, temporary restraints on truth in the cause of long-term freedom. President Franklin Roosevelt chose prominent journalists to head both the Office of War Information (OWI) and the Office of Censorship (OC), signaling that he anticipated no real curbs to press freedom. Elmer Davis, a former CBS news broadcaster and *New York Times* reporter, headed the OWI. Despite Davis's pristine professional reputation, OWI probably suffered more attacks than any other wartime agency, including accusations of partisanship, censorship, propagandizing, and just plain lying.

Davis doggedly maintained that the OWI told the truth and that the truth would win the war. "Freedom of ideas and communications is one of the things we are fighting for, and our enemies are fighting against." He denied that he was the government's press agent, morale officer, or propaganda minister. Totalitarian governments needed those things he said. Democracies did not. "We are going to use the truth, and we are going to use it toward the end of winning the war; and we know what would happen to the American people if we lose it." To even more extreme freedom-of-information purists who said wartime restrictions ruined the American way of life, Davis said, "a democracy may see fit to curtail its own liberties in its own long-term interest . . . if that curtailment should be abused, we have recourse at the ballot box."[2]

The information services adopted "truth" as their mantra. It was, they claimed, the best propaganda and a powerful weapon against fascism. Writer Robert Sherwood, who headed the Foreign Information Service, said, "truth is the only effective basis for American foreign information." Milton Eisenhower, associate director of the OWI, told a Kansas Bankers' Association in 1943 that "in the struggle for men's minds," the United States had "one great advantage, one 'secret weapon' – the Truth." Rex Stout, head of the voluntary War Writers' Board, concurred: "The truth is our secret weapon."[3]

Information services also promised that only the requirements of security would limit what the public could know. "The American people are entitled to full information – *except* information which is not known to the enemy; and which, if it were known to the enemy, would endanger American lives, American ships, or the success of American military operations." Byron Price, director of the Office of Censorship, had credentials as impressive and pristine as those of Elmer Davis. A former senior editor with the Associated Press, he headed a staff of editors from prominent newspapers and highlighted the voluntary, cooperative nature of censorship. "American editors and broadcasters really are their own censors. It is a heartening example of democracy at work." A few restrictions were necessary, Davis wrote, but we must be "wise enough to fight a democratic war."[4]

Plenty of people thought this was hooey, that all the protests about truth and democracy masked shrewd political maneuvering. The 1942 elections brought a new majority of conservatives to Congress bent on curtailing what they saw as New Deal programs masquerading as wartime agencies. The contention that honest facts would best rally the American people and aid U.S. defenses sounded like a whitewash to those who saw the OWI simply angling to gain the president a fourth term.[5] These conservatives resisted official information in principle as a totalitarian tool, and they also perceived that the OWI imposed liberal social and political agendas under the guise of the war effort.

OWI met equal resistance from other executive agencies. Secretary of State Cordell Hull thought OWI's many foreign-born writers represented security risks, and he resented the agency's policy-making ambitions. Secretary of War Henry Stimson saw propaganda as peripheral to the central military effort, and he shared the typical military allergy to publicity. Without regular information releases from the Departments of State and War, OWI also came under fire, from the private news agencies they served, as a bottleneck to freedom of information.[6]

Such resentments against government information in any form, and against the liberal OWI in particular, prompted the recruitment of executives from advertising, broadcasting, and marketing who increasingly filled the domestic branch's upper ranks in 1942–1943. Businessmen, unlike allegedly idealistic writers and journalists, were expected to keep the official programs small and to run them by efficient, "private" methods. Domestic branch chief Gardner Cowles, Jr., whose family published *Look* magazine, several newspapers, and owned a chain of radio stations, brought in several other businessmen, including William Lewis of CBS and Gilbert Price of Coca-Cola. These executives facilitated cooperation with broadcasters, Hollywood, and the War Advertising Council, which continued to mount huge public service campaigns as Congress hacked away at the OWI's domestic appropriations. The executives felt their expertise and experience in mass persuasion techniques could best keep the public rallied, whereas the OWI's intellectuals and writers, more oriented to the agency's straight news functions, held fast to the strategy of truth.

OWI writers protested the slick packaging of the war, particularly the burial of disquieting images or facts. Cowles gave priority to war production and food-rationing campaigns over depictions of fascist brutality. The writers felt that the adoption of sales techniques both perverted the strategy of truth and made a mockery of the democratic fight against fascism. To illustrate what they saw as the travesty of overcommercialism, the graphics staff produced a poster of the Statue of Liberty holding aloft four bottles of Coke, captioned "The War that Refreshes: The Four Delicious Freedoms." The quarrel became public with the resignation of many OWI writers in April 1943, including the young historian Arthur Schlesinger, Jr., who then went to the Office of Strategic Services (OSS). Their press release renewed the basic question over the proper role of domestic information programs: Should it inform the public, sell policy, or boost morale? "[T]he activities of OWI on the home front are now dominated by high-pressure promoters who prefer slick salesmanship to honest information. . . . They are turning this Office of War Information into an Office of War Bally-hoo."[7]

Ironically, antipropaganda sentiment working against a central government information agency led to abandonment of the strategy of truth. Private enterprise with its sophisticated marketing techniques emerged from the war as far preferable to any government agency, no matter how truthful. One of the OWI's private counterparts, the voluntary War Advertising Council, set the precedents and the agenda for the distribution of domestic security information in the postwar world. A *New Republic* columnist in 1944 captured the broad outline of industry's triumph: "Shouldering the OWI out of the picture paved the way for selling America all over again on the idea that industry is not only winning the war with production but is much more devoted to the public interest than is government, or than labor, which is without the funds or technique to enter the field."[8] The OWI's political failure seemed to spell the doom of large-scale government information programs.

The Brief Triumph of Voluntary Private Information

The advertising industry surpassed all other communications industries in the volume and cost of its voluntary contribution to the war effort. It purposefully blended the industry's self-interest with a notion of the public interest, so the rhetoric of the two became almost indistinguishable. Business could do the job of informing the American people better than the government. As one public service advertisement in *Fortune* proclaimed, the "U.S. system of free enterprise became 'The Fifth Freedom.'"[9]

At a joint conference of the American Association of Advertising Agencies and the Association of National Advertisers at Hot Springs, Virginia, in November 1941, the advertising industry and its big clients considered how to deal with growing popular distrust and government hostility toward advertising. A nascent consumer rights movement had recently pressured Congress to pass legislation enabling the Food and Drug Administration to prohibit misleading advertising. But some participants felt that rather than squaring off against the government in the face of imminent war, the industry should address their collective responsibilities. These two concerns swiftly became linked. A representative of the CBS radio network attending this meeting cast attacks on advertising as enemy sentiment, as part of a "vast, worldwide struggle between two philosophies, the totalitarian idea, with people as the vassals of the state against the American philosophy of free enterprise and free competition and free opportunity for the individual to realize his own destiny under free institutions."[10] Advertising went to war against the power of the state, including its own government's prospective control of information.

Immediately after Pearl Harbor, a group of prominent advertisers offered the industry's services for the domestic information program. The

War Advertising Council was created in March 1942. It voluntarily mounted more than 100 campaigns at an estimated value of more than a billion dollars. The council made immediate business sense in several ways. Public service campaign costs, donated by agencies with space donated by media companies, were fully deductible and dodged high wartime excess profits taxes. In addition, ad volume and revenue stood to fall considerably as industry mobilized to produce war goods and shortages began. Public service campaigns kept brand names alive, kept agencies busy, and demonstrated corporate patriotism.[11]

The council worked closely with the domestic branch of the OWI, which coordinated information from the diverse federal agencies and prioritized public information needs. Advertisers often heard "No soap salesmen wanted" from OWI personnel, but the industry thought that OWI stupidly neglected the technical skills and talents found on Madison Avenue. They resented the appointment of journalists, poets, and lawyers unskilled in mass persuasion to head major government information agencies, which naturally then "flop[ped] around like chickens with their heads cut off." Billing advertising as the "information" industry, the council published a brochure entitled, "This is the Army that Hitler Forgot!" One New York newspaper editor boasted that Madison Avenue put European propaganda to shame: "You can roll all the German, Russian, and English propaganda together and it won't make a squatter's shack to the Empire State Building alongside American advertising." One wonders if advertisers hesitated to make this connection between their skills and propaganda technique, a connection vehemently denied when defending the industry against charges of dishonesty. Elmer Davis, a paragon of truth, found the requirements of news and advertising, or of political speech and commercial speech, completely different. A consummate administrator, he tried to applaud the advertising industry's efforts while still fighting for the domestic OWI's life. When asked if he, as a newsman, had any objection to advertising, Davis said that was "like asking a man who is known to like music if he has any objections to beefsteak."[12]

Advertisers' frustration at being excluded from the official effort did not last long. As noted previously, businessmen with advertising experience began to take over the domestic branch of OWI in 1943. Congress gutted the branch's appropriations, reducing it to "little more than a media-oriented coordinating agency," and the War Advertising Council became the central component of the domestic information effort. The council included in a tally of its accomplishments the sale of 800 million war bonds, the planting of 50 million victory gardens, a 400 percent increase in

Women's Army Corps recruiting, and the salvaging of more than 500 million pounds of waste fat.[13]

The council certainly fulfilled its equally central goal of waging public service campaigns on behalf of business. Frank Fox suggests that its wartime success in "fighting for the American Way and winning by the American Way," settled finally the question of whether business was the rightful champion of democracy. "Put simply, the war was seen as a test, perhaps *the* test, of the American Way of Life. And if the American Way passed this test – it deserved never to be questioned again." And yet Robert Griffith has shown that in the postwar years, a renewed and expanded council worked harder than ever to identify advertising with responsible public service and a business-driven, beneficent vision of America. Still apprehensive about a renewed New Deal and worried by the spread of socialism among U.S. allies after the war, advertisers and the larger business community redoubled their efforts to sell free enterprise to Americans. Not only did it promote highway safety and the Red Cross, the Advertising Council spent millions on campaigns for the "American Economic System" and "Confidence in a Growing America." The council also swathed itself in patriotism, even adopting the 1930s folk ideology of the WPA and the Popular Front and, thus writes Jackson Lears, "did manage to conceal much of the crassness" of its commercial agenda "in a patriotic haze."[14]

The Lion and the Lamb

Despite longstanding conflicts over industry's ability to represent or defend the public interest, information experts in industry and government agreed on many fundamentals in the postwar period, especially the need to contain communism and preserve geopolitical stability. The communist threat became so overriding during the late 1940s that the lion's share of American media companies finally and reluctantly agreed that the government should control the flow of information abroad and should direct it at home.

Indeed, the Advertising Council's continuing voluntarism was emblematic of a much broader rapprochement between business and government in the postwar period, a central aspect of the so-called postwar consensus. Scholars have long marked a broad and decisive shift in American political culture after World War II that includes this new norm of business–state cooperation.[15] While the reputed harmony of 1945–1960 has been undermined by scholars pointing to the civil rights conflict, the growing dissatisfaction of women, and the persistence of both urban and rural poverty,[16] a small but vibrant literature charts the specific accommodations and collaborations between the corporate community and the federal government on regulating the economy and waging the Cold War. Robert Griffith, Elizabeth Fones-Wolf, and Kim McQuaid chronicle the systematic efforts of business organizations such as the Business Council and the Committee for Economic Development to discredit labor and New Deal liberalism in favor of free enterprise policies and ideologies and in support of the Cold War.

While highly conservative business organizations like the National Association of Manufacturers and the United States Chamber of Commerce continued to resist anything reeking of the New Deal, more progressive business leaders accepted the measures already in place as beneficial to business. These measures included federal funding of public works and management of the national debt, credit, and the money supply. But the CED, formed in 1942 to plan for the postwar economy, also wanted to prevent any further expansion of the regulatory apparatus. To the extent that planning and regulation aided economic growth, it was acceptable. Indeed, as the war wound down, many liberals concurred that wholesale reform of capitalism might not be necessary, given an expanding economy supplemented by basic social welfare and insurance. One particularly progressive business leader shocked his colleagues by suggesting that if collectivism came to postwar America, it would be business' fault for failing to prevent massive unemployment through economic planning. Such realism about government planning, argues McQuaid, paid large dividends for these corporate leaders in the form of influence over government policies.[17]

The new postwar order was grudgingly but extensively cooperative. Advertiser James Webb Young called the Advertising Council an "and/or organization": "It believes that there are some things in the public interest that business is best equipped to accomplish, some which government is best equipped to accomplish, and some which government *and* business, working together, can best get done." While resisting increased power to the state, the Advertising Council also dined annually at the White House with the president and his cabinet. Theodore Repplier, founder and long-time president of the Advertising Council, quipped, "The lion may have muttered under his breath, but he nevertheless lay down with the lamb, and you may make your own nominations as to which was which."[18]

Many executives, often funneled through the Committee for Economic Development or the Business Council, went to Washington as private consultants to help formulate policies that would regulate their industries. Voluntary advisory bodies proliferated at comical rates. McQuaid estimates that by 1952 no less than 554 such "symbiotic committees" lent their expertise to the federal government,[19] including a high-powered Broadcasters Advisory Council, whose history is told in Chapter Four. Executives routinely stepped out of their corporate careers to work as federal administrators overseeing their former industries. Questions about inappropriate influence were buried under an avalanche of praise for efficiency, cooperation, and the ability of business to regulate itself without undue government interference.

Corporations and trade organizations put extraordinary resources into selling the idea that business represented the best interests of the United States. Griffith demonstrates how the Advertising Council's public service campaigns "sought to promote an image of advertising as a responsible and civic-spirited industry, of the U.S. economy as a uniquely productive system of free enterprise, and of America as a dynamic, classless, and benignly consensual society."[20] Fones-Wolf charts a variety of methods used by corporations and industry groups, from direct lobbying in support of specific legislation to economic education programs in factories and churches. Businesses linked their vision of a successful economy with freedom and individualism, directly challenging labor and New Deal liberalism[21] and in tacit but fierce opposition to the Soviet system.

Indeed, the greatest agreement between business and the Truman administration concerned foreign policy. At least as frightening to business as the massive 1945–1946 strike wave that augured a resurgence of organized labor was the turn toward socialism among the war-devastated European allies. Growing Soviet military belligerence cemented vigorous support for a bipartisan foreign policy of containment. McQuaid notes that the business–government rapprochement was strongest on this issue of a common threat. "A federal government that had become powerful over the concerted opposition of most businessmen remained powerful, in substantial part, in order to maintain American economic, military, and political interests in strategic parts of the globe."[22]

The revolving door of business advisors to government on Cold War policies became positively dizzying. Committee for Economic Development chairman Paul Hoffman of Studebaker chaired the President's Committee on Foreign Aid, a private group that drafted Marshall Plan legislation, served on a bipartisan Congressional investigating committee charged with formulating its implementation plan, and later headed the

Economic Cooperation Administration, the state department agency that administered Marshall Plan aid. Corporate support for the Marshall Plan gave the business community access to President Truman, whose domestic policies troubled them far more than his foreign policy. Whereas deep-dyed conservatives disdained such large foreign aid expenditures, or preferred to fight Soviet imperialism with military might to wasting money on socialist-leaning regimes in Western Europe, progressive corporate support certainly smoothed the Marshall Plan's way in Congress. A nominally private group of citizens closely tied to the state department also formed the Committee for the Marshall Plan to Aid European Recovery, to sell the program to the American people through information campaigns.[23]

Government information programs made special use of corporate talents, beginning with the appointment of advertising tycoon William Benton as assistant secretary of state for public affairs in 1946 (see Figure 1). With Chester Bowles, Benton founded the important Benton and Bowles agency, was a prominent member of the America First Committee (like other liberals who feared a repeat of World War I's assault on civil liberties), and served as vice-president of the University of Chicago. *Life* called him "America's Number One Number Two Man" for all his influential work behind the scenes.[24] Benton also served as vice-president of the Committee for Economic Development. He later gained more notoriety as Joseph McCarthy's most outspoken opponent in the Senate.

Although the diplomatic corps resented Benton's Madison Avenue background, his prestige as a businessman helped him to shepherd the government's overseas information programs, transferred in 1945 to his jurisdiction in the state department, through the crucial and contested transition years between World War II and the Cold War. New Republican majorities in the House and Senate put the foreign information service through an appropriations wringer. Both foreign and domestic information programs needed leaders who could defend them as necessary and pro-American to this decidedly noninternationalist Congress, but who could also work with companies whose cooperation was crucial to the programs. Benton presided over the programs in the crucial 1946–1948 transition period.

Ironically, Benton was so familiar with the broadcasting business that industry executives perceived him as a threat. Since 1937 he had owned Muzak, Inc., the subscription radio service to businesses renowned for its somnolent background music. In November 1944, he applied to the Federal Communications Commission (FCC) for three licenses in New York City to begin three more subscription stations for home use. At five cents a

Figure 1. William Benton served as the first Assistant Secretary of State for Public Affairs, 1946–1948. With Chester Bowles, he had founded the major advertising firm of Benton & Bowles and had been vice-president of the University of Chicago. He later became Joseph McCarthy's most outspoken opponent in the U.S. Senate as a Democrat from Connecticut. Photograph from the National Archives.

day, Benton thought this alternative to commercial radio was a terrific example of the "American way" of competition, but NBC and CBS saw a grave threat to advertiser-sponsored radio. The *New York Times* said Benton's plan did real "damage to freedom" by proposing to charge a fee for the air, which the public already freely enjoyed. Benton countered that the public could pay directly for radio rather than indirectly pay advertising costs when buying products. The FCC was preparing to approve his applications, which might have profoundly changed the shape of the broadcasting industry, but in August 1945, he was nominated to be assistant secretary of state, and he withdrew the applications. Even though the networks would seem well disposed to work with a millionaire advertising executive in the state department, there remained a residual distrust of Benton as too independent-minded.[25]

The broadcasting industry had a complicated relationship with this progressive business community represented by Benton and the Committee for Economic Development. The two largest and most powerful networks, CBS and NBC, defended free enterprise vigorously when it came to programming for maximum profit against reformers who wanted to use the airwaves for educational or labor-oriented causes. Business interests since the 1920s had been immensely successful at selling corporate control and advertising as the basis for public use of the frequencies,[26] and many smaller chains and station owners continued an aggressively antigovernment stance into the 1950s and beyond. Yet because broadcasting was subject to federal regulation through the FCC, the industry generally sought voluntary, cooperative solutions to regulatory conflicts. The preeminent trade association, the National Association of Broadcasters (NAB), had successfully offered voluntary solutions to ward off increased government control since the 1920s. On the one hand, broadcasters were among the most visible and effective advocates of corporate prerogative, but on the other, they had a longstanding cooperative history that had worked to the large networks' great benefit.

NBC and CBS had an additional history of cooperation with government on national security issues, most notably in their production of programs for the official *Voice of America* broadcasting (detailed in the section, "A Market Failure"). During World War II, the chairmen of both networks, William Paley of CBS and David Sarnoff of NBC, went to work as radio experts for the psychological warfare branch of the OWI. They worked at OWI with many of their once and future employees, including future heads of their international broadcasting divisions. The government needed the experience and resources of private broadcasters during the war, and radio professionals willingly served their country in a way that also enhanced their professional lives after the war. Scores of people with careers in print journalism, film, and advertising also worked for the OWI. After the war, Benton cleverly issued certificates of merit to the employees of the wartime information program to hang in their postwar offices at newspapers, magazines, publishing houses, motion picture studios, and broadcasting stations, giving a grain of truth to the notion of a media stacked with liberals sympathetic to government. This "enlightened Mafia," as Benton called it, might be drawn into fights over legislation, and he credited them with aiding the passage of the crucial Smith-Mundt Act of 1948.[27]

In addition, at the risk of making a gross generalization, broadcasters have not embraced the First Amendment tradition as vehemently as their print counterparts. Print journalists usually summarize the conflict between public and private control of information as one between censorship and the First Amendment, or between patriotism and freedom of the press.[28] Broadcasters, whose medium itself has crucial military uses, had more often positioned themselves on both sides of this equation. They defended free enterprise as the rightful purveyor of official information and thus understood voluntary censorship as the best protector of the First Amendment. Patriotic, responsible broadcasters working with the government could best maintain freedom of the press. Broadcasters always fought for their entrepreneurial prerogatives, defending mass-market entertainment programming against the smallest hint of federal regulation. But when it came to news about war and foreign policy, regarded as security matters, they consistently cooperated with federal officials.

In the immediate postwar years, as the progressive business community sold itself as the rightful custodian of the public interest, broadcasters became embroiled in the furor between Congress and the state department over the future of overseas information programs and the role of private companies in them. Broadcasters continued to follow their pattern of cooperation on security information, but the cooling climate of international relations made their efforts increasingly inadequate to U.S. propaganda needs. No matter how willing the private volunteers were to tailor their programs to official policy, commercial broadcasters lacked the classified information and diplomatic experience that the state deemed vital to successful information campaigns. This paradox confounded the most conservative element of the business community. For a country at war to save the freedom of information, the abrupt return of control from free enterprise to the government seemed a betrayal of basic American Cold War principles.

This friction played out in two major crises in the early postwar period. In the first, the Associated Press (AP) took a hard line against any overseas government information programs, claiming that they competed with and ruined the reputations of private firms, hoping that the United States would abandon official overseas broadcasting altogether. As the conflict continued, leaders in the journalism community grudgingly admitted that the official programs were indeed necessary in the struggle against Soviet expansionism, and the AP's claim to represent the truth became an impossible ideal.

The second crisis involved the ownership and production of programs for official overseas radio, which Benton dubbed the *Voice of America* (VOA) in 1945. Congress and the state department increasingly questioned the suitability of commercial output as propaganda, and such pressure ultimately forced the networks to withdraw their participation. The entrenchment of Cold War by 1948 solidified the overseas program's future and its control by the state department (for the time being). By 1950 the United States had embarked on a full-throttle overseas propaganda offensive, yet this effort remained suspect in the era's reflexively antitotalitarian climate.

Words Are Weapons

During World War II, the three major American wire services, The Associated Press, the United Press (UP), and the International News Service (INS) all provided their services to the OWI free of charge. The OWI used wire dispatches to produce two of its major programs: a daily bulletin of breaking news for all U.S. overseas outposts, and its radio programs broadcast around the world.

When the war ended, the state department took over both of these programs. The department distributed the daily bulletin to U.S. Army-occupied regions and areas where private services were otherwise not able to operate. By January 1946, the government had ceased its service to Germany, Austria, and Japan and had scaled back its service to five remaining cities in the western Pacific in anticipation of reestablishment of commercial services.[29] Congressional resistance to information programs remained strong, but President Truman issued an executive order mandating the continuation of the VOA to present the nations of the world with "a full and fair picture of American life and of the aims and policies of the United States Government."[30] The order set up the Office of International Information and Cultural Affairs (OIC), including an International Broadcasting Division (IBD) that ran the radio operation, now called the *Voice of America*. The next section of this chapter takes up the postwar history of the VOA directly.

On January 14, 1946, AP's board of directors publicly announced that it would discontinue its service to the state department. The UP, but not the INS or the English service Reuters, followed suit, though INS urged the government to work toward its termination as well. The AP's board cited two reasons for its action: (1) government efforts competed with their own efforts to expand their commercial service around the globe, and, more importantly, (2) the use of their service by official government information programs tainted their output as propaganda. The AP's leaders saw themselves waging a worldwide crusade for freedom of the press, and they believed that U.S. propaganda programs did irreparable harm to that cause and to the AP's role in it. The UP admitted to a less high-minded motivation: They feared that the AP could tell potential clients that the UP was corrupted by being "in bed" with the government.

There is little evidence to substantiate the AP's claim that official information services posed a competitive threat to its business. Actually, the state department went to unusual lengths to facilitate private news expansion abroad. It asked Congress to exempt media corporations from the requirement that they get paid in dollars, which were scarce in Europe.[31] When Congress approved granting these exceptions to media companies, the state department asked Noel Macy, then chief of the International Press and Publications Division of the state department, to head the program within the Economic Cooperation Administration (the state department agency that administered Marshall Plan aid). Macy resigned rather than administer a program that he felt interfered with freedom of the press by selectively helping certain U.S. news outlets. In this instance, rather than competing or standing in the way, the state department pursued controversial policies to the benefit of commercial media expansion overseas. In 1939 the AP had few overseas clients, but by 1949 it served nearly 1,500 foreign newspapers and radio stations, one-third of them in Europe.[32] But the charge that the State Department competed with AP resonated with perennial antistate rhetoric that rallied Congress and the conservative business community against official information programs.

In the AP crisis, this question of competition took a back seat to the politics of propaganda. The contention that the AP's reputation for fairness would be irreparably compromised by association with the state department's information service provoked a storm of angry debate. When announcing the termination of its services to the OIC, the AP linked its own commitment to the free flow of world news to the future of humanity and peace. The AP "holds that news thus disseminated by non-governmental news agencies is essential to the highest development of mankind and to the perpetuation of peace between nations." Although granting that the Truman administration had advanced press freedom, and that some government information programs such as maintaining overseas libraries were necessary, it concluded that "the Government cannot engage in newscasting without creating the fear of propaganda which necessarily would reflect upon the objectivity of the news services from which such newscasts are prepared."[33]

William Benton issued an angry five-page press release, beginning with the bold charge that the AP's action created "an obstacle to the conduct of American foreign policy." He said the AP board was uninformed about the overseas programs and that government oversight kept VOA programs *more* impartial than privately produced programs. The *New York Times*, at the personal direction of publisher Arthur Sulzberger, printed Benton's response in full, which the AP took as an act of war. Benton also asked the American Society of Newspaper Editors (ASNE) to appoint the three distinguished editors who had made a study for the ASNE of world information the previous year to evaluate the AP's claims about OIC. The three men undertook the study.[34]

Elmer Davis, by that time a radio commentator for ABC, also condemned the AP move in his broadcast on the day following its announcement. He felt that the AP's move itself had irredeemably damaged the U.S. service's reputation, particularly because the AP continued to supply other nations' official information services, including the BBC and Tass.[35] Davis's comparison to their Tass arrangement truly angered AP executives. It was a news exchange rather than a sale, for domestic use only, and the state department had encouraged and approved it.[36]

Roy Howard of the Scripps-Howard newspaper chain, a longtime friend of Benton and defender of press freedom, pointed out that no matter how fair, any news disseminated by the U.S. government inevitably would be regarded as propaganda. "Even if it were lily white, which it will never be, if it presented both sides of every situation it attempts to cover, which it never will do, it would still, by reason of its source, be propaganda in the eyes of the world." In a speech to ASNE that prevented that organization from condemning the VOA, Benton insisted that the question was not whether propaganda was desirable but whether the United States could "solve the problem of providing the world with adequate information without engaging in propaganda."[37] Howard's faith in the commercial outfits' objectivity as key to the American image abroad would not last long.

Meetings continued into the spring of 1946 with little change and more rancor, although the AP did agree to reassess its relationship with other official news agencies. After one lengthy but apparently unproductive meeting between Benton and the AP board, Benton wrote to its chairman, Robert McLean of the *Philadelphia Bulletin*. Recounting how happy members of the board were when Benton, an industry man, took charge of the OIC, he expressed continuing perplexity as to why the AP had made its decision to terminate without consulting him. In effect, when it became clear that AP would not reverse its decision, Benton howled, "But I'm one of you!"[38]

Benton won some vindication. At the end of 1946, ASNE concluded its study of the OIC and issued a pained but sympathetic report supporting overseas programs. They observed that the commercial news services, including the AP, did not give foreign audiences an accurate picture of the United States, particularly because they did not carry enough textual information to represent U.S. policy fully. The committee hesitatingly concluded that commercial objectives did not fully align with policy goals. Plainly, the networks aired trash, and it reflected badly on the United States. In his assessment of wire service performance abroad, veteran psychological warrior C. D. Jackson worried that their dispatches allowed selection of the most sensational material about "Hollywood divorces, gangland murders, and the like" and that any story could be twisted by Communist propagandists.[39] Although it might sacrifice the popularity of trash, the overseas programs demanded more exhaustive portrayals of U.S. policy.

Although sensitive to the dangers attending government dissemination of news, not least the stigma of propaganda, the ASNE committee reported that OIC had survived the loss of the AP and UP and should continue to receive appropriations. *Houston Bulletin* executive editor Oveta Culp Hobby expressed the ASNE committee's reluctance when she wrote:

> I cannot recall a problem about which I have had as many conflicting responses . . . I am compelled to the conclusion that words are weapons in the contest of ideologies. . . . I have arrived at the conclusion that we must use the potentially powerful supplement of self-portrayal and interpretation. I abhor the necessity for it and despise the doing, but if such a program can be effective – or even partly so – it may be a partial peace insurance.[40]

Thus the Cold War began to make its mark in these debates, posing a rigorous government information campaign against increased Soviet domination as the lesser of two evils.

While William Benton was sympathetic to AP executive director Kent Cooper's "millennial hope" for international freedom of the press, he thought that the AP chief should "face the facts of life" that the postwar world was too dangerous and hostile to trust that freedom would triumph. Responding to Cooper's attacks on him as an enemy of press freedom, Benton wrote in *Editor and Publisher* in 1947: "We would be less than candid with ourselves – indeed we would be living in a world of gossamer dreams – if either of us felt we had progressed very far toward our goal."[41] By 1948 the deepening of the Cold War finally secured the future of the information services, though the withdrawal of AP made their job considerably harder. Not only did they lack the most comprehensive source for breaking information in the world; they operated under a deepened taint of propaganda. CBS and NBC had watched Benton take on the AP and decided not to test his considerable strength of will and Congressional connections in a head-on confrontation over official broadcasting.

A Market Failure

Who would run U.S. overseas broadcasting after World War II? In 1945 the answer seemed clear. Private broadcasters would operate it with assistance from the state department. Yet as the superpowers settled into Cold War, the shortcomings of commercial broadcasting for political communication became painfully apparent to the state department and Congress. William Benton, the moderate businessman in charge of overseas broadcasting, would be replaced by a career foreign service officer, signaling the full incorporation of the *Voice of America* into Cold War policy making.

The contracts to lease private facilities for the VOA ran through mid-1946. Secretary of State Jimmy Byrnes asked President Truman to extend the life of the overseas information services until the end of 1946, stressing the modesty of the proposed operation to highlight its difference from comprehensive totalitarian programs. It would not compete with private firms, it would not seek to outdo other nations, and although it was a departure for the U.S. to continue this operation in peacetime, its purpose would be "solely to supply the facts on which foreign peoples can arrive at a rational and accurate judgment [of U.S. policies and institutions]."[42] As noted above, President Truman complied, setting the parameters for a service that would promulgate a "full and fair" picture of the United States.

Benton set modest institutional goals. In 1945 he slashed the OWI's budget by eighty percent and reduced its workforce from 11,000 to 3,000 people. His budget continued to shrink from $45 million in 1946 to $25 million in 1947. But the information services sat awkwardly in the state department's structure. Foreign service officers and policy officials resented their presence and disdained information officers as "mere journalists" who could publicize policy after it was made but who should have no part in its formulation. Under Secretary Dean Acheson took this position as a means of insuring the purity of policy, saying in effect, "Let's first consider what we ought to do, what the right thing is to do . . . then we'll come back and look at it in terms of expediency." Others saw information officers as politically ignorant.[43] A succession of assistant secretaries for public affairs struggled throughout the late 1940s to get a representative on the secretary's policy staff. At first they humbly argued that the presentation of a policy affected its reception. By 1950 they boldly maintained that propaganda was a major weapon in the Cold War, and they won representation on the policy staff as well as an information officer in each geographical bureau, ironically diminishing the influence of the central information staff. By 1951–1952 the overseas programs had become a "whipping boy" for those who saw U.S. postwar foreign policy as a failure. After seven years of torment, the whole apparatus was finally moved outside the department in 1953 and set up as the U.S. Information Agency (USIA).

In 1946 the very existence of the information service was in jeopardy. To distance the VOA from the state department, and to soften the appearance of official propaganda, Benton began to advocate creation of a public corporation, financed by Congressional appropriation but run by private broadcasters. William Paley, chairman of CBS, reluctantly approved this solution, not seeing much difference between this option and a private company that sold time to the government. Paley, an OWI veteran, recognized the importance of overseas propaganda and indeed construed domestic news broadcasting to be on a continuum with it. He added that the corporation proposal needed guarantees that its board of directors would be free from political influence. Lacking his usual acumen, Paley also expected that the United Nations might soon take over all international broadcasting to alleviate the pressures of ideological warfare.[44] Benton's proposal foundered.

Throughout 1946 and into 1947, CBS and NBC supplied 40 percent of VOA's programming, and OIC produced the rest. IBD paid $4 million of its $7 million budget to private broadcasters to lease transmitters and to buy programming. The conflict over the future of "the broadcasting," as it was called, heated up with debates over the 1947 fiscal-year appropriations. Once again William Benton took the heat.

He now proposed to create an International Broadcasting Foundation (IBF; or Foundation Plan), to be run by a private board of directors appointed by the president and including the secretary of state. It would be funded by Congressional appropriation. Benton explained to Acheson that despite the policy ease of keeping the broadcasting in the department, several factors weighed in favor of separation. These included the hefty $10 million dollar budget, which would be easier to get through Congress if the VOA were privately controlled, and the desirability of a more vital set of programs, which would be better produced outside state department bureaucracy.[45]

Response to the Foundation Plan among broadcasters ranged from lukewarm support to incensed opposition. NBC and CBS went along with it, meeting continually with state department representatives on how it would actually work. Others in the industry rejected permanent government support of overseas radio as communist. In a passionate defense of free enterprise, E. J. McDonald, President of Zenith, wrote to Senator Brien McMahon even though his company had no direct interest in overseas operations. He rejected private cooperation as "sugarcoating" on a totalitarian-style government propaganda operation.[46] McDonald colorfully defended commercial broadcasting as the best possible propaganda:

> The one basic idea that the United States has to sell to the rest of the world is our American system of free enterprise. . . . What profit could there be in prattling about "the unvarnished truth" about free America when the listener knows that the programs he hears are themselves a violation of the basic principle of American free enterprise? Why should we adopt the very practices that we criticize in other governments? . . . What a revelation it would be to countless impoverished millions to hear commercial announcers vying with each other to sell more soap, candy, automobiles, watches, cigarettes, etc. etc. And what a demonstration of democracy in action it would be to hear two opposing American presidential candidates tear into each other over the radio, and then hear the election results, and learn that the loser continued to enjoy life and freedom. . . . Under the acid spur of commercial results, broadcasters will develop new technics [sic] of audience building in foreign lands that will far transcend the best efforts possible for a known government agency.[47]

The State Department felt that exactly those features that McDonald treasured as democratic in American broadcasting – salesmanship and political battles – presented a damaging picture of the United States. They dreaded distributing the image of a nation of materialist consumers; neither did they want to air the kinds of accusations and disagreements routinely featured in domestic political campaigns. McDonald had support. The trade publication *Broadcasting* also continued to defend the "free American plan radio system." But even the National Association of Broadcasters, usually among the first defenders of commercial prerogative, admitted that it was not commercially feasible for private broadcasters to fulfill the VOA's programming schedule without Congressional appropriations.[48] Despite the passion of free enterprise rhetoric, corporate control became steadily less financially and politically viable. Government had to do what free enterprise could not.

In all probability, Benton put forward the Foundation Plan in March 1947, with little hope or desire of Congress passing it, as a means of buying time while a more permanent structure could be created. By April most of the licensees believed that both a wholly government-run operation and the Foundation Plan were dead in Congress, and they feared they would be forced to take over. Niles Trammell, president of NBC, confided to Benton in May that the prospect of politicized Congressional scrutiny made him dread complete private takeover. He told Benton, "I don't want, a year hence, to be sitting in the seat you're sitting in today." Benton summed up the political dilemma for his boss Acheson: "How can the Republicans save face, and make capital out of the broadcasting, positioning themselves as against bureaucracy and for free enterprise – without risking the destruction of the broadcasting?"[49]

Legislation providing a permanent basis for overseas broadcasting had recently been introduced in the House of Representatives by Karl Mundt (R–SD) and was cosponsored by Senator Alexander Smith (R–NJ). Mundt and Smith, as with half the Congress, had traveled abroad in 1947 and witnessed apparent misperceptions of American postwar intentions. They particularly wanted to promote an American interpretation of the Marshall Plan. In hearings on the Smith-Mundt bill, the House Foreign Affairs Committee heard supportive testimony from distinguished witnesses including Generals Marshall, Eisenhower, and Bedell Smith, as well as Averell Harriman and Dean Acheson. HR 3342 passed on June 24, 1947, by a vote of 272 to 97 and was sent to the Senate. The Senate Foreign Relations Committee held hearings and dispatched it to the floor with amendments and a recommendation to pass, but it failed to come to a vote before the end of the session. In the interim, the House Foreign Affairs and Senate Foreign Relations Committees sent a joint delegation to investigate the programs in twenty-two countries. This delegation recommended swift passage of the bill, and it passed the Senate unanimously on January 19, 1948. The president signed the Smith-Mundt Act into law the following week.[50]

Officially titled the U.S. Information and Education Exchange Act of 1948, the Smith-Mundt Act put the weight of Congress behind international information but placed a greater burden on the private broadcasters. It made several specific provisions concerning the relationship of government programs to private media companies, beginning with the proviso that Congress did not intend to give the government a monopoly on shortwave broadcasting. Next it called for the creation of a United States Advisory Commission on Information (USAIC) to be made up of distinguished private citizens to advise Congress on the progress of the new Office of International Information (OII). The USAIC's main purpose was to police the effectiveness of the programs, which often meant insuring the use of private companies and corporate-style efficiency.[51] Third, it ordered the secretary of state to use the services and facilities of private press, publishing, radio, and motion pictures "to the maximum extent practicable . . . by the maximum number of different private agencies in each field consistent with the potential market for their services in each country." The act passed the Foreign Relations Committee and went to the full Senate, and NBC News vice-president William Brooks noted that the network needed to double studio time and hire forty to fifty additional people to fulfill NBC's new obligations.[52]

But during the six months between House and Senate passage of the bill, the state department began seriously to question the suitability of network-produced programming for the VOA. Kenneth Fry of IBD voiced the concern that the networks and OIC had a "fundamentally different concept of the job and how to do it." Benton asked him to elaborate. Forty-five percent of network output was music and entertainment programs, which were not, in Fry's estimation, "good or fair projections of America" and did not receive well on shortwave. But even the networks' news and commentary programming included "little Americana, few special features, few special events. In other words, they do not turn out the type of program which requires research and thoughtful presentation for background and projection of America."[53] The State Department thus began to conclude that the commercial firms, rather than sending a favorable message about the American way of life, now detracted from the overseas propaganda effort.

In August, Under Secretary of State Robert Lovett (Acheson became secretary in May) planned a meeting with top NBC and CBS officials. Lovett aimed to promote closer coordination between the department and the networks "so that a balanced and coordinated story is told." He stressed that the government had final "responsibility and authority over output," putting pressure on the networks to shape their programming according to department policy. Particularly in network broadcasts to sensitive areas such as Italy, France, and Southeast Asia, the department was concerned that "output be coordinated and guided to insure maximum effectiveness and to avoid damaging mistakes." IBD also asked that network personnel working on VOA broadcasts undergo background security checks.[54]

In September, with his welcome at the Capitol long since worn out, William Benton resigned as assistant secretary for public affairs. He sent a joint letter to Stanton at CBS and Trammell at NBC, summarizing their current agreements and understandings and reminding the executives that their broadcasts carried the authority of the U.S. government. He proposed guidelines for material to be used in VOA broadcasts to bring them closer to official output. Among other things, he urged: Avoid domestic U.S. stories, be sensitive to the target culture, highlight the president and the secretary of state's foreign policy statements, and guard against distortable stories.[55]

Frank Stanton replied that he accepted these guidelines and hoped they would prevent misunderstandings like those that had occurred in the past. But he also defended the network's record of cooperation and responsibility: "I feel that the private companies have demonstrated their fitness to discharge these responsibilities by their prewar and wartime records in this field." CBS and NBC felt increasingly pinned between a rock and a hard place, with Congressional insistence on private participation in the broadcasting and State insistence on firm policy control. Then in October, further complicating the networks' politically treacherous task, AP's board of directors voted to disallow NBC and CBS from using AP reports in preparing their VOA broadcasts, as they had earlier withdrawn their service from OIC's direct use.[56]

Just as the broadcasting received legal sanction and more secure appropriations hinging on private participation, both the state department and Congress began openly attacking the networks' output. Internal NBC correspondence just one month after passage of the Smith-Mundt Act reflects growing consternation that despite "great progress in coordinating our output" through weekly meetings between IBD, NBC, and CBS over a year, Charles Thayer of IBD had been directed to take over all programming except to Latin America. Thayer read to his network counterparts from a speech he planned to make at Yale. He said that the limits of disclosing security information to private broadcasters rendered them unable to program responsibly to sensitive areas. No matter how well staffed or willing to conform to policy, the networks by law could not have the whole picture. Information was now fully militarized. "It is a function of our foreign relations that cannot be delegated to a private agency any more than we can delegate the operations of our Army or Navy. This type of operation today is too dangerous an instrument to be used by any but those who have at their disposal the very most accurate information and who are under the immediate control of the Administration and the Congress."[57] The confirmation of career foreign service officer George V. Allen as Benton's successor as assistant secretary in February confirmed the trend toward more internal policy control. The future of the overseas information service now seemed to hinge more on its acceptance by the foreign service than on cooperation with private communications companies.

Still, Benton and others resisted the trend and looked for help on Capitol Hill. Benton wrote to Representative Mike Mansfield (D–MT) that "the present hope of the Department, as well as of Congress – and I know how many members of your committee share this hope – is that private industry in the United States will do a much bigger job in this area." Aligning information with the foreign service would also complicate already excruciating appropriations battles. Edward Barrett, assistant secretary for public affairs from 1950 to 1952, explained the advantage of "itinerants" coming in and out of government: "You've got to have somebody who's dispensable. Only a guy who's a non-career officer can tell a Senator to go to hell, and they needed it, sometimes." Some of Thayer's IBD staff also resisted the move away from private cooperation and received Thayer's approval to express their dissent. One VOA programmer told NBC representatives that he believed "the Government should not do the job alone on the grounds that it smacks too much of un-American, totalitarian propaganda methods."[58]

But by June 1948, a strident Congressional investigation led the networks seriously to doubt that they wanted to continue programming for the VOA. Congress had monitored VOA output sporadically since the war. One congressman insisted on receiving transcripts of every VOA broadcast, every day, after one show made a slightly derogatory reference to his home state of Nebraska. The State Department Subcommittee of the House of Representatives' Committee on Expenditures in the Executive Departments, known as the Chenoweth Committee, began active "surveillance" of the VOA in March 1948. By May they held public hearings with their Senate counterpart because they judged that both the networks and the state department had failed to live up to their responsibilities under the Smith-Mundt Act. Specifically, they charged that the networks produced programs unflattering and dangerous to the United States and that the state department failed to police network output. Despite an extreme personnel shortage, IBD then began to monitor the political content of domestic radio programs shortwaved abroad by NBC and CBS.[59]

One broadcast in particular provoked grief. An NBC Spanish-language series for broadcast in Central and South America, *Know North America*, was written by a Cuban and produced by a Venezuelan. One of the programs included the line, "Don't you have a saying that Texas was born in sin but New England was born in hypocrisy?" Another, about Native Americans still living in the trans–Mississippi West, reported, "Our Indian maidens run in races dressed in nothing but feathers." The committee judged that this and other passages from the series lied about and ridiculed the United States and were "vulgar and misleading." Tracing the problem to the use of inexperienced, disloyal personnel who were not U.S. citizens, the committee lambasted NBC as incompetent if not traitorous. "[I]f there did not exist a deliberate design and intention on the part of some employee, or employees, of the National Broadcasting Company to sabotage our efforts to promote international understanding and goodwill, those employees of the Company were ignorant of the intent and purpose of this phase of the foreign information program as authorized by Congress."[60]

In defense of the network, Charles Denny, vice-president and general counsel of NBC, reminded the committee that the short passages on six programs they found objectionable constituted a small fragment of NBC's weekly VOA output of 272 programs in twenty-one languages. He also recited the history of NBC's extensive cooperation in international broadcasting since 1929. He blamed the recent slips on "a basic weakness in the present procedures for administering international broadcasting – the lack of a centralized responsibility for programming" and hoped the hearings would help to eliminate this weakness.[61]

They did. Wanting no further investigations into their programs or hiring practices, NBC and CBS decided that the government should take full responsibility for VOA programming, and they canceled their contracts. During a three-month period between July and September 1948, the networks arranged to transfer all their operations to the state department, which offered to provide first employment opportunities to the network personnel previously involved in this work. Again in the transitional period, George Allen castigated NBC for inappropriate broadcasts, particularly one French-language broadcast describing the overly extravagant wedding reception of celebrities Lana Turner and Bob Topping. "The script writer's declaration that 'Hollywood is not all of America' was insufficient to prevent the program from leaving the impression on the listener that the events described were typical of the U.S."[62]

Thus we see three distinct approaches to VOA content in these debates. William Benton, Elmer Davis, and their allies in the state department prized a sober and serious approach to truth that they felt the government could best achieve. The Associated Press believed that only private news organizations working without the taint of government propaganda could represent the truth. Finally, Congress preferred a sort of unsullied mythological truth about America, handled with the political control of a government operation but the flare of commercial distribution. The networks tried to please everyone – and failed.

Diehard defenders of free enterprise lamented the withdrawal of private broadcasters from the overseas information campaigns. Conservative and progressive critics of government propaganda alike were concerned about the trampling of freedom by a nascent national security state, but the most vocal opposition centered only on the threat to corporate prerogative. In mid-1949 the NAB's Advisory Committee on International Information sent a report to the United States Advisory Commission on Information, the watchdog group set up by Smith-Mundt to oversee the VOA for Congress. This report expressed the fear that such "inroads of the U.S. Government" contravened the intent of Congress and the people of the United States. The committee recommended that, with proper policy coordination, the shortwave operations should be operated "under private management methods." They stressed that "the American *method* of broadcasting is just as important as the message which is transmitted through the shortwave facilities."[63] While this component of the broadcasting industry continued to trumpet free enterprise, most people directly involved with the overseas information program, including the two most powerful networks, agreed that private efforts would be inadequate.

Although the networks severed their institutional contracts with the VOA, individual broadcasters working for the networks continued to record programs for shortwave transmission for many years. When members of Congress criticized this practice, Allen's successor as assistant secretary of state for public affairs, Edward Barrett, replied that the practice fulfilled the Smith-Mundt Act's specific directions to the secretary to use private services whenever practicable. In 1951 at the height of McCarthyite hysteria about communists in the state department, CBS correspondent Eric Sevareid became embroiled in a controversy over his being "in the pay of the Dean Acheson group." Broadcasters received $50 apiece for recording commentaries for the VOA, well below their market rate. CBS News president Ed Chester formulated a policy that said if a U.S. agency asked a CBS correspondent to perform such a task, he could. "CBS Radio does not want to deny the newsman to perform a patriotic service if he desires to do so but it does feel that since the motivating force is patriotism, the work should be performed gratis or not at all."[64] The deeper the United States sank into Cold War, the more members of Congress whipped up fears about domestic communist subversion, the less likely private broadcasters could or would participate in overseas information programs.

Managing the Marketplace of Ideas

Between 1946 and 1952, the consensual answer to the question of who should control international information shifted 180 degrees. In 1946, the Advertising Council's success and AP's unilateral withdrawal of its services from the state department signaled that all overseas information would be distributed through private channels. But by 1948, the view that the United States needed to manage the circulation of ideas in the international arena was fairly well accepted in the Departments of State and Defense, Congress, and the most powerful networks. All information had military implications. The Cold War made propaganda an integral part of American foreign policy and took as its casualty confidence that the United States would triumph in the marketplace of ideas. As Margaret Blanchard summarized the mood in 1948, "Americans repeatedly said that they were willing to have American ideas meet in free combat with ideas from other nations, for they were secure in the knowledge that American views would triumph. Now, an American victory in the free interplay of ideas no longer seemed so sure."[65]

The drive for greater policy control and for aggressive anticommunist tactics extended to the domestic arena as well. In the Cold War of words, wrote C. D. Jackson, "all our writings, all our publications, all our expressions of thought, must be weighed according to their propaganda impact."[66] Not only did information specialists caution that domestic stories could be manipulated for communist purposes abroad; they argued that the will of the American public was central to winning the Cold War. But the government could not simply take over the domestic information market as it had the overseas programs, and the state department had no designs on running domestic broadcasting. The rhetoric of free enterprise persisted and even became more adamant as the United States increasingly defined itself as the enemy of Soviet totalitarianism. Government information programmers looked to broad cooperation and voluntarism from private broadcasters to provide ideological coordination of domestic news with overseas propaganda needs.

Still, the vehemently probusiness contingent that opposed any government involvement in overseas information feared that the state would next take over domestic broadcasting. In 1947 NAB president Justin Miller had warned against a domestic totalitarian future unless private broadcasters ran the overseas programs:

> [T]he future of free broadcasting in this country is largely dependent on what happens during the next few years at the international level. . . . [T]he free broadcasters of America should be helping to shape public opinion concerning them and helping the people to decide the question properly, instead of leaving the question to our State Department and to representatives of government broadcasting throughout the world.[67]

Miller's call to the purposeful shaping of public opinion by broadcasters on their own behalf undermines his defense of commercial broadcasting as free. Although this argument utterly failed to prevent the expansion of both overseas and domestic propaganda operations, his insistence on private broadcasters' voluntarism remained central to both propaganda efforts.

In 1953, the conservative Hearst-owned *New York Daily Mirror* published an editorial that summarized the remaining political opposition to information programs, in both small government and pro-capitalistic terms. It also invoked the strategy of truth on the side of free enterprise, claiming that U.S. policies should be self-evidently righteous and should not need further explanation or packaging:

> This is a capitalistic country of individual enterprise and freedom, and any government agency which is afraid – or ashamed – to say so is misrepresenting America and its people. . . . If this country acts properly and honorably, in accordance with the vital principle of enlightened self-interest, we will not need to "sell" our story with an interminable flow of words, words, words, at the taxpayers' expense and in violation of the Jeffersonian precept that the best government is that which governs least.[68]

Despite the continuing potency of such language, the U.S. government had already adopted an aggressive propaganda program and would not relinquish it anytime soon. Even so, those Americans most closely identified with the propaganda effort insisted on portraying the American approach to information in terms of a free marketplace of ideas. As Barrett's book title *Truth is Our Weapon* suggests, they often forgot that it was their own tactic.

The voluntary cooperation that failed in overseas broadcasting became the norm in the nascent domestic television industry. Information officers and media representatives alike boasted that this system worked better than any other. Andrew Berding, who served as a high-level information officer in both the Departments of State and Defense in this period, wrote that the "first principle" in disseminating foreign policy information to the public was to rely on mass media, "as contrasted with government created and financed dissemination of information." The selling point was always business's efficiency. "I was confident that these public media could do the job better than government distribution, and at comparatively little expense to the government, and that the government could not and should not try to compete with them."[69]

The overseas propaganda value of such voluntarism, and the negative associations of official control of domestic information, often took precedence in debates about control of domestic information. Theodore Repplier of the Advertising Council urged the state department to advertise "the unique method that has grown up in the United States of distributing public information voluntarily" at the United Nations in 1948. He listed five propaganda advantages, explaining that "because this is entirely voluntary, it is a good example of how a Democracy handles a problem by cooperative effort. . . . It shows that people do not need compulsion to act in a Democracy but they will act in concert when they are given the facts."[70]

Officials in the state department and the Central Intelligence Agency (CIA) were so taken with the notion of private broadcasters disseminating pro-U.S. information that in 1949 they created and funded an imitation "private" radio station to broadcast to countries behind the Iron Curtain. The CIA ran Radio Free Europe (RFE) but created the illusion of private ownership to bolster the appearance of spontaneous anticommunism on the part of the U.S. public. The station would not be constrained by the diplomatic attention focused on the official VOA. The CIA also created a domestic fundraising arm for RFE, called the "Crusade for Freedom," to defray the agency's costs – "Radio Free Europe is a private American enterprise, it depends on voluntary subscriptions" – and as a propaganda campaign to rally the American public behind the ostensibly private anticommunist effort.[71]

The architects of Cold War information policy received remarkable cooperation from the nascent television industry in putting the desired information before the American public. Broadcasters believed both in fighting communism and in their own continued control of information as a guarantor of democracy. Chapters Three through Six detail their cooperative efforts with the state department, the White House, and the defense department. But first, Chapter Two looks at the advent of television in American political culture, and how the question of control, so hotly debated when it came to overseas information, disappeared entirely in the domestic arena.

CHAPTER TWO

A WEAPON FOR TRUTH: DEMOCRACY AND THE ADVENT OF TELEVISION NEWS

Federal information officials decreed that domestic news about the Cold War should be "coordinated" at high levels, but they also recognized that the American public would never accept news that smacked of propaganda. We saw in Chapter One that the networks, as part of the progressive business community, cooperated with the state to help secure domestic support for the fight against communism. Members of Congress and conservative business leaders continued to voice outrage about overseas propaganda, yet considerable government control of domestic information never became a political issue. How did the collaboratively produced programs described in the following chapters, which seem to violate the canons of professional journalism and the public's expectations for an independent news media, instead seem to fulfill the networks' public service responsibility? We must look at long-term cultural constellations around capitalism, professionalism, and technology to explain the public's unquestioning acceptance of these programs.

The ownership of television by private corporations signaled that it would manifest the marketplace of ideas and serve democracy at least as well as commercial radio or privately owned newspapers did. Television shared in the legitimacy of capitalism itself. Yet to be accepted as serious journalists, news broadcasters also had to be protected from undue influence by capitalist owners and advertisers. Journalists' professionalism provided this assurance in the ideology of a strict objectivity that would keep an inappropriate corporate slant (and political biases of all stripes) out of the news. So television news gained legitimacy *both* from its proximity to markets and its insulation from them. In addition, television technology promised to democratize government as never before by bringing it directly into the home. On all these counts, the public welcomed the advent of television news.

Number of televisions sold and TV households in the United States,
1949–1959

Year	Number TVs Sold	Total Sold to Date	Number of TV Households	Percentage of Households with TV
1941–49		3,600,000		
1950	6,100,000	9,700,000	3,900,000	9.0
1951	5,900,000	15,600,000	10,300,000	23.5
1952	6,100,000	21,800,000	15,300,000	34.2
1953	6,400,000	28,200,000	20,400,000	44.7
1954	7,300,000	35,500,000	26,000,000	55.7
1955	7,400,000	42,900,000	30,700,000	64.5
1956	6,800,000	49,700,000	34,900,000	71.8
1957	6,600,000	56,300,000	38,900,000	78.6
1958	5,100,000	61,400,000	41,900,000	83.2
1959	5,700,000	67,100,000	43,900,000	85.9

Adapted from Cobbett Steinberg, *TV Facts* (New York: Facts on File, 1985),
85–86.

Yet the introduction of new technologies and modes of discourse is
never so easy or seamless. The medium also prompted fears, protests, and
ambivalence. Its commercialism made many people scoff. The marketplace of ideas was a fine ideal, but people also worried about cheapening
the public sphere with so many crude commercials and cheap entertainments. Journalists dismissed television news as mere show business. Also,
fears of domestic subversion dampened the allure of the technology. Such
a powerful, decadent medium in the heart of the American home would
seem to make an appealing tool for secret communists seeking to undermine American resolve in the Cold War.

This chapter examines these lines of contention about the legitimacy of
television news as it was invented before an audience that leapt from five
to forty-five percent of American households between 1948 and 1953. In
each case, the news divisions' difficult position could be negotiated by reporting closely and without comment on the activities of high-ranking officials, the very practice federal information officers most wanted. This
practice provided the networks with a public service defense against
charges of overcommercialism, followed strict guidelines for professional

Number of television stations affiliated with networks, 1949–1959

Year	NBC	CBS	ABC	DuMont
1949	25	15	11	45
1950	56	27	13	52
1951	63	30	14	62
1952	64	31	15	62
1953	71	33	24	133
1954	164	113	40	195
1955	189	139	46	158
1956	200	168	53	
1957	205	180	60	
1958	209	191	69	
1959	213	193	79	

Adapt from Cobbett Steinberg, *TV Facts* (New York: Facts on File, 1985), 405–6.

objectivity, and guarded against communist use of the airwaves. In addition to these implicit satisfactions of the public's fears about television, the networks also developed overt campaigns to demonstrate their correctness along these fault lines. In each case, they used language laden with the perils of communism and the delights of consumerism so potent at the opening of the Cold War.

In cultivating legitimacy through these avenues, the networks directed attention away from the ultimate question of who controlled broadcasting. While pointing to the incredible potency of the medium itself, they imputed powerlessness to its owners and operators. Disinclined to question corporate control itself in the midst of the postwar boom, the public never looked very hard at the institutional nexus producing their television news programs. Corporate-owned and commercially sponsored television was fully naturalized as the only kind of television. This fog surrounding who controlled broadcasting, and to what ends, left television news' collaborations with the national security state unseen in American culture.

An X-Ray and a Mirror

In January 1948, nineteen commercial television stations broadcast to an estimated 175,000 sets. The largest network, the National Broadcasting Company, linked stations in only four east-coast cities: New York,

Philadelphia, Washington, D.C., and Schenectady.[1] Still a high-risk venture, television lost money every year. The four networks together lost $25 million in 1949.

James Baughman has shown that cultural observers predicting television's impact alternately celebrated it as a force for enlightenment and truth and feared it as an instrument of propaganda and nonsense.[2] In its earliest years, denigrated by print and radio journalists, television struggled to establish itself as a legitimate news medium. On the one hand, the technology promised to enhance democracy. It offered unprecedented access for citizens to see government officials at work, to observe their faces, and to evaluate their character. On the other hand, television threatened democracy because it concentrated so much power to shape public opinion into such few hands. Both these sets of expectations encouraged broadcasters to focus with little comment on the activities of government officials, the very practice defined and defended as highly objective news reporting. The networks cultivated access to high-ranking government officials but distanced themselves from association with any discernibly partisan set of political positions. Highly circumscribed routines for objectivity helped. They simply parroted official information.

In 1947–1948, television journalists faced considerable challenges in providing any coverage whatsoever of national politics. Many experienced print and radio hands doubted that television would become a major news medium. An editor told reporter Don Hewit, who went on to produce *60 Minutes* and earn almost a billion dollars for CBS by 1991, that television was a passing fad. When Reuven Frank, later NBC News president, was first hired by that network in 1950, his boss told him, "Nobody in radio who is worth anything thinks [television's] gonna last."[3]

To begin with, technology clearly limited the medium's power to report news. Coverage of the 1948 party conventions was limited to the northeastern states by the reach of coaxial cables. The networks had no camera crews of their own until the early 1950s, and they relied on newsreel companies to provide film.[4] Nightly news programs consisted mostly of readers stringing together wire service dispatches and film that had to be flown to New York from where it was shot. There was no remote reporting unless scheduled in advance. These programs did not become the news divisions' flagship programs until the mid-1960s, when video and other technologies made more immediate coverage possible. Until 1963, they lasted only fifteen minutes on CBS and NBC, and until 1967 on ABC.

The category "news" itself has evolved according to the limits of technology: In 1952, NBC's press panel program *Meet the Press* won the

Peabody Award for the year's outstanding news program. Panel discussion and interview programs seemed more timely than nightly news because they featured newsmakers and were broadcast live. These programs particularly fostered an equation of news with newsmakers' statements rather than contemporaneously broadcast events. The guests almost always came from Congress or the executive branch of the federal government. During the 1950s, eighty-five percent of the guests on *Meet the Press* were government officials.[5]

The technology's unfamiliarity and demands alienated newsmakers and other journalists. Broadcasters had to establish themselves as practicing journalists just to win camera access to scheduled political events like speeches and press conferences. Film equipment, by its sheer mass and the hot lights required before the advent of video, dominated any event it covered. James Reston of the *New York Times* called the televised news conference "the goofiest idea since the hula hoop." When broadcaster Leonard Reinsch was appointed to run President Harry S Truman's "press" conferences, print journalists ridiculed him and his efforts to turn them into "news" conferences. Reston's colleague A. M. Rosenthal complained, "The paraphernalia of TV – the glaring lights, the cameras, the portable power machines, the huge coils of cable and the strong-arm men of the crew – force the newspaperman to work in a hectic, noisy movie-set atmosphere." CBS's very first network television editorial, delivered in 1954 by its president Frank Stanton, pleaded for electronic journalists to have the same access to Congressional hearings that print journalists enjoyed.[6]

Not just the disruptiveness of television technology but the perennial critique of its staple entertainment programming undermined its credibility in news broadcasting. Intellectual elites, no matter how much they approve of capitalism as an economic system, routinely denigrate popular journalism as "mere show business." Rosenthal, then the *New York Times* United Nations correspondent, judged, "Television is not interested in news but in entertainment." NBC Washington correspondent Ray Scherer wrote, "The writing gentry tended to look down upon us as fugitives from show business or radio correspondents down on their luck." This disdain of TV news as "mere" entertainment, particularly from those most immediately inconvenienced and displaced by the medium, has been the most persistent criticism from 1948 until the present day. *Sponsor* magazine concluded in 1952 that TV's "hottest" problem was its "battle for respectability."[7] With such resistance to the very establishment of television as a news medium, access to high-ranking public officials provided a straight path to credibility.

TV pioneers envisioned limitless possibilities for transmitting news, generating extravagant hopes for democracy. They equated the visual access to government officials that television offered with public participation in the televised event. This greater participation would enhance each citizen-viewer's knowledge and stake in government and increase government accountability. Even sixty-three *New York Times* reporters polled in 1951 agreed that television stimulated interest in local and national politics and that discussion and interview programs contributed to a "more enlightened public opinion."[8]

The novelty of viewing public figures live became something of an obsession during the early years of television. Programs entitled *Meet the Boss, Meet the Champions, Meet the Masters, Meet the Professor, Meet the Veep* (featuring Vice-President Alben Barkley), *Meet Your Congress, Meet the Press, Meet Your Cover Girl,* and *Mrs. Roosevelt Meets the Public* played upon the excitement surrounding this new accessibility. Lynn Spigel observes that television offered *hyperreality*: not just transmitting spectacles into the home but transporting viewers into the public arena.[9] In its early years, television thus promised to involve private citizens in political events rather than, as many critics contend happened instead, isolating them in their living rooms and encouraging them to become spectators to public life instead of participants.

The mere existence of television seemed to ensure honesty in government. On the 1951 premiere of his benchmark series *See It Now,* CBS broadcaster Edward R. Murrow remarked, "No journalistic age was ever given a weapon for truth with quite the scope of this fledgling television." Early broadcasters felt they delivered on the medium's promise simply by showing politicians at work. The service television offered to high-ranking officials by granting them immediate access to large audiences soon made earlier predictions of the failure of television news sound like sour grapes. Broadcasters earned acceptance as news gatherers, if not credibility as journalists, partly by making themselves indispensable to prominent public figures.

Broadcasters used two metaphors with astonishing consistency to describe television's impact on democracy. First, they portrayed its effect on politicians as that of an X-ray revealing the subject's essential character. Second, they depicted television itself as a mirror held up to society, adding no selective or distorting effects of its own. Both of these metaphors manifest a belief in the technology's almost magical potency. Both metaphors also so entirely deemphasize the role of those controlling television that one would think the technology operated itself.

The X-ray metaphor promoted the notion that it was impossible to deceive the camera. This magic would immeasurably enhance the visual access to government that television provided. Walter Cronkite ascribed to television an "X-ray quality." Founder, producer, and panelist of *Meet the Press*, Lawrence Spivak said, "TV has an almost infrared quality of getting beneath the skin of an interviewee." News producer and writer Henry Cassirer elaborated on the effect: "No radio interview can give you the intimacy of television, the familiarity not only with the view, but with the total personality of the guest, his looks, his gestures, his human qualities. They usually remain more unforgettable in the mind of the audience than any statement he may have made."[10]

This excitement, like much of the scholarship that television has since generated, focused predominantly on its role in portraying candidates before elections. Sig Mickelson described his colleagues' exultations: "We . . . [were] convinced that we had the most magnificent new device that had ever been created, a device that would bring politics literally into the living room, a device that could make candidates become real human beings." When presidential aspirant Dwight D. Eisenhower resisted campaigning on television in 1952, a prominent advertiser cautioned him that the medium with its "triple advantages of sight, sound, and motion" could already "make or break" a candidate. *New York Times* television critic Jack Gould declared in 1955 that "TV has done a most useful job in disposing of some poseurs."[11] If it was impossible to deceive the camera, what negative effects could television possibly introduce to the democratic process?

To this day, broadcasters invoke the mirror analogy for television. This analogy, even more explicitly than that of the X-ray, denies the power exerted by television's owners or operators in deference to the power of the technology itself. In 1954, CBS president Frank Stanton denied that cameras selectively chose or framed events, claiming that cameras were "the public's mirror reflecting things exactly as they are. To blame radio and television for blemishes or excesses makes no more sense than to blame a mirror because you do not like the reflection which you see in it." Stanton maintained that television cameras did not change the way politicians presented themselves, because they were always far too busy and preoccupied to play to the cameras. He dismissed criticism that broadcasting created "spectacles or circuses" by saying that radio and television didn't "compel people to show off or misbehave." Broadcasters themselves thus exerted no power and bore no responsibility for the shape of political debate. The NAB publication "Free Television" likewise boasted that television could overcome the limitations to objectivity imposed on written news reports. These "second-hand" accounts from town criers and "pad-and-pencil newspapermen" of what happened at public meetings always reproduced the limitations of the individual's viewpoint, but television was unencumbered by such restrictions.[12]

Given such enthusiastic faith in television's power to unmask any lie and to broadcast only undistorted truth, self-conscious public officials shied away from it at first. The exposure was too unrelenting: If you spoke badly or too candidly, there was no recourse. Candidates and elected officials, more than appointed officials, risked such intense exposure. Diplomats and military officers, those most closely associated with Cold War policies, judged the potential losses of excessive candor far greater than any potential gain. They especially avoided unscripted press panel programs as too confrontational. Yet officials soon learned to set parameters for their appearances. Where they could control the interview, they gained easy exposure. A newspaper reporter pinpointed the new calculus at work in 1953 between reporters and delegates to the United Nations:

> We [print reporters] talk to him [a delegate]. We want news, answers. He knows that. And he knows that we'll check up on him, go after other sources, dig around a little, maybe develop a story. But look at that [television] program. No embarrassing questions, a chance to tell the world why he is heaven's gift to diplomacy, a big audience; painless. He's smart. What does he want to talk to newspapermen for?[13]

By the late 1950s, Harry Rasky, producer of CBS's interview program *UN in Action* could joke, "It's much tougher to find a shy diplomat than to find a shy calendar girl."[14]

Industry experts soon formulated techniques for effective campaigning on television. This advice simultaneously subscribed to the X-ray analogy that TV saw through any artifice while listing techniques for simulating sincerity. In 1952, the NAB published a television edition of its radio primer for candidates entitled, "Is Your Hat in the Ring?" It advised wholesale changes in campaign style to suit this intimate medium. Flowery oratory should be replaced by informal, sincere conversation. "Remember," the brochure urged, "your *eyes* as well as your voice reveal your sincerity to the viewer." After several pages of do's and don'ts on movement, makeup, lighting, scripts, timing, keeping the audience's attention, and the crew's activities, the pamphlet concludes, "Above all else – relax, be natural, be friendly." Both President Truman and Secretary of State Dean Acheson received coaching on their television technique from CBS executives.[15]

By the mid-1950s, broadcasters no longer needed to struggle for access to officials. Television appearances became routine. A mutual dependence between broadcasters and officials, each seeking legitimacy through the other, fostered the equation of news with official information. Yet broadcasters could not get too close to any one politician, agency, party, or position. In the politically charged atmosphere of the Second Red Scare, the safest course was a carefully modulated but unassailable anticommunism. It was better to emphasize the technology and draw attention away from the network's keen but unremarked powers of selection, valuation, and interpretation.

Reluctant Partners[16]

The X-ray and mirror metaphors certainly reflect television broadcasters' excitement at government's new visibility. The alternate set of expectations greeting television news stemmed from fears of TV's ability to distribute propaganda and to concentrate political power. President Harry Truman wondered and worried about what fascist demagogues like Father Charles Coughlin or Adolf Hitler would do with the medium.[17] Like television's happier prospects, these fears also encouraged a narrow focus on official information.

Of course, the fear of communism far overshadowed fear of fascism in the postwar period. The apparent military force of the Soviet Union and the threat of internal subversion made many Americans wary of any institution with the potential power of television. The *American Mercury* cautioned against leftists seeking to invade television: "Video is the answer to the thought-controller's dream." Frank M. Folsom, president of the Radio Corporation of America (RCA), NBC network's parent corporation, averred in 1951 that television served a vital patriotic function by supporting federal institutions "when swiftly changing events may otherwise cause confusion and alarm to the detriment of unity of purpose in safeguarding the democratic institutions of our land." A widely distributed comic book, "This is Tomorrow," portrayed communist control of mass communication as one of the most catastrophic outcomes in a projected Soviet takeover of the United States; the communists dictate the news to the press associations, nationalize the telephone system and forbid international calls, and block overseas broadcast signals (see Figure 2).[18]

Figure 2. A forty-eight–page comic book entitled "This is Tomorrow" begins, "It wasn't long after the end of the Second World War that Communist forces in America seized their chance." It was published by American Business Consultants, the same firm that issued *Red Channels,* the primary blacklist for the broadcasting industry. Original at the Harry S Truman Library.

Television historian Erik Barnouw emphasizes that the industry matured at the height of the Second Red Scare and was dominated by anticommunist hysteria. "Evolving from a radio industry born under military influence and reared by big business, [television] now entered adolescence traumatized by phobia. It would learn caution, and cowardice."[19] The networks scrupulously avoided programming that could bring charges of disloyalty or partisanship. Simple reporting of official pronouncements – whether from red-baiting Congressmen, defensive state department officials, or the alternatively popular and reviled president – filled the bill for strict objectivity. Despite the networks' consistent cooperation with blacklisters, they portrayed themselves as victims, or at worst as reluctant partners, in the political sanitization of the airwaves, again denying their own power.

Anticommunist organizers targeted the entertainment industry because of the alleged danger of thought manipulation by leftists. The Mundt-Nixon Bill of 1947 specifically disallowed communists from using the broadcast frequencies for what Senator Mundt described as "treachery, propaganda, and sabotage." J. Edgar Hoover of the FBI urged station owners to root out the inevitable secret communists in their employ. While the networks promoted the belief that their strict objectivity excluded all forms of opinion, an article in the *New Republic* as early as January 1947 entitled "Thought Control – American Style" noted the disappearance of many leftists from radio broadcasting, though the networks claimed to be uneasy with opinion in general.[20]

For-profit loyalty investigators policed the industry. In 1947, Alfred Kohlberg, an importer of Chinese textiles and ardently anticommunist member of the "China Lobby," funded three ex-FBI investigators to found American Business Consultants. They published *Counterattack, The Newsletter of Facts on Communism*. Subscribers to *Counterattack* were offered special reports, including the well-known *Red Channels, The Report of Communist Influence in Radio and Television*, issued in June 1950. Soon nicknamed "the Bible of Madison Avenue" for its ubiquity with networks, sponsors, and advertising agencies, *Red Channels* listed 151 people in the radio and television industries who were allegedly linked to "Communist causes."[21] Among network news personnel, *Red Channels* listed only William Shirer, Alexander Kendrick, and Howard K. Smith, all of CBS, but blacklisting created a pervasive climate that set unspoken codes for hiring and for news content.

American Business Consultants represented an extremist group of corporate and ex-government personnel. These relentless anticommunists, not secret communists, managed to exercise inordinate control over the broadcasting industry by their control over its advertisers. Lawrence Johnson, a zealous anticommunist who owned a chain of supermarkets in upstate New York, provided mechanisms for control. He wrote to manufacturers, threatening boycotts, or he displayed their products with a sign indicating that the manufacturer supported communism if they did not withdraw sponsorship from programs he deemed un-American. The direct liaison between the sponsors and American Business Consultants was Jack Wren, a former naval intelligence officer who oversaw "security" at the advertising agency of Batten, Barton, Durstine and Osborn. *Counterattack* tried at least once to get President Truman to intervene in network programming directly. Truman's press secretary equably informed its managing editor, "I am sorry, but it would be out of line with White House policy for the President to attempt to influence the programs of the radio networks, no matter how good the cause."[22]

CBS and NBC responded to the accusations that they harbored secret communists by instituting their own internal security systems. NBC had required its new employees to sign loyalty oaths since the mid-1940s, delegating the investigation of alleged risks to its legal department. CBS created a new vice-presidency for this purpose. In December 1950, CBS also began to require loyalty oaths of its employees on the model of the federal program instituted by President Harry Truman. CBS Chairman William S. Paley instituted the oaths after he heard that FBI Director J. Edgar Hoover referred to the network as the "Communist Broadcasting System."[23] Visceral anti-Semitism against Paley and RCA Chairman David Sarnoff probably also contributed to fears that the networks purveyed covertly un-American fare.

The networks walked a political tightrope. They were (unreasonably) suspected of harboring subversives, and they needed access to high-ranking officials to counter that suspicion. Yet if they got too close to the Democratic administration or to the Republican majority in the Senate, they risked alienating the other group. The narrow strictures of early Cold War objectivity mitigated this challenge, allowing them simultaneous proximity to government officials and distance from the particulars of their positions. The closer each collaborative program's ties to the executive branch, the more difficult this became. Chapter Four examines Republican objections to the joint NBC–White House series *Battle Report*.

As discussed in the Introduction, the especially close collaborations between the networks and the reviled Truman state department might seem surprising in this context. Network co-productions flourished at the height of McCarthyite charges of subversion in the department, despite the well-founded expectation that the networks would recoil from association with anything redolent of disloyalty. Certainly the networks covered Congressional allegations of communism in government in other formats. Yet longstanding friendships between public and private information personnel, as well as broadcasters' own indignation at charges of secret communist influence on the television industry, suggested to the networks that the charges had little merit. Giving a forum to state department officials provided the department a chance to prove its loyalty and competence (although, as we shall see in Chapter 3, they failed to formulate a winning strategy on that score), maintained the important long-term institutional relationship between the networks and the department, and allowed the networks to boast of their access to the heart of the alleged problem. By both covering the charges of subversion and providing a forum for their rebuttal, the networks actually pursued a consistent and prudent business course of trying to alienate no one.

An NBC spokesman characterized the networks' participation in blacklisting not as political concurrence but as "a business safeguard" when the network's advertisers were being squeezed by *Counterattack* and the like.[24] Daniel T. O'Shea, who oversaw the oaths and investigated controversial personnel for CBS, also saw the network's motives as economic rather than political:

> They didn't do the blacklisting because of what people had done; they did it because of business. Shows were beginning to cost more. A client would say, "Listen, we can't have this. We're spending forty or fifty thousand dollars for good will. We don't want to be identified with this. . . ." I kept some people off the air. Never deliberately unjustly. It wasn't that I felt myself in the middle of ridding the world of Communists – rather of some group or another who were affecting CBS's business.[25]

Thus, these spokesmen admitted that the accuracy of each accusation was unimportant to the networks because the negative impressions created by false accusations still alienated their source of revenue, sponsors. As the networks first pursued and won wide audiences, a group of well-placed extremists was able to exclude everyone but avowed anticommunists from the broadcasting industry by their manipulation of the industry's profit base. This uncomfortable fact was virtually eclipsed by the shadow of Tass.

By saying they suffered through blacklisting as a matter of business survival rather than political assent, the networks helped to maintain their legitimacy as the guardians of free speech in the marketplace of ideas. Many broadcasters personally condemned the climate of fear despite their employers' acquiescence. NBC News Producer Pat Weaver told a group of Dartmouth students on the program *Youth Wants to Know* in 1955:

> [T]he basic [advertisers] management groups in large part are very conservative and . . . do not wish to associate the sale of their product with anything controversial. . . . Those of us who run communications know that America is based on the sanctity of dissent, that anything which pressures uniformity or conformity is a block that is building a wall that ends our whole way of life. I think generally speaking . . . the attitude of [network] management is one for dissent and for the unpopular idea and for the use of controversial issues.[26]

By arguing that profit motives rather than political complicity inspired the networks to cave in to the blacklisters, broadcasters could imply that they had not renounced the First Amendment. They had just temporarily abandoned it to stay in business, and business was the bulwark of freedom. Individual broadcasters were then victims of the blacklisters rather than their conspirators, reinforcing the paradoxical illusion of network powerlessness. William Boddy argues that the networks "generally succeeded in presenting themselves as victims of, or at worst, reluctant partners in, program censorship and restrictive employment practices."[27] While requiring their employees to sign loyalty oaths and forcing out anyone with alleged leftist sympathies, the networks managed to present themselves as the champions of free speech, the powerless victims of patriotic, if overexuberant, anticommunists.

"Free Television"

Perhaps the most important cultural context to explore in understanding the acceptance of network–government collaborations to produce news are American attitudes toward capitalism itself, specifically corporate control of information. Although deeply felt sentiment in the United States had long associated capitalism with liberty, another long, if more peripheral, tradition suspected and condemned corporate power as contrary to the average person's freedom. The networks ceaselessly promoted the notion that corporate control of the frequencies constituted a free and democratic marketplace of ideas. At least since the 1930s, the networks had conducted campaigns that, as Robert McChesney puts it, "successfully attach[ed] commercial broadcasting to the ideological wagon that equated capitalism with the free and equal marketplace, the free and equal marketplace with democracy, and democracy with 'Americanism.'" The longstanding, fundamental critique of capitalism largely disintegrated in the face of the postwar middle-class boom and the array of consumer goods signaling the arrival of the good life. Television's innumerable critics have focused ad nauseam on the medium's (over)commercialism but have sought to redress it in voluntary standards such as limiting the amount of ads in children's programs – not through a fundamental restructuring of the industry. Corporate ownership and sponsorship of network broadcasting itself, let alone its relationship with the national security state, has remained virtually invisible, naturalized, or "off limits" since the 1930s.[28]

But the networks did not, as they claimed, represent an equitable and democratic radio market of free individuals engaged in debate. The networks successfully sowed rhetoric about the free marketplace, but that highly sanitized version of American capitalism belied the actual status of the broadcasting industry. Rather, the broadcasting industry represented a highly skewed market, giving nearly exclusive access to powerfully established corporate interests.[29] In the mid-1940s, more than ten major companies planned to launch television networks. Had more succeeded, the marketplace of ideas would certainly have been better served than by the oligarchical structure that prevailed for three decades. The most powerful segment of the industry deterred or bankrupted most of their competitors and at the same time sold themselves as committed to free debate and the openness of the marketplace. They succeeded in part because they linked alternatives to totalitarian communism.

The Radio Corporation of America (RCA), the manufacturing parent company of the NBC network, exerted the most influence over electronics manufacturing because of its near monopoly on broadcasting patents. Indeed, in the 1940s and early 1950s, major profits in the television industry came from sale of sets rather than from sale of programs to sponsors. Network television broadcasting lost money until 1951. Revenue from manufacturing sales (RCA, DuMont), AM radio (RCA, CBS), and all the networks' owned and operated stations offset network losses until then and outpaced network profits until the late 1950s.

In the late 1930s, several competing television technologies were under development. The Federal Communications Commission (FCC) refused to select one for immediate commercial activation, waiting for a clearly superior system to emerge. RCA seized the public's imagination with a television demonstration at the 1939 World's Fair and began marketing sets before the FCC endorsed a technology. *Fortune* said RCA's false start "was grabbing for power and control of television too."[30] But when the FCC condemned the move and resolved to reconsider its own position, Congress condemned the FCC as hostile to American business. In 1941, the FCC endorsed standards that gave thirty-six percent of the usable spectrum to the very high frequency (VHF) stations, channels 2–13. NBC held the important patents for sets built to receive these stations, and this decision solidified the company's dominance of the new industry.

Then in 1943–1944, the FCC considered reallocating the spectrum for high-contrast black-and-white or color broadcasting. NBC's principal competitor, CBS, pressed for a high-contrast black-and-white system that would entail a shift to the ultra high frequency (UHF) band. Its allies consisted of companies without extensive investments in television technology or patents who were looking to break into television: Zenith, Cowles, ABC, Westinghouse, and IT&T. Those companies with substantial investments in VHF technology, particularly RCA, but also Farnsworth, General Electric, and DuMont, vehemently opposed expansion into UHF. They protested that the sets already sold would become obsolescent if a new system was approved and the spectrum reallocated. RCA executives also argued that their technology would be ready for consumers at the end of World War II and would help prevent a return of the Depression. "Television has the power to create consumer demand and buying of goods and services beyond anything we have heretofore known."[31]

In May 1945, the FCC ruled again for VHF broadcasting pioneers. This far-reaching decision effectively limited television service to the VHF band, creating an artificial scarcity of television broadcast licenses. Extremely well-capitalized corporations controlled these licenses and were able to decimate their smaller competitors. Over a battle for FM radio frequencies with a similar outcome, Senator Charles Tobey said of the FCC, "The bit was in their mouth and they 'geed' and 'hawed' for many in the industry."[32] In 1946, CBS again pushed the FCC for reallocation, this time for a modified color broadcasting system, but the commission again rejected its proposal. FCC chairman Charles Denney resigned shortly thereafter to become an NBC vice-president, with a 300 percent raise.

But even with such succor from the FCC, the VHF-dominated industry did not seem to be living up to its promise. By the end of 1947, only sixteen commercial television stations operated in the United States. *Fortune*, which had shared RCA's optimism that television would lead the postwar consumer boom, now blamed CBS and its allocation fights for threatening to turn television "into the biggest and costliest flop in U.S. industrial history."[33] The future was so uncertain that even RCA, so far the big winner through its VHF patents and stations, cut its own risks in television by scaling back investments.

Then came the freeze. The 1945 allocation plan had required stations broadcasting on adjacent frequencies to be located at least 85 miles apart, and those on the same frequency to be 200 miles apart. In May 1948, the FCC reduced these distances to 75 and 150 miles. This caused so much interference and alarm that the FCC announced a temporary freeze on license approvals for new stations until the problem of frequency interference could be resolved. It was supposed to last six to nine months, but then the FCC decided to reopen the issue of color broadcasting. Instead, it lasted almost four years, from September 1948 until April 1952. Boddy notes that the term "freeze" is misleading because the number of stations on the air actually rose from 50 to 108 due to previously approved licenses. Sets also flew out of stores; the number sold swelled from 1.2 to 15 million, representing a jump from four-tenths to thirty-four percent of American homes.[34]

The freeze greatly benefited entrenched VHF interests, which now included CBS. In 1947–1948, CBS had gobbled up five owned and operated VHF stations and affiliated many more,[35] but NBC was still dominant, with the only station in a majority of markets. During the freeze, 108 stations broadcast to sixty-three markets. Forty cities had one station, eleven had two stations, eight had three stations, and only three had four or more stations. Allen DuMont, who played a significant role in the development of television but whose company, DuMont Television Network, was continually marginalized by FCC decisions, claimed that CBS distracted the FCC with the color question to prolong the freeze to the advantage of the two dominant networks. He told the FCC, "the freeze reserved to two networks the almost exclusive right to broadcast in all but twelve of the sixty-three markets which had television service."[36] Boddy concludes that due to the freeze, Mutual, Philco, and Paramount dropped their plans to launch television networks, and ABC and DuMont almost went bankrupt. DuMont did fold in 1955 after the FCC approved a merger between ABC and one of DuMont's principal investors, Paramount. In effect, the FCC sacrificed DuMont to ABC "in order that at least ABC might survive and prosper to offset the obvious dominance which NBC and CBS had gained in the industry during the freeze years."[37]

Those hurt by the freeze attacked NBC and CBS in antimonopolist language, appealing to an earlier, more entrepreneurial capitalism. One of DuMont's allies prepared a memo for President Truman, saying that the

high barriers to entry combined with the FCC's policies would result in
television being "monopolized by very wealthy groups. . . . This will result in a concentration of control of this valuable new media in the hands
of a few instead of in the hands of those who have built the broadcast industry."[38] This plea appealed to a smaller-scale capitalism, with more pronounced notions of individual ownership and fairness.

NBC and its allies fought back by portraying themselves and their business practices as the best servants of the American people. Although, in
this instance, they stopped short of explicitly linking the alternative of a
more competitive capitalism with communism, they cast opposition to
VHF as opposition to the American way. C. B. Jolliffe, who left his post as
head engineer for the FCC to become vice-president in charge of RCA
Laboratories, denied that a move to the more capacious UHF band would
enhance the marketplace of ideas or be a blow to RCA alone. He told a
Senate commerce committee:

> There appear to be some who would block the progress of television with
> charges which misrepresent the purpose and leadership of RCA and NBC in
> bringing television to the American people. One of these misrepresentations is
> the assertion that all television should be moved into the higher frequencies. Let
> us make no mistake about this. If such a move were made at this time, it would
> not mean more television. It would mean no television at all.[39]

Jolliffe thus linked the future of television – all its allure to consumers, and
all the jobs and wealth it could create – with the future of RCA's plans,
and he predicted the demise of the industry if RCA failed. RCA said, in effect, "oligopoly or nothing." A more competitive and perhaps diverse television industry was lost in the rush to commercial development, aided by
successful promotion of the notion that large corporations best served the
public.

A 1950 *Television* editorial linked threats to the large networks directly
to communism. "Threat to Our Economy" called on the industry to fight
any questioning of their profit-making prerogatives by the FCC. The
writer F. A. Kugel urged broadcasters to rally to the defense of the big
VHF broadcasters against FCC commissioners who questioned their mo-
nopolistic practices. They should

> strike out against the menace of socialism which is steadily creeping into every
> phase of our economic life. . . . When men like Commissioner Jones and Com-
> missioner Johnson can talk in terms of "vested interests" and "profits for the
> few," we have, right in the open, the kind of thinking that can ruin our country.
> The very basis for free enterprise is profits.[40]

By 1950, such strictly antistate sentiment had been abandoned by most of the business community and even by the networks in favor of cooperative, voluntary solutions to regulatory problems. But the rhetoric still proved potent and expedient because no one in government or industry could afford the taint of socialism in 1950, even those who simply defended a more competitive, smaller-scale capitalism. The phrase "right in the open" amply demonstrates the equation of big corporations with righteous anticommunism.

NBC even used the sentiment that corporations could best enlighten the public as a 1951 sales strategy to get advertisers to sponsor public affairs programs and to better its reputation for public service. "How pleased the Communists would be," chided a draft sales memo written by network vice-president Davidson Taylor, "if television, with its great power to command attention, spent all its time amusing the American people, and never brought them information or made them think." Taylor hastened to tell the sales force to assure potential sponsors that the network would not minimize entertainment but that it was vital that "the techniques of entertainment showmanship be applied to the purpose of enlightenment." Doing their part against communism would improve sales in the Sunday public affairs programming ghetto! The memo offers three strategies toward the end of such strategic enlightenment: to make news and public affairs programs jazzier, to add covert instruction to entertainment programs, and for each regular series to offer a special educational broadcast twice a year. This last proposal was given the military title, "Operation Frontal Lobes." Even *Time* magazine was skeptical that television could become primarily an educational medium. "Getting culture into the Milton Berle show might have daunted even hardier men than NBC's executives."[41]

If they managed, by pulling the anticommunist trump card, to legitimize large-scale corporate ownership for television, the networks were less successful at fending off criticism of their prime-time entertainment schedules' commercialism. Even in the alleged "Golden Age" of live drama, this was a constant refrain. Dismay at the perceived vacancy of television programming crystallized and culminated toward the end of the decade. In 1958, CBS broadcaster Edward R. Murrow made a widely quoted speech to the Radio and Television News Directors Association decrying the "decadence, escapism, and insularities from the world in which we live."[42] This speech did not attract as much attention or precipitate as much dismay at the networks as FCC commissioner Newton Minow's

1961 "vast wasteland" speech, but then Murrow had no regulatory jurisdiction over the industry. He embodied CBS News integrity and would finally signal his despair by leaving the network and commercial broadcasting to head the USIA during the Kennedy administration.

A 1958 publication by the National Association of Broadcasters entitled "Free Television," if not a direct response to Murrow's speech, was a
contemporaneous attempt to rebut growing criticism of the medium's
overcommercialism. The pamphlet is a straightforward public relations effort to portray the network oligarchy and its basis in corporate advertising
as responsible for the good life in America. "The U.S. has the highest standard of living in the world. It also has the best and most advertising in the
world. These two facts are directly related." "Free Television" explains
that advertising enabled mass production and low prices for consumer
goods, paid the bills for television entertainment, and disseminated "commercial news" about the latest products and styles, vital to "make life easier for the housewife." In news and public affairs, the NAB explicitly
linked the information flow vital to democracy to the networks' wealth
rather than to its public service ethic or objectivity. "Americans are the
best informed people in the world. Free television spends millions of dollars a year to help keep them that way."[43]

The networks rarely defended the innate worth or integrity of their programs but rather cited their high ratings as evidence that the people
wanted this type of programming, equating consumer choice with democracy. The allure of the marketplace-of-ideas metaphor obscured the ways
that rules of the market differ from rules of a free debate between equals,
not least in the depth of the resources available to the networks for pro-
mulgating ideas useful to them. The metaphor is in many ways "too cunning about democracy,"[44] confusing it with marketing. But its tenacity
bought the networks astonishing license to program without hard
scrutiny, including collaboration with federal agencies to produce news.
Corporate control of broadcasting was celebrated as good and democratic, even if its price included the purging of leftists, the uncritical par-
roting of official information, and often insipid programming.

The History of Objectivity

If the first bedrock belief that legitimized public–private collaboration to
produce news was faith in the benevolence of the market, the second,
paradoxically, was the network news divisions' supposed insulation from

the market in the form of journalists' professionalism. At the heart of any news organization's legitimacy is the journalist's professional code of conduct, specifically the standard of objectivity. Corporate ownership ostensibly protected the flow of vital information from undue influence by the state. But to earn acceptance as professional news organizations, the news divisions also had to prove themselves protected from the undue influence of corporate owners and advertisers. Joint state–network programs fit neatly into an extremely circumscribed ideology of objectivity that prevailed in the postwar period, requiring only a strict accounting of who, what, where, and when.

Historians have correlated the rise of the journalist's code of objectivity to the rise of commercial news media in the mid-nineteenth century. The advent of penny papers in the 1840s led to the abandonment of partisan journalism and a new concept of straight information. Advertisers steadily replaced political parties as newspapers' primary patrons. This disengagement of information from partisan sources was augmented by the rise of wire services.[45] Fundamentally, objectivity emerged as a sales strategy to increase the client base for any one news outlet across the political spectrum.

The meaning of objectivity, and the forms of journalistic routines that meet it, vary according to political, economic, and cultural tides. In the early twentieth century, objectivity looked differently at newspapers owned by the Hearst, Pulitzer, and Ochs families. It also evolved significantly through time. Dan Schiller argues that during the heyday of the penny press in the mid-nineteenth century, objectivity meant a democratization of information. Michael Schudson asserts that in the wake of World War I, with the public reeling from disclosures about the Creel Committee's propaganda, objectivity meant providing explanatory context for potentially misleading facts. Also in the 1920s, journalism embraced a fully realized scientific paradigm, or as Walter Lippmann called it, "the habit of disinterested realism." The professional code of objectivity helped legitimize the commercial press as the "protector of the public good" even as the news industry became increasingly concentrated throughout the twentieth century.[46] Americans believe so reflexively in a wall of separation between editing and publishing that they are more likely to perceive news bias flowing from individual journalists' opinions, despite these strict professional codes of practice, than from media corporations' institutional interests.

Most journalism historians agree that the code of objectivity as insistence on "hard facts" reached its apogee during the early Cold War. Daniel Hallin writes:

> From about World War II through the early 1960s, objectivity was assumed to require strict separation not only between fact and value but between fact and interpretation. This was the heyday of straight journalism; news analysis for the most part was restricted to the signed column, and the ordinary reporter was to tell "who, what, when, where" and leave it at that.[47]

Hallin and others correlate this narrowing of the routines of objectivity to the intensity of the postwar consensus. Exclusive reliance on official sources in foreign policy reporting signaled elite agreement on the outlines of policy. When elites disagree over a policy, as they did over Vietnam with great vehemence after 1967, journalists follow different procedures to signal objectivity, principally balancing opposing sources. But when consensus is as strong as it was during the early Cold War, we can expect close adherence to the official line, and the possibility for credible opposition diminishes. In such times, observes Hallin, "the political discourse that filters through the media to the public does come very close to the one-dimensionality described by Marcuse."[48] In this way, we can correlate the standards of objectivity with the boundaries of political orthodoxy. Bedrock beliefs about the superiority of capitalism have figured in such orthodoxies throughout American history, providing a firm foundation for the commercial strategies of news corporations that trade on their claims to objectivity.

The fledgling news divisions gained legitimacy in the eyes of the public from their proximity to government officials at a time of extreme deference to military authority, ascendant corporate prestige, and strict consensus. By doing so they also fulfilled a set of conditions for professional objectivity linked to that consensus and thus gained legitimacy with the journalistic community. Collaboratively produced programs did not seem to surrender television's public service responsibility. Indeed, the networks construed the programs quietly co-produced with the government as the exemplary *fulfillment* of their public service responsibility and as evidence of their highly detached professional objectivity.

During the early Cold War, a historically specific and overriding faith in the marketplace as objectivity's guarantor against expansionist communism discounted the otherwise obvious notion that network television represented powerful and particular interests. This simultaneous faith in the market and insulation from the market was a hallmark of the mid-century anticommunist brew. Chapter Seven looks at explicit statements of broadcasters' objectivity codes from the 1950s, how broadcasting performed according to those codes, and how the codes connected to broader tides of postwar intellectual history.

Invisible Power

Each of these cultural constructions – around television technology, capitalism, and objectivity – shared an awe of television as a very powerful medium. They portrayed the technology as remarkably potent but paradoxically rendered its owners, their institutional interests and alignments, and the constructedness of television news itself, so remarkably invisible as to be seemingly powerless. Television's ability to influence politics for the better seemed to flow from the technology itself, and its capacity to influence politics for the worse seemed to flow from the secret schemes of individual broadcasters but never from the industry's broad institutional structure. For all these reasons, the information professionals working both sides of the public–private divide could justify their joint operations to themselves and to the public. But enough introduction. Let's look at what they did.

CHAPTER THREE

CLEARER THAN TRUTH: THE STATE DEPARTMENT'S DOMESTIC INFORMATION PROGRAMS, 1947–1953

The Department of State took the brunt of public frustration over communist gains beginning in 1947. From the "loss" of China, to the explosion of the first Soviet atom bomb, to war in Korea, Americans watched the rise of an even greater threat to the United States than Nazism. How could world communism triumph so decisively without help from inside the U.S. diplomatic corps? The department was accused of active subversion, harboring dissidents, gross incompetence, and effete arrogance. With varying success, its public affairs staff attempted to sell the Truman administration's Cold War policies and to reclaim public trust in the state department itself as a loyal, competent agency. They succeeded in selling their Cold War policies far better than they did in reinstating public trust in the state department.

Diplomatic reporting had long been dominated by informal insider journalism, where reporters and senior officers cultivated one another in background briefings and at private clubs. This certainly continued. But the technological hurdles of early television production required more systematic cooperation, allowing officials greater control over the final product. Television thus became the primary outlet for the department's growing interest in active domestic information management. The fledgling television news operations, in need of cheap programs, access to newsmakers, and demonstrations of their public service, offered thorough cooperation.

Not a Friend in Sight

In 1945, the Department of State subsumed remaining personnel from wartime information agencies. Three services under the new office of assistant secretary of state for public affairs (ASSPA) were created: for international information, international education, and (domestic) public affairs (PA). Archibald MacLeish was the first ASSPA, followed by William Benton in 1946, George V. Allen in 1948, and Edward Barrett in 1950. Between 1947 and 1952, the number of staff members the department devoted to domestic information ranged from 215 to 264.[1]

PA faced opposition on just about every front. Overseas information operations became a particular target of the Republicans in Congress who charged disloyalty and incompetence in the Truman state department. Although the national security leadership deemed overseas propaganda a primary weapon in the Cold War, Congress allocated little money for it. Benton wrote: "Notably in our overseas activities, but domestically as well, we continue to operate in terms of pennies in contrast to the dollars we spend for the more orthodox forms of national defense."[2] Domestic information, as a legacy from the OWI, was tarred with the brush of totalitarian or wasteful propaganda or was seen as a public relations machine for the Democratic Party.

The foreign service shared one sentiment with Congressional conservatives: They too disdained the information services. Benton believed this hostility stemmed from simple resistance to new ways of doing things. But even overseas psychological warriors ridiculed domestic programs as impossibly constrained by politics. C. D. Jackson judged a young *Fortune* ad salesman to have a "hole in his head" for wanting to "devote himself to interpreting the Department on American foreign policy to the American people," calling it "the zeroest of zero jobs." Congress formally restricted the executive branch's prerogative to disseminate information at home. The Smith-Mundt Act of 1948, which gave permanent authorization to postwar overseas programs, prohibited the executive branch from spending money to influence Congress. Later that year, a subcommittee of the House Committee on Executive Expenditures investigated whether the department had illegally tried to influence Congress to pass the Marshall Plan. The state department public affairs staff noted that they more often sustained the opposite criticism, that they disseminated too little information about foreign policy. As the postwar programs took shape around the Marshall Plan in 1947, they professed to "follow a middle line" between the two poles of withholding information and "attempting to force its views . . . upon the American people."[3]

In its attempts at self-definition, PA contorted itself to appear as both a truthful, democratic information agency and as a hard-hitting anticommunist weapon indispensable to prosecuting the Cold War, a fundamental contradiction in its mission. Secretary of State Dean Acheson claimed that the service distributed accurate information and left the public to its own

Figure 3. Francis Russell, director of public affairs for the Department of State, 1945–1953, held a purer view of public information than most of his superiors. Photograph from the National Archives.

conclusions: "The domestic information function of the State Department is to report facts and report the Department's own thinking. It is then up to the public to formulate its own views."[4] Yet the department was rarely so confident of garnering support for its policies. PA's function clearly also included managing and shaping public opinion. That was, after all, their expertise. The service continually published confidential directives with titles such as "Psychological Objectives for the Next Three Months," "Domestic Information Objectives," "Domestic Information Objectives for the Rest of 1950," and "Measures for Promoting National Unity and Confidence in the Government," enumerating points for senior officers to emphasize in their public statements and speeches.

Housing domestic and overseas operations in the same branch sharpened the dilemma. Francis Russell (see Figure 3), the director of public affairs from 1945 to 1953, struggled throughout his tenure to define the differences between ostensibly truthful domestic programs and admittedly manipulative overseas operations. During periodic reviews of the branch's administrative structure, Russell argued that both operationally and politically, the two needed to be kept separate. To begin with, the government owned the distribution facilities for overseas programs but relied on private media at home and thus required very different planning. Russell also maintained that policy goals at home and abroad varied so widely that "a single information policy 'line' for both overseas and domestic operations is worthless as it has to be too generalized to be applicable to both."[5]

But the political reasons to keep them separate were overriding. The free press was a crucial element in the U.S. self-definition – in contrast to what George Kennan called (in "The Sources of Soviet Conduct") the "secretiveness, the lack of frankness, the duplicity" of Soviet policy. Their claim to truth had vital propaganda uses both at home and abroad, and Russell wanted to protect it:

> The Cold War has reached a point where propaganda abroad is indispensable. Up to now, however, the Department has diligently cultivated the concept of PA as a service to the American people, a place where the public can come to obtain information and to present their views to the policy makers. If the American people ever get the idea that the same high-powered propaganda machine (same General Manager, same planning and programming) that has been built up to work over the Russians is also at work on them, the result will be disaster for both the domestic and overseas programs.

In an oral history twenty years later, Russell maintained that the domestic programs remained faithful to democratic ideals: "We hewed as exactly to the line separating lack of information from propaganda as I was able to determine it." In contrast, Edward Barrett (see Figure 4), who relished wartime excitement, admitted, "We really tried to stick to the truth and tell nothing but the truth, but we didn't always tell the *whole* truth."[6]

To forestall charges of impropriety or propaganda, a minimally private organization closely tied to the state department took over the work of selling the Marshall Plan at home. An elite group of citizens formed the Committee for the Marshall Plan to Aid European Recovery, which one historian described as an "external propaganda agency acting on behalf of the European Recovery Plan." Delegating this work to unofficial bodies dodged both Congressional limitations and the broader cultural sensitivity to propaganda. Other minimally or ostensibly private groups, such as the Committee on the Present Danger, the National Committee for a Free Europe, and the television networks "spontaneously" supported Cold War

Figure 4. Edward Barrett, assistant secretary of state for public affairs,
1948–1950, believed that "truth is our weapon" (the title of his 1951 book)
against communism, and he enjoyed a remarkably varied career in public and
private information. Before his tenure at the Department of State, he was head of
domestic information for the Office of War Information and executive editor of
Newsweek. He went on to become a publicist at Hill & Knowlton, and dean of
the Columbia School of Journalism. Photograph from the National Archives.

policies, added to the appearance of popular consent, and affirmed Cold
War axioms about democratic government.[7]

Russell pointed to the watchdog role of the private media as a guarantor of government candor, insisting that journalists would "resent any
type of operation premised upon the assumption that their output was to
be 'planned.'" Occasionally, the press did get indignant about being propagandized. In 1951, *U.S. News and World Report* printed an article,
"How U.S. Tries to Influence You: Government Spends Millions to Tell Its
Story," that surveyed the domestic information bureaus in many departments but spotlighted the state department. A cartoon depicts the ten-step

procedure on "How Government Conditions the Public to Ideas It Wants to Put Over." Stories are "planted" with the press, thousands of officials take up the new "line," "opponents are driven to cover," and the public gets the new view "hammered in" (see Figure 5).

Stripped of its scandalized tone, the piece presents a fairly accurate picture of domestic information operations. But it fails to acknowledge how much reporters relied on bureaus like PA every day for their routine stories. A photograph accompanying it shows reporters scrambling to get government press releases. While right- and left-wing critics of the Truman administration's Cold War policies disdained PA as a Democratic Party propaganda machine, reporters from both the *Chicago Tribune* and the *Daily Worker* depended on it for their bread-and-butter stories. During crisis periods such as the one that followed the Chinese intervention in the Korean War, Secretary of State Dean Acheson met with reporters and columnists every day for weeks on end. PA suffered the occasional indignant exposé, but reporters usually courted them as the primary source of diplomatic information in the capital. Broadcasters could afford to alienate them even less than they could print reporters.

No matter how politically embattled the Truman state department became, the information procedures and politics of the national security state bred broadcasters' deference to authority. The state controlled virtually all breaking security news, strict codes of objectivity excused journalists from evaluating official statements, and anyone who contradicted policy statements risked charges of subversion. Television news fit more nearly into the model of quasi-official information organizations – like the Committee for the Marshall Plan, the National Committee for a Free Europe, and the Committee on the Present Danger – than it did into the tradition of an independent or adversarial press.[8]

The First Programs

From television's inception, PA gave it special attention. The very first nationwide television broadcast – the signing of the Japanese peace treaty in San Francisco on September 21, 1951 – was a diplomatic milestone. The department favored television because it did "a better job than any other medium at depicting Foreign Policy in action." Their broadcasting experts recommended using it to defend against charges of disloyalty because it was a "personal vehicle to stir confidence in officers." Television presented exposition of policy poorly, but PA presumed that the more educated, affluent citizens interested in detailed exposition were mostly Re-

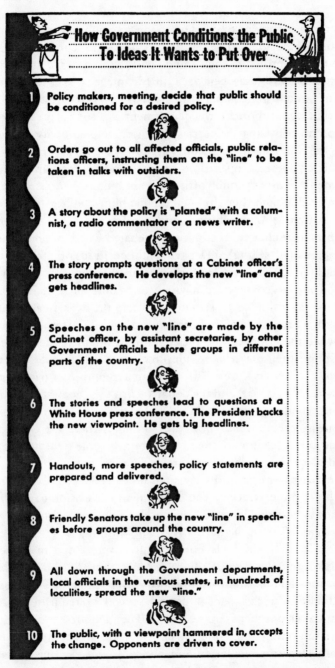

Figure 5. This illustration accompanied a *U.S. News & World Report* article called, "How U.S. Tries to Influence You: Government Spends Millions to Tell Its Story," published June 15, 1951. Copyright 1951, *U.S. News & World Report.*

publicans already hostile to the department. They believed that the Democratic working-class constituency, "the people who repudiated Dewey because he was identified in their minds with big business" and who voted for Truman because they believed "in his integrity as a man and as an American," watched the popular medium of television. Therefore, the best way to stimulate support for the department was for the president to "use the radio and television in a series of basic, simple down-to-earth statements of the problem that confronts us, and what we are trying to do."[9]

Organizing domestic operations to run smoothly took an extended period of trial and error. Senior officials feared making fools of themselves on live television, and they shunned the medium's undignified show business associations. PA lacked funds and personnel, so their early programming efforts were clumsy. In 1947, they debated whether they should "undertake aggressive 'selling' of Departmental positions or stick pretty much to its publicly-stated policy of servicing media and groups at their request."[10] They largely serviced media groups until early 1950, when reticence to use television aggressively aggravated the department's public relations crisis brought on by Senator Joseph McCarthy. PA had more success when they went on the anticommunist offensive themselves, using broadcasting to sell the arms buildup recommended by NSC-68 and galvanized by the war in Korea. The growing acceptance of overseas propaganda to wage Cold War, and the department's own domestic political embattlement, finally prompted PA to sell themselves and their positions more aggressively at home. They courted diplomatic correspondents with access and influence in exchange for more favorable treatment, and they produced programs for the nascent television medium.

In its earliest ventures into television, PA established production guidelines with private producers. The department's television career began in 1948 when American University proposed to produce a program entitled *Your Foreign Policy* for the ABC affiliate in Washington, D.C. Discussions on "Greek-Turkish Aid," "Is European Recovery Road to Peace?" and "Who Makes Foreign Policy?" aired in March and April. Later that year, the university and the department refined the program for WTTG, the DuMont affiliate. The department named several prerequisites for "more than nominal Department cooperation." They required wide distribution ("network or nothing"), ideological control ("treatment must be in accordance with Department dignity and policy"), and exciting visuals (cartoons or "cheese cake gal doing three-dimensional displays such as piling up blocks, etc.").[11] The DuMont and NBC networks deferred, but the

NBC affiliate in Washington aired two programs on the Berlin crisis and the North Atlantic Pact under the title *World Spotlight.*

Director of Public Affairs Francis Russell made some suggestions to Bill Wood, the director of the Radio, Television, and Visual Media branch, in case the department attempted future telecasts of this kind. The program should look less like a government production and more like a penetrating inquiry:

> 1. The introductory placards and announcements on the program might state that "NBC *Interviews* the State Department" rather than that the program is "in cooperation with the State Department." This would get the thing off in an atmosphere of the Department being interrogated rather than an atmosphere of the Department trying to put over some ideas.
> 2. In discussing the "questions of the week" it should not be stated that the questions are based on anything done by the State Department or any information emanating from the State Department as it looks as though the questions were framed. Wally Deuel might just state on his own authority or on the basis of inquiries that he has made around the country that "more people asked these questions this week on this subject than any others."

World Spotlight was thoroughly scripted and rehearsed, but from this earliest effort to present state department policies on television, PA cultivated the appearance of spontaneity.[12]

During their early years, the television networks needed cheap programming. The networks rarely sent their own news crews outside the United States, but government agencies operated film crews throughout the world. State department agencies with film units included the Mutual Security Administration, the Federal Security Agency, and the Economic Cooperation Administration. They produced films for propaganda use in nations receiving foreign aid and lent these films to broadcasters for free. The networks aired them in little-watched portions of their schedules. CBS, NBC, and DuMont aired the films intermittently and distributed them to affiliated stations for local scheduling. DuMont showed several films about overseas psychological warfare under the series title, *Our Secret Weapon – The Truth.* ABC gathered Federal Security Agency films into a series called *Everybody's Business.* As late as 1954, ABC, the least financially secure network, continued to air state department films in summer replacement series.[13]

In order to prevent charges that they intruded on the prerogatives of private broadcasters, public affairs officials required stations formally to distinguish government films from independently gathered news reports. In January 1949, the International Motion Picture (IMP) section of the state department formulated a general policy for the use of its films by television broadcasters: "For use of IMP films for television or other domestic interests it should clearly be stated that they are being shown in the interest of helping the American people understand the overseas information program and should not be competitive to the private efforts in this country."[14] Yet these disclaimers, flashed briefly on the screen at the end of government-produced programs, attracted little notice. IMP seemed more worried about appearing to encroach on business than on appearing to propagandize. Later programs, where final responsibility rested with the networks but which were produced with substantial government assistance, did not carry the same disclaimers.

In addition to airing government-produced films in the absence of their own news-gathering teams, the networks also bought news film from independent production companies. The state department exerted control over these film makers by lending selective assistance and access to their personnel and contacts abroad, and their film archives at home. Officials helped film makers who they considered reputable and who would make films congruent with their policy interests. In 1949, Eric Pommer, an independent film maker who was until 1948 an official with the motion picture branch of the U.S. military government for Germany, proposed to make a series of thirteen films for use on U.S. television, telling the story of Germany from Potsdam to Bonn. He promised to emphasize U.S. operations and accomplishments and to begin each program with a statement from a leading military or state department official. Department representatives stressed that the programs should not be so positive that the American public would not understand that many problems remained unsolved. Pommer received a letter providing that the department would lend, at least, "moral assistance and unofficial guidance."[15]

However, the department refused similar assistance to an unknown film company producing a series to be titled *Meet the Americas*. After determining that the firm was most likely "very small and operating on a speculative basis," an official in the Bureau of Inter-American Affairs recommended a blanket excuse, indicating that department policy was "not to endorse programs of any kind,"[16] although its collaborations on other projects went well beyond mere endorsement. The department selectively accorded access to its archives on the basis of the film maker's friendliness and reputability.

Several PA officers believed that they made their first big mistake with television when the Soviet Union ended its boycott of the United Nations Security Council in August 1950. The networks provided hours of uncut coverage of Security Council deliberations that first summer of the Korean War. The council was chaired by the Soviet ambassador to the UN. Jacob Malik, moaned Russell, became "a figure and a byword in every community to which television extends. . . . Probably there has never been a single factor that has influenced public thinking on a matter of international policy as has the television coverage of the Security Council." Rather than insisting that a major speech by Secretary of State Acheson to the General Assembly be aired in its entirety, PA decided excerpts edited for the nightly newscasts would be more effective. Afterward, Russell lamented that NBC and CBS "failed completely to get across the force and color of the speech" and that the networks had to do a better job promoting U.S. policy. "I think we should raise hell with the networks about this and bring home to them the fact that their cooperation on a thing of this importance is indispensable if we are going to lick Soviet propaganda."[17]

Even the most established and supportive producers occasionally broadcast programs that chagrined the department. PA addressed these incidents through personal contact with media executives. During the San Francisco conference for the Japanese Peace Treaty in 1951, special negotiator John Foster Dulles complained to Edward Barrett that the *March of Time* was showing films of Japanese war atrocities on TV and newsreels. Barrett responded, "I share your regret that such material has been exhumed at this critical time but agree that there is no official action possible to stop it. I suggest, however, that a note from you to the publisher of the *March of Time* and the sponsor of the Ford Television Film Playhouse might be effective." In a postscript, he added that he would "mention it informally to 'Time' also."[18]

PA climbed a steep learning curve in its early television ventures. Personal, informal contacts brought the most effective avenues of control, but most importantly, they learned to pay obeisance to the trappings of journalistic independence.

"The Attack of the Primitives"[19]

This method for amplifying the official point of view worked well enough when news originated in the department. PA had far less success controlling press coverage when members of Congress attacked the department.

Senator Joseph McCarthy launched an unprecedented crisis for PA when he made his infamous speech in Wheeling, West Virginia, on February 9, 1950. McCarthy claimed to have a list of 205 names "known to the Secretary of State as being members of the Communist Party and who nevertheless are still working and shaping policy in the State Department." PA officers mobilized their personal connections with editors and journalists to control the story, but senior officers' failure to mount a dynamic defense left the advantage to McCarthy and his allies.

In the first week of March, Russell and Barrett reported to Under Secretary of State James Webb that media commentary, public opinion surveys, and the statements of major organizations warned of "increasing public pressure, which could become dangerous, for some sort of bold action." Webb declared that the department would initiate a "strong, affirmative public relations policy," yet he failed to provide specifics. He invited the leadership of the State Department Correspondents Association and the most prominent diplomatic reporters to give advice on what to do.[20]

The department initially tried to refute McCarthy's points one by one and to expose his use of half-truths and innuendo. Lloyd Lehrbas, special assistant to the under secretary and a former senior Asia correspondent for the Associated Press, attended the April 20, 1950, meeting of the American Society of Newspaper Editors where McCarthy spoke. Based on his conversations with editors both friendly and hostile to the senator, Lehrbas recommended stressing that McCarthy discredited himself by "his refusal or inability to produce any documentary proof of his charges." Yet a defensive strategy based on McCarthy's lack of proof could never offset the damage done by McCarthy's dynamic attacks. As Ruth Montgomery of the *New York Daily News* reminded McCarthy on national television, "The denials are never given as much attention."[21]

The department used personal contact, already useful for news management, as a means of damage control. Barrett, the former head of the overseas information division of the Office of War Information as well as former editorial director of *Newsweek*, was upset with that magazine's criticism of the department's loyalty programs following McCarthy's Wheeling speech. He wrote a "strictly personal" letter to *Newsweek* editor Kenneth Crawford, stressing the commonality of their endeavors: "I believe I am looking at this just as much from the standpoint of *Newsweek* as from the standpoint of my present job." He judged that the magazine's coverage of McCarthy was "falling a little short of your own standards of objectivity" and that "the tone of the *Newsweek* pieces is really an injustice to the Department."

Barrett then made an offer of extraordinary access:

> I may be wrong, or I may be naive, but I would like to make this suggestion: That you personally come down here for a day or two and take a thorough look-see at the Department's loyalty setup, the procedures followed and the way individual cases are handled. I think it is sound and effective. If it isn't, we would like to have someone with your well-grounded skepticism take a look and make suggestions.

Barrett offered access and influence in policy making to secure more favorable press treatment. This gesture became standard procedure. PA set up "information" circuits (quotation marks were used in the source) where radio commentators rotated visits to department officers, and their output was then monitored to see if it became more favorable.[22]

In March 1950, Barrett and Russell debated whether a TV appearance by Secretary Acheson was advisable. McCarthy made regular appearances on interview programs. Russell contended that the department underutilized both radio and television and conducted a thorough survey of department–broadcast relations to aid in determining an appropriate forum for Acheson's television debut. Should it be a "straight talk" or an interview, live or filmed in advance? Russell anticipated that television could offset McCarthy's attacks on Acheson because it could "humanize the Secretary and take him visually as well as audibly into the U.S. family circle." Barrett advanced his own "brainwave" idea to improve Acheson's image: a nonexclusive version of the famous candid interview between Harry Truman and Arthur Krock. Correspondents from the four television networks could jointly submit a list of long-term questions. "There would be no holds barred. Even the Hiss case could be brought up. The Secretary, having time to prepare and think through his answers in advance could undoubtedly do an admirable job."[23] They reached no decision and postponed Acheson's television debut.

To devise appropriate responses to ongoing charges of disloyalty and incompetence, Barrett formed the Public Relations Working Group (PRWG) on March 24, 1950. Its function eventually broadened "to serve as a strategy board, a public relations staff for the top leadership of the Department, to recommend the pattern of the strategy of the Department's public relations program and to follow up on the execution of the strategy by specific measures." By August 1950, the PRWG decided that point-by-point responses to McCarthy's repetitious charges served only to keep his allegations in the news longer, "but if he comes up with anything really new, the Department will reply."[24] They thus abandoned their minimal defensive strategy as well as any offensive one.

Russell's broadcast study revealed distrust and distaste for television among senior department officers. They claimed they were too busy or that the issues facing their sections were too hot to discuss on such an uncontrolled medium. This reluctance fueled McCarthy's claims that the department had something to hide. Still, William O. Player, Jr., a special assistant to Barrett, recommended that the department continue its prudent policy of avoiding "highly controversial programs on radio or television or those in which newspaper reporters are free to probe Department policies for the purposes of highlighting intra departmental differences and other matters which might prove embarrassing to the Department." Player urged Barrett to encourage senior officers to appear on shows that gave "adequate opportunity for exposition of the Department's point of view."[25]

Russell defined acceptable programs as those scripted in advance. Senior officers generally refused to participate in forums that more nearly approximated the ideal of free inquiry. Lawrence Spivak of NBC's *Meet the Press*, known as a combative questioner and ardent anticommunist, complained to Russell that no one accepted his invitations because they had to "be 'cleared' before they could be heard in public." Between 1950 and 1953, three ambassadors and the head of internal security were the only state department personnel to appear on *Meet the Press*, compared with thirty-three U.S. Senators. The radio-TV branch preferred more dramatic appearances, such as the ceremony for the Japanese Peace Treaty, where the Kremlin spokesmen played their parts as "consummate villains" opposite Acheson's "shining hero." They avoided talk programs because "without conflict the TV audience would have been confined to a small segment of the population . . . those seriously interested in being informed and improved." Spivak acknowledged that they had a strategy but judged it a failure: "You fellows may know what you're doing but the results have not been too good from a public relations point of view."[26]

The senior officers' unwillingness to risk getting "down and dirty" with McCarthy, particularly on live television, and their failure to put the senator on the defensive, doomed their attempts to put themselves in a favorable light.[27] In 1951, PA even revived the longstanding idea of an anthology series dramatizing the foreign service along the lines of the current live drama *Treasury Men in Action* to gain sympathy and recognition from the public. The advertising agency Foote, Cone, and Belding interested Pepsodent in sponsoring the series, but it remained undeveloped. Most likely, senior officers felt it was too commercial for the department's dignity. In 1949, Campbell's Soup had offered to sponsor a television version of the radio program *Tales of the Foreign Service*, but Russell had torpedoed it. "It seems to me that there are some distinctions between soup advertising and State Department public relations. . . . In my opinion the State Department should be less willing even than the White House or the Supreme Court to have itself commercially sponsored by a private company, no matter what the company's products or interest."[28]

But where the department sought dignity, it conveyed only arrogance. The personal reputation of Dean Acheson and public perceptions of the state department remained awful for many years. The networks offered their support through their jointly produced series but not particularly on this issue of internal security. They gave a forum to McCarthy elsewhere in their schedules and sought to maintain their high-level access in the state department.

If PA failed to salvage the department's image, it became more experienced and adept at selling its policies as the second Truman administration progressed. They went on the anticommunist offensive themselves.

A Scare Campaign

Ironically, while the department faced widespread condemnation for softness on communism, the now famous joint State-Defense Study Group headed by Paul Nitze formulated a policy directive that recommended massive militarization in the fight against communism. When a draft of NSC-68 came to Edward Barrett for his comments in April 1950, he called it "magnificent" and noted the scope of the policy change it represented. He expressed reservations about the ability of a democracy to maintain a long-term arms race without a public relations campaign to enlist public support:

> I think that, however much we whip up sentiment, we are going to run into vast opposition among informed people to a huge arms race. We will be warned that we are heading toward a "garrison state." Moreover, even if we could sell the idea, I fear that the U.S. public would rapidly tire of such an effort. In the absence of real and continuing crises, a dictatorship can unquestionably out-last a democracy in a conventional armament race.

Barrett thought PA could overcome public resistance to astronomical expenditures and to the creation of a garrison state by emphasizing the menace of expansionist communism. He alternatively called the projected operation "building public awareness of the problem" and a "psychological 'scare campaign,'" showing that he equated public information with pro-

paganda. He was also confident that he could "whip up" public sentiment.

This campaign, which would presumably be conducted through private
media, would be followed closely by publicity about the government's
programs to meet the threat:

> The first step in the campaign is obviously building up a full public awareness
> of the problem. This might take three months or it might require no more than
> ten days. My hunch is that it will be nearer ten days. We must be sure that the
> Government is in a position to come forward with positive steps to be taken
> just as soon as the atmosphere is right. It is imperative, for both domestic and
> overseas reasons, that there should not be too much of a time lag between the
> creation of a public awareness of the problem and the setting forth of a positive
> Government program to solve that problem. In other words, we should have at
> least the broad proposals for action well in hand before the psychological
> "scare campaign" is started.

The program should highlight the U.S.'s "natural superiority" in science,
technology, and psychological warfare, as proven in the Marshall Plan
and Point IV programs. Barrett concluded that Americans "could be sold"
on a massive weapons program that brought together the nation's "scientific brains to launch the greatest new weapons research program in
history." Francis Russell added that although the majority of Americans
believed that the United States should continue to fight expansionist communism, public acceptance of NSC-68 would hinge on the degree that
U.S. security seemed threatened, the amount of personal sacrifice involved, and the projected effectiveness of the measures proposed.[29]

Consultants to the State-Defense Policy Review Group emphasized the
need for private groups to aid in this propaganda effort. Chester Barnard,
chairman of the Rockefeller Foundation, recommended that a group of independent citizens be given access to the same sources as the authors of
NSC-68. They would (of course) certify its necessity. Robert Lovett suggested using schools, colleges, and churches as well as well-spoken officials and elder statesmen to get the message out once a "group of para-
phrasers" turned "what it is we have to say to the American people into
understandable terms for the average man on the street." Among those
Barnard mentioned was Harvard president James Conant, who, along with
atomic scientist Vannevar Bush and former under secretary of the army
Tracy Voorhees, founded the first Committee on the Present Danger. Like
the Committee on the Marshall Plan, the Committee on the Present Dan-

ger served as an external propaganda agency advocating immediate European and American rearmament. Barnard later became a member.[30]

A month after the consultants recommended popularizing NSC-68, President Truman and Dean Acheson each made major addresses to the American Society of Newspaper Editors meeting in Washington. Both speeches were broadcast on nationwide radio, and both stressed the crucial role played by private groups in the propaganda war against communism. Truman gave his famous "Campaign of Truth" speech, which he began by noting that democracy hinged on the quality of information provided to the people by news media. The U.S. defense against Soviet propaganda was "truth – plain, simple, unvarnished truth – presented by the newspapers, radio, newsreels, and other sources that the people trust." Truman spoke mostly about false conceptions of the United States held by people overseas due to communist propaganda. He told of directing Acheson to wage a campaign of truth that "will require the imagination and energies of private individuals and groups . . . to use fully all the private and governmental means that have proved successful so far – and to discover and employ a great many new ones." A major part would be played by "our great public information channels – newspapers and magazines, radio, and motion pictures."[31] The president explicitly asked the editors for ideological support for the national security state. None of them blanched at the enlistment to propagandize.

Acheson's speech carried out Barrett's plan to mount a psychological scare campaign coupled with government initiatives to meet the proclaimed threat. He began by sounding the alarm, "We are faced with a threat not only to our country but to the civilization in which we live and to the whole physical environment in which that civilization can exist." The *New York Times* entitled its lead story the following day, "Acheson Declares U.S. Is in Danger as Kremlin Target" and described the speech as Acheson's "most comprehensive statement on the position of the United States in the world today and the role Government and citizens must play to preserve their freedom." His six-point plan to defend freedom stressed the role of private news media in representing the United States to the world. He told the editors that they shouldered the responsibility for global freedom.[32]

In perhaps the most famous passage from his memoirs, Acheson rationalized the exaggerations that accompanied the drive to get support behind NSC-68: "The task of a public officer seeking to explain and gain support for a major policy is not that of the writer of a doctoral thesis. . . .

If we made our points clearer than truth, we did not differ from most other educators and could hardly do otherwise."[33] Acheson had little respect for the intellect of the public he served, but he was confident that he represented their interests by sponsoring such "enhancement."

Learning to Work the Networks

The key for getting airtime from the networks was to offer enough newsworthy information without revealing more than was prudent. PA wanted exposure for high-ranking department officials, who it saw as the best spokesmen for government competence and policies, but not overexposure or leaks of sensitive information. The networks wanted newsmaking announcements on their programs. But as the 1950s progressed, even splashy revelations did not suffice to keep these programs in prime time.

In spring of 1950, just after the announcement of the "Campaign of Truth," the department introduced a television program that sold the militarization of U.S. policy. *The Marshall Plan in Action* aired on ABC from June 1950 through February 1953, changing its title to *Strength for a Free World* in January 1951. Produced by the Economic Cooperation Administration (ECA), the state department bureau that administered Marshall Plan aid, the program aired sometimes twice a week on thirteen ABC stations. Until early 1952, ABC re-edited old Mutual Security Agency (MSA) films to fit the thirty-minute format. Titles of individual episodes included, "Year of Decision," "Story of Recovery," "Free City," and "A General Comes Back."[34]

When the program debuted on June 24, 1950, its opening narration characterized the Marshall Plan as a European rearmament plan: "Marshall Plan aid has laid the economic foundation in Western Europe for new military strength. Economic strength is military potential." The Korean War began the following day, and thereafter ECA administrator Paul Hoffman added the Far East to his opening gambit. "The Marshall Plan is helping to build up the economic strength of more than 20 free nations in Europe and Asia, so they can resist the danger of Communist aggression such as has already started in Korea."[35]

The program pleased no one at the state department or ABC and relatively few in the television audience. In 1952, it had an estimated audience in six cities of 426,000, compared with 30 million for the top-rated *I Love Lucy*. ECA director of information Robert Mullen wrote: "I feel compelled to state once again my strong belief that the program should be taken off the air. In my opinion it is actually doing harm." The ECA then contracted with European-based film companies for the production of programs produced specifically for television. The information section of the Office of the U.S. Special Representative in Europe also began to edit old MSA films into thirty-minute segments for use on the show. Either way, the author of a 1954 doctoral dissertation on television programming practices dismissed the show as propaganda, a synonym for bad television, but not particularly harmful because he assumed no one would watch it.[36]

As the network secured more sophisticated programs and sponsors for them, cheaply produced government films became less attractive, and the programs's declining importance to the network became clear to the state department. For most of its run, *The Marshall Plan in Action* aired in the 9:30–10:00 P.M. Sunday slot. In April 1952, ABC moved it to Tuesday night at 8:00, opposite the most popular program on television, NBC's Milton Berle show. DuMont's *Life is Worth Living*, with Bishop Fulton J. Sheen, new to television but rapidly gaining an audience, and Frank Sinatra also broadcast programs in that time slot. Despite their own dissatisfaction with the program, the switch angered ECA and SRE officials, one of whom wrote: "I am frankly of the opinion that we are being used by ABC to fill a half-hour of their time when it would be impossible for them to put anything else on the air that could stand up to the competition at that time. Since they are getting our show free of charge, it is rather obvious what they are doing."[37] Unless ABC agreed to change the time, the ECA planned to scout options with other networks or independent stations.

Frank Freeman, ABC's assistant director of film who supervised the series on the network end, reassured Harrison McClung at the MSA office in Paris. He said ABC moved the program to Tuesday at 8:00 because it was the only available timeslot with a Washington, D.C., pickup for the ECA administrator's appearance. The program was moved twice more before ABC canceled it in 1953, and it never earned a significant audience. PA learned that old films gained them nothing with the networks or the television audience. To get noticed, they needed to deliver top policy makers for timely, news-making appearances.

The department's most successful television program during this period grew out of Russell's March 1950 study of the department's use of broadcasting to ease its public relations crisis. Russell undertook to find network series time for a round table program on foreign policy to be produced by the department. When he talked to the networks' Washington, D.C., affiliates, they showed interest but the program could not appear to be a state department production. "All respondents emphasized the need of finding an able moderator who was not identified with the State Department to avoid charges of airing a 'loaded' show."[38] The affiliates particularly feared Republican backlash for giving air time to the Democratic administration. While the program *Overseas Press Club* took a summer hiatus, CBS offered its Sunday evening timeslot to the department for a program called *World Briefing* and then *Diplomatic Pouch*. It would imitate a department briefing session.

Even in so controlled a forum, policy officers resisted public exposure. Assistant Secretary of State for German Affairs Henry Byroade was scheduled for the August 19 show. In the week before the broadcast, Byroade tried to beg off, apparently because he did not want to have to answer questions about German rearmament or the proposed European army. But CBS personnel accommodated this reluctance. "[Barrett] assured Byroade that questions that would be embarrassing could be discussed in advance with Quincy Howell [*sic*] and avoided." Byroade directed his staff to come up with questions and brief answers to be used on the program. One loyal viewer called Byroade's appearance "the best so far."[39]

The PA senior staff wanted Secretary Acheson to appear on the last scheduled episode of *Diplomatic Pouch* on September 10. By August 29, Under Secretary Webb and the White House had approved his participation, but Acheson had not yet been asked, perhaps because he was preparing for a "Big 3" meeting where he would broach the subject of German rearmament. Barrett reminded Webb that the secretary was regarded as "somewhat stiff and aloof" and that an informal television presentation would help offset that image. The perception of candidness might also counter more substantive criticisms. "In the present public opinion and Congressional situation it is most important that the Secretary be given a series of frank questions to which he could give frank answers." Barrett also urged that their delivery of such a high-ranking officer for a CBS show "should be used as a chip in efforts to get CBS to continue series, possibly in some other form or at some other time."[40] (It didn't.) Acheson consented, and Margaret Carter of the Division of Public Liaison and Francis Russell scripted the "frank" questions and answers.

The September 10, 1950, program opened with a voice-over, "What happens abroad, happens to you. The war in Asia is a war on the whole free world of which we are a part, and so foreign affairs are American affairs." The questions from CBS correspondents Charles Collingwood, Edward R. Murrow, and Griffin Bancroft set up the secretary to deliver apparently rehearsed speeches. The correct maps "spontaneously" materialized when his remarks turned to those areas of the world. The broadcast made page one of the *New York Times* the following day with Acheson's prediction that the People's Republic of China would not enter the Korean War.[41]

Accomplished and respected commentators suspended their professional autonomy on *Diplomatic Pouch*. Collingwood asked a rather naive question for a network White House correspondent, "You've often talked about situations of strength. Is that a part of our foreign policy?" Smiling, the usually dour Murrow asked, "What are the odds of us getting into a shooting war with the Soviet Union? Do you think it's inevitable?" Murrow later broached a difficult subject, criticism of the conduct of the Korean War in the press, "even from radio." Four weeks earlier, CBS had suppressed one of Murrow's own broadcasts for being too critical of U.S. policy (see Chapter Four). But rather than asking Acheson to respond to the criticisms, Murrow grinned broadly at the secretary and asked, "What do you do for relaxation and relief from this constant tension?"[42] Presumably the answer to this question was designed to counter the secretary's image as "stiff and aloof." The *New York Times* printed a sidebar to its front page story, "Acheson Is Bearing Up By Forgetting Criticism." This episode of *Diplomatic Pouch* performed doubly well, as a smooth television production and by attracting attention in other media.

Acheson enjoyed playing his role on *Diplomatic Pouch*. Ironically, he deemed that in the future he would prefer to prepare for such appearances with a press-conference style briefing book rather than a script. Barrett agreed but emphasized that this should not open the door to unrestrained debate. "It would be desirable to get the correspondents to agree to bring up no questions they had not raised in the form of queries submitted in advance."[43]

Disaster in Korea

The Korean War presented an even greater public relations crisis for the administration than attacks by Congressional conservatives. When the People's Republic of China decisively intervened in late November 1950, the Truman administration appeared unprepared and bumbling. The initial rush of public support for the war waned from sixty percent approval of U.S. entry in August 1950 to thirty-seven percent in October 1952. Edward Barrett found only one benefit from the war: "It shows up to intelligent people on both sides of the Iron Curtain the rank hypocrisy of the Kremlin's so-called peace initiative."[44]

Barrett formulated measures to shore up support but identified a conflict between domestic and overseas psychological strategy. At home he counseled a show of anticommunist muscle to alleviate the perception that "Washington leadership is utterly confused and sterile. [The American people] are saying, in effect: 'Don't just sit there; do something.'" But for U.S. allies "frightened to death that we are going to bluster into a general war," he prescribed a peacekeeping posture. He proposed a way to bridge the two, especially given the recommendations of NSC-68. "We know we are bound to embark on a huge mobilization program; hence it should be quite possible to use that fact in a way that will meet the psychological crisis we face." The message should emphasize massive armament: "We are not going to be rushed into any foolish international action; we are going to husband our resources; but we are going into a gigantic mobilization in the belief that it is the one way of preserving the peace." PA sold deterrence because it filled the need to appear both belligerent and benign. Barrett recommended that President Truman make a speech presenting the world situation as outlined in NSC-68 and ordering measures to accelerate war production and enlistment. The following week, the president gave a major radio address doing just that.[45]

Early in the war, C. D. Jackson, the *eminence grise* of psychological warfare, made several unsolicited suggestions to Barrett for dramatizing "the coming victory" in Asia and the United States. An unrepentant booster, Jackson first recommended that "the U.S. Government . . . proclaim 'Korea Day,' during which what Koreans we can muster in this country should be on television, should be speechifying, should be dancing in costume." Next, General Alfred Gruenther's son, a captain in a joint Korean-American division, "could be flown back to this country and paraded as an example of Asia-American military unity." The event would be "merchandisable up to the hilt in Asia." If they could add a Negro division, and some marine, navy, and air force personnel, "you would really have something that this country and the rest of the world might get hopped up about." Barrett failed to implement Jackson's suggestions, but this memo demonstrates how Jackson applied overseas propaganda techniques to domestic information problems. Francis Russell, more of an information purist concerned with departmental dignity, probably found the memo entirely inappropriate.[46]

The Public Relations Working Group and Barrett's staff tried to attend to long-term needs as well as brushfire crises in public opinion. The war drew attention away from other arenas in the struggle against communism. Some officers voiced concern that Europe would be left underdefended. To keep the menace of world communism in the public eye, the PRWG advised the senior staff that "it would be beneficial for the Assistant Secretaries to make radio speeches regarding malevolent Communist activities in their areas." Barrett also prepared information contingency plans when truce talks began in 1951 in the event they were succeeded, dragged on, or failed.[47]

By April 1952, with presidential elections approaching, deputy (and acting) ASSPA Howland Sargeant recommended a massive campaign to "correct the trend in public opinion in this country that the whole Korean venture has turned out badly." He recommended a stress on the United Nations' political and military gains, particularly that the war "stopped the aggression and cleared the Republic of Korea of enemy forces," accomplished a great military feat against tremendous odds, showed the power of unity in the free world, and prevented a consolidation of Soviet power in the Far East. Sargeant had long contended that the greatest obstacle to effective state department public relations was the diffusion of responsibility among the ASSPA, the Office of Public Affairs, advisors to the regional bureaus, and special assistants to the secretary and under secretary. He now advised Acheson that the most efficient way to regain public support would be to appoint a committee chaired by Joseph Short, the White House press secretary, with information specialists from the state and defense departments, the Mutual Security Agency, the National Security Council, and the Psychological Strategy Board. Only such a unified group could secure the cooperation of the president, cabinet officers, and members of Congress needed to sustain a massive public relations blitz on the war's successes.[48] Acheson failed to act on Sargeant's recommendation; he was likely more concerned with making policy than with selling it.

Clearer Than Truth

In assessing PA's programs, we can cite a public opinion report prepared for PA by the National Opinion Research Center (NORC) in 1951 describing a troubling paradox. Most Americans approved of most individual U.S. foreign policies, but they distrusted the overall foreign policy of the United States. NORC suggested reasons – that the public approved the principle but not the execution, or that disapproval carried over from domestic policy, or that the public failed to see consistency[49] – all of which danced around the fundamental problem that the Truman administration had irretrievably lost the public trust. PA succeeded in selling their policies but utterly failed to sell themselves.

Edward Barrett resigned in January 1952 after a vicious appropriations battle. Senator William Benton tried to enlist C. D. Jackson to become assistant secretary of state for public affairs, but Jackson laughed, "I would not touch Ed Barrett's job with a 20-foot pole." He cited the fundamental contradiction of an information policy that claimed to be truthful and also to wage psychological war:

> I have always felt that if the U.S. wanted to commit itself to an aggressive, effective propaganda operation, that operation simply could not be centered in the State Department. There is a built-in contradiction in the present situation which I know I don't have to spell out to you. On the other hand, if the most that the U.S. officially wished to commit itself to is news, information, and cultural dissemination, such an operation could remain within the State Department. Today, it is neither one nor the other; hence the present problems and difficulties.

To ease the appropriations struggle, when Barrett left, his job was split in two. Businessman Wilson Compton took charge of the International Information Administration, which was finally moved outside the state department in 1953 as the United States Information Agency (USIA), greatly reducing political friction surrounding the overseas programs. Barrett's deputy Howland Sargeant became assistant secretary for public affairs, a job that was redefined as "staff officer to the Secretary on information matters," more of a public relations adviser than a chief information officer. In the Eisenhower administration, Sargeant became advisor on National Security Affairs, a position also held by C. D. Jackson and Nelson Rockefeller, integrating "what we liked to call in those days the psychological factors" into policy formulation and implementation.[50] Information finally became integral to Cold War policy making but only when distanced from the state department.

PA's selling function became less apologetic under the Republicans, who had so long blasted it under the Democrats. Early in his tenure in the new Republican administration, Sargeant's successor as ASSPA, Philadelphia newspaperman Carl McCardle, showed that the apparent contradiction of his mission with democratic principles would not trouble him. He said, "In the process of operating our domestic information program we will – as we have in the past – be referred to as 'propagandist.' That's a chance we'll have to take." In 1955, C. D. Jackson likewise dismissed the "self-consciousness and fear that any organized attempt at orchestration will be attacked as administration propaganda." Even in a secret paper, Jackson invoked the hyperbolic rationale for uninhibited propaganda. "In the context of the vast and dangerous game which is being played, this is utter nonsense . . . for what we are dealing with is . . . a victory or defeat in the most titanic struggle in which this nation has ever found itself involved."[51] Such pronouncements had become utterly axiomatic, even among those who had first implemented them as a strategy. As Deborah Welch Larson has written, "The requirements of policy legitimation cannot explain why U.S. policy makers internalized their own rhetoric."[52]

This puzzle lies at the heart of the Cold War consensus. Even when studying its most self-conscious designers, we find it tricky to separate deliberate manipulation from avowed doctrine from embedded culture. This seamlessness might suggest authentic belief, but the very formulations of democratic truth and totalitarian distortion that seem so fervently felt became the very rationale that government information officers used to abandon candor as their guiding policy. In their war for hearts and minds, they embellished the truth in order to save it, but they seem to have forgotten that they did so.

CHAPTER FOUR

READY, WILLING, ABLE: TELEVISION RESPONDS TO THE KOREAN CRISIS, 1950–1953

The broadcasting industry rallied to the cause of the Korean War in unprecedented ways. Government officials who privately briefed the broadcasters on the world situation, including the president and the secretaries of state, defense, and commerce, stressed that broadcast news played a crucial role in the outcome of both hot and cold wars, reinforcing the obligation to cooperate at every step. The industry's self-interests dovetailed with the state's immediate needs, and television's cooperation supported the Cold War assertion that the private sector and the public freely supported use of the military to contain communism.

The Truman administration welcomed the broadcasting industry's voluntarism for a variety of reasons. First, centralizing domestic information and morale services outside the government averted the political imbroglios that had plagued the Office of War Information during World War II. Broadcasters' Korean War service protected the executive branch from charges that it propagandized the public or Congress. Above all, the embattled Truman administration welcomed any offer of public relations assistance. Cabinet members used their meetings with broadcasting executives to ask for coverage that fostered wartime solidarity against the communist menace but that also showcased their competence against the partisan and disabling charges of their domestic Republican adversaries. The administration quietly brought broadcasters on board for the war effort with confidential briefings and praise for their patriotism, hoping for more sympathetic treatment.

This chapter describes the extent of the industry's wartime voluntarism, showing how mutual self-interest propelled government–industry cooperation. At the outset of the war, several threats seemed to face the broadcasting industry: a financial crisis, the threat of government seizure of all broadcasting facilities in the interests of national security, and the specter of censorship. The National Association of Broadcasters (NAB) organized the Broadcast Advisory Council (BAC) to work out cooperative resolutions to the problems posed by those threats. The BAC also volunteered to channel and promote official information through an unprecedented public service campaign tying together the Advertising Council, the NAB, and individual stations. As the limited war effort grew less urgent and less popular, broadcasters' support also waned. The industry's voluntarism, though linked to the fight against a mortal enemy, always hinged on the effort's enhancement of its public relations.

A Brief Panic

At the outset of the Korean conflict, the broadcasting industry feared that the war would jeopardize television's commercial development, and even its very existence as a private industry. World War II had suspended the first growth of the industry in the United States. In 1942, television manufacturers began retooling to produce military electronics, the construction of television stations stalled, and many existing stations were summarily silenced for the duration.

In June 1950, when the North Korean army crossed the 38th parallel into South Korea and President Truman committed American troops, broadcasters feared another postponement to the growth of their medium. An array of possible threats to their business, already curtailed by the FCC's freeze on granting new licenses, loomed: a shortage of parts, advertiser flight to radio, or an overall scarcity of consumer goods that would dry up advertising revenue. Industry leaders kept vigilant watch and took proactive measures to ensure that the war would not interfere with their business.

The outbreak of war precipitated an immediate financial crisis. Network stock prices dropped abruptly. *Broadcasting* reported that the stocks of radio and television manufacturers fell because investors feared that profits would suffer in plant conversions to military production. In July, NBC monitored reports that the state department would recommend to the president that he order television plants to convert to radar production.[1] The stocks of the networks whose parent companies did not manufacture receivers dropped also, from fears that advertising revenues might diminish.

Presuming the public would rely on radio for war news as it had during World War II, industry analysts forecast sponsor flight from television. Before the war began, radio advertising revenues were falling while high-priced television time was selling out completely. *Variety*, the daily trade journal of the entertainment industries, headlined the coming of the Korean War as "RADIO'S BIG SECOND CHANCE." In its trademark telegraphic style, *Variety* proclaimed, "Ascendancy of TV as the new giant of show business during the past three years looks certain to be arrested." Contrary to these expectations, NBC's internal studies found that in the first six weeks of the war, radio listening increased but not at the expense of television viewing.[2] Television owners wanted more war news. The initial panic over television's future soon tapered off.

Still, the war would likely create shortages of consumer goods to be advertised, including home electronics. If television manufacturing and sales stalled due to a shortage of electronic parts, "sponsors might question the feasibility of spending TV's heavy coin requirements to reach a limited market, particularly when they themselves might be short on consumer goods." Norge, Inc., a consumer products division of the military contractor Borg-Warner, canceled a $15,000 contract for thirty minutes on NBC because "they felt that this is a bad time to be entering a major advertising effort." But *Variety* reported that this was the only cancellation due to war concerns, and Nescafe immediately bought the Sunday night slot.[3]

Some advertisers did shift their emphasis from selling consumer goods to emphasizing their corporate patriotism. Institutional advertising actually began during World War I, when manufacturers lacked stock but wanted to keep brand names alive. During the Korean War, public affairs television programs took on new appeal for institutional advertisers. In September 1950, the Revere Brass and Copper Corporation bought the panel discussion *Meet the Press*, and Acadia Life Insurance contemplated buying *American Forum of the Air*. Several clients of the McCann-Erickson advertising agency expressed interest in a weekly recap of United Nations activities.[4]

The most serious hindrance to the industry came from the loss of personnel to reserve duty or the draft. By December 1950, NBC had twenty-four men called for reserve or national guard duty, and twenty-seven called by the selective service. But in the end, the rate of television set manufacturing continued to grow during the mobilization, and some manufacturers had foreseen shortages even before the war began. Even eighty percent of the projected 1950 output for new televisions topped 1949 figures. Industry spokesmen agreed that production figures would continue to grow but that prices of new television sets would no longer decline.[5]

In the end, 22 million televisions were sold during the war, bringing the total sold in the United States to 28 million sets, representing nearly half of American homes. The collective income of the four television networks went from a $10 million deficit in 1950 to a $71 million profit in 1953, and broadcasters were acclaimed for the public service they provided during the emergency.[6] All in all, the industry's growth continued apace, but the initial war scares still precipitated bold action.

Voluntarism Defined

One tried and true method for preventing government regulation of business is to form private advisory committees to solve problems without resort to "government bureaucracy." During and just after World War II, as we saw in Chapter One, organizations such as the Business Council and the Council for Economic Development worked closely with federal agencies to develop voluntary business standards. The external threat posed by communist aggression in Korea momentarily rallied this progressive business community to a fever pitch. The number of industry advisory committees spawned by the Korean War indicates the scope of the Cold War consensus between business and the state. At the end of 1950, 68 such committees dispensed private wisdom to public officials; by 1952, 554 groups offered their expertise. The corporate quid pro quo for supporting "limited war"' traded government price controls to prevent crippling inflation for continued rollback of New Deal–style regulation.[7] Broadcasters, who mediated information reaching every other industry, organized early and received special attention from the Truman administration.

From the earliest days of commercial radio, broadcasters preferred to cooperate with government regulators than to be subject to restrictive legislation. Founded in 1922 to protect the rights and interests of the broadcasting industry, the National Association of Broadcasters routinely proposed industry self-regulation, through adherence to NAB codes of practice, as an alternative to mandatory government measures that might curtail corporate prerogative. The industry has followed this pattern in times of both external and internal crisis, from World War II through the quiz show scandals of 1959–1961 and periodic Congressional inquiries into sex and violence in programming beginning in the 1960s. It has promised more public service programming, a family viewing hour, and warnings to precede explicit programs.[8]

The NAB's innovative cooperation with the executive branch during the Korean War consolidated its position as the television industry's primary trade organization. At the outset of the war, only two of the five radio and television networks were affiliated with the NAB. By the end of the war, all the major networks had joined, and station membership had risen. By 1957, one analyst called the NAB "one of the most effective trade associations in the United States."[9]

During the early Cold War, the NAB's self-interested voluntarism took on the urgency of anticommunist mobilization. The industry emphasized its centrality to national security and morale, casting its mobilization in the idiom of patriotic duty. NAB president Justin Miller wrote to Dr. John Steelman, assistant to President Truman (the equivalent of today's chief of staff): "We realize that the essential medium which we represent – capable of conveying to our people, instantly, messages of information, advice and instruction in times of extreme necessity – is so vital to the preservation of our way of life, that anything less than readiness for complete self-mobilization would constitute serious dereliction of duty."[10]

Industry leaders repeatedly pledged their willingness to cooperate with the government in every feasible way. In July 1950, RCA chairman Brigadier General (Army Reserve) David Sarnoff telegraphed his congratulations to President Truman for his initial war speeches to Congress and the American people. Sarnoff pledged RCA's "fullest cooperation" and put the corporation's considerable resources at the president's disposal. Norman Chandler, owner of the *Los Angeles Times* and the CBS affiliate in Los Angeles, KTTV, made an offer to his friend Secretary of Defense Louis Johnson in August 1950. "I would like to make available to our government the facilities and personnel of Television Station KTTV for whatever purpose our government might feel they would best serve." Chandler suggested several services that KTTV could offer, including "trained personnel for research, electronic equipment for development, and programming facilities for civilian defense instruction and for relaying government messages." Johnson found Chandler's "most generous offer . . . indeed heartwarming" and directed two defense agencies, the Joint Armed Forces Public Information Office in Los Angeles and the Department of Defense Research and Development Board, to follow up. Stations in Cincinnati, Columbus, and Washington, D.C., also offered their services and facilities to local defense authorities.[11]

Prior to June 1950, the White House's John Steelman and NAB public relations director Ralph Hardy had discussed plans for a council of broadcasters to participate in military planning. When NAB president Justin Miller contemplated forming such a "Defense Council of Broadcasters," he jotted down the various hostilities within the industry that could hamper its formation: "networks jealous of each other; nets [*sic*] and affiliates at arms length; nets like to pretend 'no unaffiliated'; affiliated and unaffiliated jealous and competitive."[12]

The war would help override these jealousies. The NAB moved to consolidate its position as industry representative by gaining recognition from the executive branch as such. In mid-July 1950, Hardy asked John Steelman for a letter "requesting NAB to head [an] organization [of the] entire radio and TV industries." Steelman consulted with President Truman, who was reportedly "very impressed with NAB's taking leadership and volunteering to take over this job." NAB vice-president Bill Ryan cabled his boss Justin Miller in California that their move succeeded in preempting network mobilization:

> Following some plotting . . . Steelman promised Hardy that from now on NAB will get first consideration in all plans re radio and TV while emergency situation exists. . . . Networks immediately took hold and indicated they would like to take leadership. However, we are way ahead of them, and Steelman's letter settles the issue.

For this end-run to succeed, it had to appear that the White House had approached the NAB. Miller's notes included the strategy to "advise President of our availability and await instructions" and that Steelman's letter should "speak in terms of 'government request for action.'" Steelman played along generously, writing for public consumption, "I hope you will not consider it presumptuous if I ask that the National Association of Broadcasters take immediate steps to organize the entire broadcasting industry in some manner in which it would be instantly available to the government as required." An NAB press release, dated the same day as Steelman's letter and reproducing it, previews the formation and function of the council. Top officials recognized that the impetus came from the NAB.[13]

Much later Steelman still claimed that organizing the industry for wartime service had been his own idea. He portrayed it as an effort to keep the public apprised and to prevent the spread of rumors: "I foresaw the power that radio and television was [sic] going to have in America, the influence it was going to have. I thought there ought to be an organization that paid attention to responding correctly to that big responsibility. It should have standards, etc. about the facts." But at the time, privately, Steelman minimized the significance of the NAB group from the White House's vantage. When the federal security administrator suggested likewise unifying foreign language broadcasters as had been done during

World War II, Steelman brushed it off. "The meeting we had with the National Association of Broadcasters has been overemphasized, I fear. Ever since [World War II], the NAB has sent out regular mailings to all radio stations in support of various government programs. The object of this meeting was to tighten up the whole operation."[14]

Divergence between the aims of the principals led to disagreements over the BAC's function. The NAB sought to strengthen itself through preemptive public relations, whereas the White House wanted an expedient means of disseminating information. The first draft plan for the BAC, prepared by Bill Ryan, proposed six advisory panels made up of industry executives "acting as liaison groups between the government and the broadcasters in circulating quickly and effectively to stations information about Government needs, policies, programs, etc." They included panels for civilian and military manpower, security, civil mobilization, informational services, and morale services. But the White House worried that these panels would have nothing to do and would "detract considerably from the enthusiasm" of being involved in the war effort. Jackson proposed instead one large committee that could appoint subcommittees as the need arose. The NAB submitted a plan for five slightly different panels and a distinguished advisory board in late September,[15] but most of the time the group acted as a whole.

On August 7 and 8, 1950, the twenty-seven–member NAB board convened in Washington, D.C. They met with Steelman and Jackson at the White House, and with FCC chairman Wayne McCoy. At both meetings, the officials assured the industry representatives that no restrictions would be imposed on broadcasters beyond the voluntary measures implemented during World War II. NAB president Miller praised Steelman for his "recognition of the principle that voluntary effort by [public] media during time of emergency is the fundamental pattern to pursue in a democracy." Jackson specified that civil defense or censorship measures affecting broadcasters would be formulated "only after a lot of conferences with a lot of people, including the broadcasters."[16]

Given these assurances, the NAB board unanimously passed a resolution declaring the broadcasting industry "ready, able and willing" to support the government's national security aims:

> Whereas, broadcasting has a definite and unique function in the pattern of national defense and,
>
> Whereas, the broadcasters are fully cognizant of their essential service and responsibility voluntarily to perform that function as evidenced by the industry

record during World War II which has been strongly attested by the President and other high Government officials,

Therefore, be it resolved that the broadcasting industry is now in every respect ready, able and willing to take its full part in effectuating all measures necessary to insure the national security and to achieve those objectives to which our country is committed.[17]

At the August 7 and 8 meetings, the board also began to consider the composition of the Broadcasters' Advisory Council. Justin Miller appointed the board, which included himself as NAB president, the presidents of the Radio-Television Manufacturers Association, the Television Broadcasters Association, the National Association of Educational Broadcasters, and the presidents of the five major radio and television networks. On November 17, 1950, Miller appointed an additional ten members, broadcast station operators from around the country. Miller also appointed NAB public relations director Ralph Hardy to be the council's secretary. Hardy already served on the Advertising Advisory Committee to the secretary of commerce and on the board of directors of the Advertising Council.[18]

Other industry groups resisted the constitutive power taken by the NAB, claiming that the council did not represent non-NAB members. The vice-president of WTOP in Washington, D.C., an unaffiliated station, wrote to John Steelman that although only half of the nation's commercial radio stations were affiliated with the NAB, thirteen out of fourteen station presidents serving on the BAC came from NAB stations. The National Association of Radio News Directors also asked for representation on the council. By January 1951, the BAC had tabled requests for expansion of the group until "more definite specifications of the functions of the BAC are worked out."[19] Before any of the unrepresented groups mounted a substantial challenge to the BAC, it had fulfilled its goal of consolidating the NAB's position as industry leader, and the domestic war effort was dwindling with the stalemate in Korea. No one pursued a battle over membership in an outmoded organization.

To Withstand Attack

Perhaps the most alarming threat to broadcasting early in the war stemmed from the strategic importance of the frequencies. Many people feared an imminent invasion of U.S. territory and noted that enemy planes could use broadcast signals for navigation. As operators of such sensitive electronic equipment during wartime, broadcasters were subject to federal seizure. Expanding government regulation gravely concerned industry executives because it could last beyond the immediate war crisis and curtail corporate control.

During World War II, the NAB leadership had likewise feared that the government would use that conflict as an excuse to "move in" on private broadcasting. Two industry veterans wrote: "The future of American radio under free enterprise was clearly at stake." This threat had resurfaced in the months before the Cold War turned hot in Korea. President Harry Truman appointed a Temporary Communications Policy Board in February 1950 by executive order. He charged it to study the allocation of the frequencies and to propose international communications policy and guidelines for the relationship between government and private communications operators. The board was composed of respected engineers, including the presidents of the Massachusetts and California Institutes of Technology. From January to June 1951, *Broadcasting* and *Variety* reported rumors that the board would recommend the establishment of a permanent agency on the level of the FCC to allocate broadcast frequencies. In January 1951, however, the Temporary Communications Policy Board "suddenly put a lid on information about its activities."[20] Presumably, the BAC had taken up its concerns in the emergency, and no such agency was created.

President Truman specified broadcasters' civil defense responsibilities in September 1950 with the publication of the comprehensive report, "United States Civil Defense." In the event of an atomic attack on the United States, the report called upon radio and television to warn and aid the target area. The media were also asked to inform and educate the public in advance of an attack as to the importance of civil defense and cooperation with civil defense agencies. However, the proposed legislation that accompanied the president's report, the "Model State Civil Defense Act," provided for state seizure of communications facilities in an emergency. The apparent blanket powers that this item gave the president alarmed broadcasters.[21] The networks individually and the BAC committed themselves to cooperation with the government, but they lobbied hard against the bill.

The potential enemy threat to broadcasting facilities provided an opportunity for members of Congress to trumpet their anticommunist vigilance. When the Model State Civil Defense Act reached the Senate, legislators called attention to the "serious dangers" that could result from enemy seizure of media in an attack. Senator Brien McMahon (D–CT) warned, "It is quite possible that Communists even now are organized to seize a ra-

dio station when an enemy attack may occur, and to broadcast messages
generating panic and chaos among the populace. . . . An irresponsible and
reckless use of communications facilities could greatly impair our capacity
to successfully withstand a surprise assault."[22] McMahon and others
played upon public fears of infiltration and propaganda. The bill stalled in
Congress.

The People's Republic of China entered the war in late November
1950, ending hopes for a quick victory and reigniting domestic defense
planning. In January 1951, Assistant Secretary of Defense Marx Leva
asked for legislation giving the president broad powers to control radio
and television during emergencies, or "periods of critical international relationships," to prevent the use of signals as navigation aids by enemy
planes. The "Electromagnetic Radiation Control Act" shortly came before
the Senate Interstate and Foreign Commerce Committee. The NAB and its
member stations reacted fiercely to this proposal. Agreeing to find a technical solution to the signal problem, one television executive wrote: "It
seems to me most extraordinary that anybody in the U.S. should talk of
closing down broadcasting in the event of war." Senator Edwin C. Johnson (D–CO), chairman of the Senate Commerce Committee, said he was
"not convinced the legislation is good or necessary and that he would in-
sist on full hearings,"[23] which were conducted before Johnson's committee
on February 21.

Justin Miller, a former federal judge, attacked the language of the bill,
which granted the president power to control broadcasting "in time of
war, national emergency, or whenever the President deems it advisable in
the interest of national security." If used in a time other than war, Miller
argued, the bill "would probably be unconstitutional, as a violation of the
First Amendment." He proposed slight amendments to Section 606 of the
Federal Communications Act, which served as the guideline for government powers over broadcasting during World War II. Miller also proposed
that station owners should be compensated if their equipment was "controlled, used, or closed," but he did not convince lawmakers. NAB engineering chief Neal McNaughton and public relations director Ralph
Hardy also testified before the Senate Commerce Committee. Turning the
pervasive anticommunist rhetoric to their advantage, they argued that
shutting down broadcasting stations would give the enemy an opportunity
to use the frequencies themselves. "Enemy agents, planning in advance,
could establish secret transmitting stations throughout the country. These
could be planned to provide enemy planes with directions needed to send
them to their targets."[24] They proposed instead a cooperative effort be-

tween the government and broadcasters to work out a signal pattern that would confuse enemy attempts to navigate by them.

The language of the bill, adopted on October 24, 1951 as Public Law 200, finally gave the president powers to regulate or close stations "upon proclamation of war, disaster, etc. and if he deems it to be in the public interest." Yet several agreements softened that threat. Two months later, during a week of BAC meetings, President Truman issued an executive order amending the law to prohibit the government from interfering with program content or from using or removing any equipment if stations were seized.[25]

The problem of enemy navigation was solved by a cooperative effort between the FCC, the Air Defense Command, the Office of Civil Defense, and broadcasting executives and engineers. It was called CONELRAD (Control of Electromagnetic Radiation). The plan was announced to broadcast licensees by the FCC in April 1951, including the provision that the procedure would be overseen by a joint government–industry Board of War Communications similar to the one created during World War II. Asked by station operators whether participation was fully voluntary, FCC officials admitted that "stations have a choice of going along with the plan or shutting down should an air raid occur." By December 1952, 1,000 stations had volunteered to participate and had spent $1.5 million of their own funds on equipment. After receiving approval from the secretary of defense and the chairman of the National Resources Security Board, the plan was successfully tested in May 1953. When the Air Defense Command proclaimed an air raid alert, FM and TV stations would go off the air, and AM stations would stagger five to fifteen seconds of broadcasting on the same two frequencies, thwarting attempts to navigate on continuous signals.[26]

The industry prevented the imposition of government regulation by voluntarily contributing extensive corporate resources to the military effort. Like corporate leaders in virtually every industry, broadcasting executives entered a discreet symbiosis with their government counterparts, as long as they remained in control of corporate assets.[27]

Asking for Censorship

Industry representatives worked with military officials on another potential threat that the war posed to network operations: censorship. Both officials and broadcasters characterized censorship as a security issue; they both sought to prevent disclosure of information useful to the enemy.

Yet throughout American history, war journalists have rarely disclosed classified military information that endangered American troops. Dean Rusk, secretary of state for the Kennedy and Johnson administrations, later could "recall no disclosure of national security information by a reporter that led to serious harm to the nation." As the editorialist for the print trade journal *Editor and Publisher* wrote, "American newspapermen are Americans first and newspapermen second."[28] Broadcasters have supported national security policy even more steadfastly than have print journalists.

At the beginning of the Korean conflict, General Douglas MacArthur gave the responsibility for determining whether or not military information was classified to the journalists in the field. Lacking consistent guidelines, correspondents daily had to choose between withholding and disclosing sensitive information or between getting scooped and getting thrown out of Korea. Divulging military secrets was not the only grounds for getting thrown out. The high command also forbade "criticism of command decisions or of the conduct of Allied soldiers on the battlefield." *Editor and Publisher* remarked in July 1950, "It makes a pretty impossible and ridiculous situation when there are no censorship limitations on war correspondents but they are told they might be silenced if they write something that headquarters doesn't like." Yet the military was satisfied. When MacArthur reflected on this period of voluntary censorship, he praised the press corps' restraint: "I have never seen the desired balance between public information and military security so well achieved and preserved as in the course of the Korean campaign."[29]

The state department's Public Relations Working Group, as well as a committee of newspaper and broadcasting executives from the American Society of Newspaper Editors and the National Association of Broadcasters, recommended adopting a voluntary censorship code based on the Office of Censorship's guidelines from World War II, which left responsibility with each correspondent. At the outset of World War II, the radio branch of the war department had asked the NAB to call together industry representatives to formulate a voluntary censorship code. Broadcasters, print journalists, generals, and information officers all praised the voluntary "velvet glove" system implemented during World War II, supervised by Byron Price's Office of Censorship. The broadcasting division of the Office of Censorship never employed more than six people at a time, attesting to the cooperation it received.[30]

But the situation on the ground in Korea in July and August 1950 made voluntary cooperation impracticable. The Department of Defense provided only one phone line for more than 200 accredited American reporters. The reporting of defeats suffered by the United Nations forces into September led military information officers to complain that the coverage was excessively critical, especially of command decisions. Army public information officer Colonel Marion P. Nichols charged correspondents with "lack of decency, honesty, and regard for procedure," as well as "inaccurate and irresponsible reporting." Two wire service reporters were sent back to Tokyo for "reorientation."[31]

The BAC reminded John Steelman at the White House to include them in any censorship planning. "Broadcasters who know and understand their medium's influence for good certainly comprehend the perils inherent in its use. They understand it better than anyone else. They have demonstrated this understanding through the application of voluntary censorship in a previous conflict. In the field of security, therefore, it is essential that media be consulted before steps are taken."[32]

Voluntary censorship left room for disputes between correspondents and their editors over what constituted damaging reports. When even the most seasoned and patriotic war correspondents could not muster the support that had prevailed in World War II, network management resorted to self-censorship. The dean of news broadcasters, CBS's Edward R. Murrow, traveled to Korea in mid-July and found nothing that resembled World War II. His CBS colleague Bill Downs greeted him, looking shaggy and yelling, "Go back! Go back! It ain't our kind of war!" Murrow was unprepared for the confusion of a civil war where he could not clearly identify the enemy. The brutality (six American journalists died in Korea in July 1950 alone) and the refugees shocked him. One night Murrow and three colleagues, along with their Korean drivers, were held at gunpoint for several hours by a squad of American marines who were convinced that the journalists were North Korean infiltrators. Only the recognition of Murrow's voice by their commanding officer saved their lives. Friendly fire caused two deaths that night.[33]

Even so, at the outset of the crisis, Murrow's radio broadcasts espoused Cold War orthodoxy: "If southern Korea falls, it is only reasonable to expect . . . that there will be other and bolder ventures." His biographer Ann Sperber captures Murrow's point of reference, "Asia, 1950, viewed through the lenses of Europe, 1938 . . . South Korea as a sort of Asian Czechoslovakia." But Murrow reported each strategic failure and interviewed shell-shocked troops. A rumor circulated that MacArthur had petitioned CBS to remove him from Korea.[34]

In mid-August, Murrow stopped in Tokyo on his way home for the start of the September broadcast season. His last report from Asia contrasted optimistic reports from Washington forecasting an early conclusion to the war with dire assessments from the field. Mindful of MacArthur's prohibitions, Murrow began, "This is a most difficult broadcast to do. I have never believed that correspondents who move in and out of the battle area, engage in privileged conversations with commanders and with troops, and who have access to public platform [sic] should engage in criticism of command decisions or of commanders while the battle is in progress." He then described a "meaningless" offensive that cost hundreds of lives and drained vital supplies. "Experienced officers, some of them wearing stars, called it folly. . . . This was not a decision that was forced upon us by the enemy. Our command took it, because, in the words of one officer who was in a position to know – 'We decided we needed a victory.'"

He concluded:

> But when we start moving through dead valleys, through villages to which we have put the torch by retreating, what then of the people who live there? They have lived on the knife edge of despair and disaster for centuries. Their pitiful possessions have been consumed in the flames of war. Will our occupation of that flea-bitten land lessen, or increase, the attraction of Communism?[35]

When the story came over the wire in New York, Ed Chester, the CBS director of news, took it upstairs to confer with CBS chairman William Paley, president Frank Stanton, and corporate legal counsel. Someone on Murrow's staff called Chester's attention to members of Congress making similar statements. On the Senate floor, Republican Styles Bridges said that people will be "appalled when they know the truth."

"It's killed," Chester pronounced, on returning to the newsroom, for violating MacArthur's prohibition of criticizing command decisions, and for giving comfort and propaganda to the enemy. In addition, Chester questioned the reliability of Murrow's sources, "casting doubt where it had never been cast before."[36]

Murrow drafted a letter of resignation but decided not to send it. CBS killed three other cables that week, filed by Bill Downs and Bill Costello, on MacArthur's censorship and other defense department information policies. Lacking explicit military guidelines, network owners resorted to self-censorship to avoid charges of aiding and abetting the enemy. *Newsweek* aired the discontent at CBS, captioning a grim picture of Murrow, "Censorship started at home."[37]

The situation was untenable and occasioned one of the strangest actions in the history of war journalism. One month into the war, the 700-member Overseas Press Club and many senior correspondents actually requested the imposition of formal censorship.[38] The correspondents' need for clear guidelines on the classification of military information outweighed their reluctance to submit their dispatches to formal review.

Then in September, before the army responded, conflicts over allegedly negative reporting diminished. The war turned around with the spectacular and successful Inchon harbor invasion masterminded by MacArthur. The BAC censorship panel was defined as once again "pursuing aggressively the program for a voluntary type of censorship, should any become necessary."[39] But when the People's Republic of China entered the war in November, ending MacArthur's "Home by Christmas" campaign, army–press tensions once again escalated. Criticism of the president and senior military staff mounted as the United Nations forces retreated to the Pusan perimeter on the southern tip of the Korean peninsula during the first two weeks of December.

At that demoralizing moment, Secretary of Defense George Marshall invited representatives of the three largest news services, the American Society of Newspaper Editors, and the BAC to the Pentagon to discuss "the best means to handle news coverage of the combat zone to eliminate stories of value to the enemy." On December 18, Justin Miller, Ralph Hardy, and Robert K. Richards of the NAB, along with nine representatives of the print media, met with the secretary of defense, the director of the Office of Public Information in the defense department and the army's chief of information, to discuss the imposition of formal censorship in Korea. The industry representatives echoed the Overseas Press Club's request for censorship, resolving that "the security of information from the combat area is the responsibility of the military,"[40] not correspondents in the field, their editors, or their companies' executives.

MacArthur later defended his information policies by claiming that the participants at that meeting "made it unequivocally clear that military censorship should be imposed." The general added, "It is indeed a screwy world . . . when a soldier fighting to preserve freedom of the press finds himself opposed by the press itself."[41] Veteran Korea correspondents, especially those working for the wire services, reflected that although censorship violated their first amendment sensibilities, it eased the daily struggle to get their stories out under impossible conditions.[42]

On December 19, MacArthur created a press advisory division to help correspondents check security clearance. The next day he announced that

all print stories, broadcasts, and photographs concerning military operations would be screened in Korea or Tokyo before dispatch. By December
26, full censorship was in effect for stories originating at Eighth Army
headquarters.[43]

Whether or not reporters found their jobs easier, the effect of formal
censorship on war news was not to increase security but to give the military more control over content. The censors deleted not only military information that might compromise the war effort; they also excised "comments indicating a low morale or poor efficiency on the part of United
Nations troops," the word "retreat," and any information that would "in-
jure the morale of our forces" or "embarrass the United States, its allies or
neutral countries."[44] In a cold war, their reasoning went, security means
eliminating not only classified information but embarrassing information;
in such a propaganda war, good morale is itself a victory as well as a
means to victory.

The threat of censorship, like the other threats that broadcasters faced
during the war, was resolved by consultation rather than edict. But censorship, unlike financial hardship or government takeover, was enacted
rather than averted.

The Defense Bulletin

During World War II, the OWI chose and prioritized the government's information needs, and the Advertising Council, among others, carried out
the campaigns. The council, rather than the OWI, would serve as a precedent and model for the BAC, and its status would be preserved. The BAC,
like the Advertising Council, "was dedicated as much to showing ad
power and shoring up a shaky political position as it was to the selfless
public service it proclaimed." When he formed the BAC, Justin Miller immediately consulted Theodore Repplier, a founder and president of the
Advertising Council.[45]

The White House also saw the BAC as an efficient vehicle for distributing information without resort to a central government agency like the
OWI. In 1950, the state department's foreign and domestic information
agencies together with the Advertising Council administered most of the
OWI's former functions. Steelman's assistant Charles Jackson (not to be
confused with C. D. Jackson, then serving as publisher of *Fortune*), an
OWI veteran, served as the government's liaison to the Advertising Council. Jackson felt that war information could be handled by just a little
more coordination between the information directors of individual de-

partments on the government side and through the BAC at the station level.[46]

Steelman and Jackson hoped that broadcasters would distribute information on war production, civilian and military recruiting, and civil defense. They could help both in small ways, by preventing shortages of specific war materials, and in large ways, to shore up morale. In return, the White House promised to centralize government public relations, which would result in better cooperation from senior officials as well as a more coherent public information campaign. According to the NAB's minutes, Jackson proposed a simple quid pro quo:

> The Government will undertake to "control the brass," if the broadcasters will control the civilians. He said they realized the desire of the "brass," both military and otherwise, to put the best foot forward in order to secure a good public opinion; that sometimes there is serious competition between different governmental agencies and that it is necessary for overall control to be exercised in order that there be no talking about things "that ain't in the book."[47]

In other words, Jackson would use the White House's authority to secure cooperation from the state and defense departments if the broadcasters would get station managers to whip up morale with a flurry of public service advertising and war programming.

The NAB envisioned a more ambitious reworking of government–broadcast relationships under their control, but the White House kept them in check. Jackson responded promptly to the initial draft proposal for several ambitious BAC panels with the message that many of the proposed relationships were already in place. "Currently, all networks are in almost daily contact with all Government departments. Certainly this relationship should not be disturbed." He also noted that individual agencies were already supplying networks and stations with programs. "The most important thing this committee can do is to make sure that the various messages appear on the air. This would involve personal contact with hundreds of station managers and definitely tying them into the operation."[48]

At its initial White House meeting, the NAB board agreed to issue a regular *Defense Bulletin*. Jackson would direct the old OWI task of gathering information from government agencies that the White House wanted publicized. The NAB's public affairs department would distribute it to all stations, whether they belonged to the NAB or not. They expected extensive assistance from the Advertising Council in developing the texts of public service announcements. The BAC adapted the council's criteria for weighing proposed campaigns. The project should be nonpartisan, not designed to influence legislation, national in scope, and serious and important enough to justify national play.[49]

Each *Defense Bulletin* bore the NAB seal with a ribbon running through it, inscribed, "America's Broadcasters, Ready, Willing, Able." One issue, dated September 25, 1950, and titled "Guide for Public Service Activity on Behalf of Defense," addressed four issues: armed forces volunteers, United States savings bonds, the "Crusade for Freedom," and United Nations Day. A brief analysis of each "problem" preceded suggestions for public service activities and scripts for public service announcements. To promote savings bonds ("saving for a sunnier day," "saving for your future independence"), the *Bulletin* also offered several series for local broadcast and sponsorship featuring celebrity bond pitches. The issues of the *Defense Bulletin* extant in the NAB Library, Justin Miller's papers, and the Truman Library highlight the NAB's voluntarism as much as they provide a guide to public service on behalf of defense. One issue chronicles the formation of the BAC; another reports on a civil defense drill conducted by New Jersey broadcasters at their own expense.[50]

By December 1950, it was clear that the BAC would not approach even the limited filtering function that the official OWI had performed. The Departments of State, Commerce, and Agriculture, as well as the marines, navy, army, and coast guard, still sent requests for public service announcements directly to stations.[51] Although a voluntary arrangement avoided the pitfalls of an official information agency, it could not command the participation of all the federal bureaus looking for publicity.

The intent of those present at the August board meetings was to publish the bulletin at least three times monthly, but it never reached that goal. The latest reference to it that I found is a memorandum prepared for the September 22, 1951, edition.[52] By then, the war had become a bitter stalemate, and the industry's voluntarism no longer seemed so necessary, or even desirable. Given the Truman administration's plummeting popularity, continuing association brought broadcasters no public relations benefits.

We Must Unite Our Forces

The personal reputations of Harry Truman and Dean Acheson were tied to the success of the war effort, and by late 1953, none of the three enjoyed wide support. Senior government officials appreciated the gathering of broadcasters at BAC meetings as an opportunity to give veiled comments on the fairness of their own coverage. They stressed the gravity of the international situation and asked the broadcasters to build public morale by instilling confidence in the nation's leaders. Again and again they stressed that giving air time to the administration's critics undermined the war effort. Morale had become a partisan political issue.

In the crisis atmosphere of mid-December 1950, the BAC met with an array of high government officials "in order that we can understand more thoroughly those national problems in which broadcasting can contribute its assistance as an industry." The council began at 10:15 A.M. at the state department with a meeting with Secretary of State Dean Acheson. Acheson began with the sentence, "We are facing a situation of possible 'all-out' war," and he argued that the attack in Korea showed that the Soviet Union was willing to use deadly force in dealing with the West. After a lengthy briefing on the USSR's intentions in Europe and Asia, he concluded by pleading for national support of the president and his cabinet in wartime. He called for circling the wagons:

> What we have to realize is that we live in a time of very great danger, we cannot run away from it, we can't appease it. What we must do is roll back our sleeves and go to work. It's easy to criticize the other fellow and to attack the Administration and the Cabinet. The point is that the President was elected by the people, and the Cabinet selected by the President is the best we have got now – poor things – and I think it is important that we let them get on with the job. We must not let ourselves say things to frighten one another. We must unite our forces to face the grave dangers that threaten us.

An NAB press release dutifully reported that Acheson "solicited the aid of broadcasters in relating the character of the world situation to the nation's listeners in truthful, dispassionate fashion."[53]

Acheson's aides followed his briefing with a request for the speedy creation of "methods to create closer liaison between state department activities and the nation's broadcast media." The department's public affairs staff followed up with a report saying that BAC could best serve them by giving more air time to senior officials. That same week, NBC made a generous offer to give Acheson thirty minutes on its radio and television networks. The state department's public affairs staff found the session so successful that they recommended quickly scheduling an additional meeting with more broadcasters and another with "top flight" print editors and publishers.[54] The senior staff treated these meetings as a personal public relations tour.

The council next met with President Truman in the Oval Office for twenty minutes. The president reassured the broadcasters that he anticipated no controls of the media beyond the voluntary measures in place during World War II. Like Acheson, he asked that the industry do their best to preserve the high morale of the American people, by promoting rather than undermining confidence in their leaders. "He expressed the opinion that the people do not mistrust him, but when [journalists] question the loyalty and motives of those who serve with him, they are undermining him. Broadcasters could do much, he thought, by being objective in their reporting of events, and in presenting both sides of every story."[55] No senior officer showed enough pique as to call their coverage unfair but rather asked for more loyal and patriotic war news.

The meetings continued with lunch at the Department of Defense, hosted by the newly appointed director of the Office of Public Information, Clayton Fritchey, a former reporter for the *New York Times* and editor of the *New Orleans Times-Picayune*. Secretary of Defense George Marshall briefly joined the group to address the importance of morale on the home front as well as among the armed forces. Justin Miller had written to Marshall in advance, asking for a few minutes to receive his advice on how to serve the military better. "It seems essential at this time that this great and swift medium of mass communication should place its services at the disposal of those who are in the front lines of defending our nation." The secretary dwelled on the broadcasters' role in fostering unity and morale. He gave homage to freedom of the press but expressed concern about giving too much information to the enemy. He said, "We must learn how to preserve these things without letting them destroy us."[56] This meeting occurred during the same week that ASNE, BAC, and wire-service representatives asked for formal censorship in the combat theater.

In return for their voluntary efforts, broadcasters received exclusive information. In an off-the-record session after the meeting with Marshall, army, navy, and air force information officers briefed the council on the current military situation in Korea. They screened unreleased films of warfare, including captured Russian air force flight films. The council then moved on to the Department of Commerce, where they met with Secretary of Commerce Sawyer and the administrator of the National Production Authority, William H. Harrison. Both stressed the need to bolster confidence in public officials and asked for ongoing contact with the group. The BAC met briefly in executive session at the end of the day, concluding that restraint should be exercised in setting up channels for official information. They agreed to reconvene shortly.[57]

The BAC performed quite an array of services during the Korean conflict. It worked out a voluntary solution to securing broadcasting facilities from enemy attack, consulted on the imposition of formal censorship in the combat theater, and created a voluntary system for the distribution of war information. Its most crucial legacy is that it helped avert the reenactment of an official wartime information agency, proving that corporate voluntarism sufficed as a method for disseminating domestic propaganda that was still formulated by the state. The most publicly visible manifestation of that voluntarism is chronicled in the next chapter.

CHAPTER FIVE

CLOSER TO YOUR GOVERNMENT: THE WHITE HOUSE AND NBC PRESENT *BATTLE REPORT – WASHINGTON*, 1950–1953

The North Korean invasion of South Korea in June 1950 actually brought a feeling of relief to many Americans. It clarified communist intentions, which often seemed shrouded in secrecy. Now a war could be declared and an enemy vanquished. Joseph C. Harsch, Washington bureau chief of the *Christian Science Monitor* for twenty years, observed, "Never before in that time have I felt such a sense of relief and unity pass through the city."[1] But simple victory receded like a carrot on a stick. Within weeks, United Nations forces fell back to the southernmost Pusan perimeter. General Douglas MacArthur's bold waterborne invasion at Inchon turned the tide of the war in September 1950, but his insistence on bringing the war to the doorstep of the People's Republic of China brought its army into the conflict in late November. President Truman and Secretary of State Dean Acheson bore the brunt of the public's frustration with waging limited war. When Truman dismissed MacArthur for insubordination in April 1951, anti-administration talk escalated calls for impeachment.

As discussed in Chapter Four, television broadcasters expected the public to turn to their radios and newspapers for war news out of habit from World War II. Until the summer of 1950, even though television executives "have beaten their brains and tapped their tills until it hurt," according to *Editor and Publisher*, "folks just seemed to prefer variety entertainment on the screens and news in newspapers or via radio."[2] Korea provided television news with a chance to prove itself. In addition to their behind-the-scenes support through the Broadcasters Advisory Council, the networks rushed to perform voluntary public service by adding war news programs to their schedules. These programs clearly and loudly defended the war effort. The administration's critics also found ready access to the airwaves on regularly scheduled programs, yet an array of special series dedicated themselves to shoring up morale. NBC's television offering *Battle Report – Washington* was an official weekly report to the nation on the progress of the war and was an undeniable public relations boon to the besieged Truman administration.

Special programming on both broadcast media took a distinct tone and approach from World War II news. The contest between armies provided some breaking news, but the war did not play out in a series of dramatic battles. The coverage instead emphasized the clash of ideologies between the United States and the Soviet Union, which was not a declared belligerent in the war. It demonized a subhuman enemy, showcased American efforts to contain the communist threat, and advertised the beneficence of American institutions. No one would mistake these broadcasts for objective news reports, but very few critics called for a more evenhanded approach. The Truman administration hoped to unify the nation against an external enemy and lead the nation in war to save the future of Western civilization.

The networks clearly stated their patriotic purposes. CBS produced a radio program entitled *One Nation Indivisible* that premiered on August 20, 1950. CBS president Frank Stanton announced, "In these broadcasts we feel it is important to discuss the conditions which the American people must face as our country prepares itself for an indefinite period of partial or total mobilization and the sacrifices that they must make in order to strengthen themselves for this ordeal."[3] The program's declared purpose was not to distribute objective information but to strengthen the American will to fight.

On television, CBS likewise aired *The Facts We Face* beginning in August 1950. It started as a five-week series to chart the progress of the war in Korea but soon broadened to cover all aspects of U.S. mobilization in the Cold War; it lasted for a year. CBS president Frank Stanton wrote to John Steelman, assistant to President Truman, that the goal of this series was to demonstrate U.S. military strength to unify the public and to deter U.S. enemies. It aimed to show the specific steps that the government was taking "to make the nation's defenses so strong that no enemy will dare to strike." The White House routinely approved the show's scripts.[4]

NBC showcased Pentagon announcements on the progress of the war every day, from 5:15 to 5:30 on their radio network, to an estimated audience of 20 million listeners.[5] The DuMont network imitated *Battle Report* with its series *Pentagon*, featuring interviews with defense officials detailing their efforts toward U.S. security. *Pentagon* aired on Sunday nights at 8:30 and on Mondays at 8:00; it lasted for a year and half beginning in the spring of 1951. Television's war coverage adhered closely to the administration's line.

Good Play

NBC beat its competitors soundly in the race to provide high-profile war news on television with *Battle Report – Washington*. The program was produced in the White House office of John Steelman, who appeared at the beginning and end of each episode. He began by announcing that its purpose was to give "the people of the United States a firsthand account of what the Federal Government is doing in the worldwide battle against communism." He introduced a broad array of federal officials who briefed the public on every aspect of the war effort and on what was expected of the citizenry. On the premiere, Steelman promised the show would "bring you closer to your government. . . . Through the magic of television, we hope we can bring millions of our citizens in close touch with official Washington. You will both *hear* and *see* the men who are working *for you.* . . . These intimate meetings with government officials are indeed – Democracy in Action."[6]

The program employed varied formats, from stock government documentaries to news footage shot specifically for the show. Steelman's staff assembled officials connected with the mobilization, and government information officers wrote their scripts. NBC provided technical support at a cost of $1,000–$6,000 per episode. The program lasted more than two years. Its ratings varied with its time slot (first Sunday at 8:00, then Friday at 9:30) but grew steadily with the number of TV markets it reached. In late 1950, the government estimated that *Battle Report – Washington* achieved a local rating of 10 in each of 22 markets, or an average audience of 50,000 homes, which officials deemed "quite good for this type of show." It reached 36 markets by mid-1951. NBC estimated that with thirty percent of sets in use, twenty-five percent of those would be tuned to *Battle Report*, with 2.4 viewers at each set, for an audience of 1.8 million.[7]

Steelman recalled the genesis of *Battle Report – Washington*: "The idea was to get people in the know to appear with me every Sunday. I interviewed generals, admirals, people from the State Department. It was a very popular program. At the time, it was the longest feature of its type ever on TV." He claimed that he originated the idea for the series and that it stemmed from the success of annual White House conferences where senior officials briefed civic and business leaders on the state of the nation. These meetings were a perfect emblem of state–government cooperation in the early postwar years but also a straightforward public relations practice for the Truman administration. The guests felt close to power and were less likely to lambaste the administration publicly if they saw themselves as insiders. *TV Guide* chirped about Steelman, "Sold on the idea of an informed America, he recognized television as the perfect mass communications medium to permit – not a mere 100 – but literally millions of Americans to attend his White House conference, not annually but weekly." The program would personalize the government and let the public see competent officials in command of their areas. *TV Guide* concurred that it worked, advising its readers, "You owe it to yourself to see *Battle Report*. It doesn't indulge in flag-waving, but we guarantee you'll feel a new pride in your country – and your government."[8] In the context of *Battle Report – Washington*, it is impossible to separate Steelman's commendable public service from his promotional expertise.

NBC also undertook the series for the praise it brought the network. Internal NBC correspondence indicates that the idea for the series originated not with Steelman but with network executives. The successful premiere "fully justifies our interest in going to the government with this proposal. In addition we got a good play in the news sections as a follow up on the show." In periodic reviews of the program's performance, executives first and foremost evaluated its public relations yield. In September, the program "seemed to reaching some of its public relations objectives" when a member of the House of Representatives read praise for NBC's public service into the *Congressional Record*. It reads in part:

> Mr. Speaker, I know of no agency of Government, research institute, or any other type of private concern in these United States that is making a greater contribution to the vast problem of informing our people as to current affairs than the National Broadcasting Company is doing in projecting this series of broadcasts. . . . The show is a definite must for all Americans – completely frank, unbiased, bipartisan, it is a news event broadcasted by video by Americans and for Americans. . . . The contributions that the National Broadcasting Co. is making to this nation become crystal clear.

The program merited nine mentions in the *Congressional Record* in its first year on the air, a conspicuous dividend with a crucial constituency.[9] But not everyone found it unbiased or bipartisan, as we shall see.

The public relations points that accrued to NBC were closely tied to the course of the war. Barely a month into production, its director of television production told Steelman, "It seems to me that as we get deeper and deeper into the Korean War – both on the fighting front and on the home front – it becomes increasingly important for the people to get information about their responsibilities first hand from top level officials." Although he promised Steelman to continue the series "until such time as your people decide the need for it no longer exists,"[10] NBC became notably less generous as the war grew less exigent and less popular.

For its part, NBC initially asked only that the government deliver high-ranking officials – at the assistant secretary or ambassador level if they came from the state department – and that they "break" news on the program. The state department indeed delivered the secretary, the under secretary, and every assistant secretary. As time went on, securing such prime guests became difficult to guarantee because, according to someone trying to book them, "these people are among the most overworked, and understandably, are reluctant to forego a few hours of leisure on a Sunday afternoon." In the summers, the program had to be moved to weekdays because "the people who should appear on the show are often away from town."[11] The opportunity to see such high-ranking officials was the program's principal attraction and purpose.

Officials' reticence to appear increased just when tricky domestic political situations most begged for their visibility. To renew interest in *Battle Report – Washington* and support for the war as both flagged in late spring 1951, Steelman rounded up all the officials in charge of U.S. mobilization for a special broadcast. It had such an official imprint that NBC offered it to stations affiliated with other networks. But at the last minute, Secretary of Defense George Marshall, Mobilization Director Charles Wilson, and Economic Stabilization Administrator Eric Johnston pulled out, citing "pressure of work and other commitments," and the episode was canceled.[12] They decided that exposure would be a greater political liability than seclusion.

Bookings were indeed a headache. Like diplomats, Pentagon officials avoided television. Army, air force, and navy personnel declined to appear on the program during the early months of the war because they felt the military situation was too sensitive. Any remarks that defense department personnel made required security clearance, which sometimes made for last-minute dashes from the Pentagon to the NBC studios at the Wardman Park Hotel. In the weeks leading to the show's premiere, Charles Jackson, Steelman's assistant, requested that DOD's Office of Public Information (OPI) provide a regular spokesman who could come with maps and charts to summarize the week's military operations. OPI's radio-TV branch chief Charles Dillon concurred because operations personnel would be perennially reluctant to appear.[13] But in the end, due to pressure from the White House, more than a hundred generals, admirals, veterans, and high-ranking Pentagon civilians did appear on *Battle Report – Washington.*

Misunderstandings arose because the White House produced *Battle Report,* but many of the guests came from cabinet departments. Dillon complained that his office received word from NBC that Pentagon personnel had been designated by the White House to appear. The White House and the defense department each lined up sufficient guests for one show. Dillon also warned his superiors that the show's White House connection would ultimately cause a backlash. "Sooner or later the White House and Department of Defense are going to get in trouble with the other three networks because their requests for the same people may be turned down, while the NBC bid may be accepted because of the White House cache." When CBS started *The Facts We Face,* no doubt as its answer to *Battle Report,* Steelman's assistant Charles Jackson took over the government's liaison to CBS to avoid booking conflicts with *Battle Report.* NBC did indeed draw criticism for its close ties to the White House, but the biggest challenge facing *Battle Report's* producers in the government and at NBC was to keep the audience/public tuned in. They experimented with various ways to "beat the drum" for *Battle Report.*[14]

The Fabulous Jones Boys

To add glitz to an undeniably stodgy program, NBC created the first overseas network camera crew for *Battle Report.* A network press release announced that in February 1951 the "fabulous twin newsreel photographers" Gene and Charles Jones would make a three-month European tour visiting fifteen countries. They would provide the footage to illustrate reports to the nation aired on *Battle Report,* which now covered world events as well as the war in Korea. The twenty-five–year-old Jones twins, marine combat photographers during World War II, earned White House and Congressional accreditation at age sixteen.[15] The press release promised that they would shun "rear echelon comfort and safety" as they had in the past at Iwo Jima and the landing at Inchon, where Gene took shrapnel.

Although they were courageous and technically proficient, the "Jones boys," as they were called, were very young and politically naive. Davidson Taylor, the network vice-president, wrote them a gung-ho letter when their assignment was approved. He clearly worried that they lacked diplomatic skill and sophistication but hoped they would gain experience as they pioneered overseas television broadcasting:

> I am counting on you to be the first real political and feature television reporters with sound cameras developed by NBC for foreign coverage. . . . You have the skill and the courage required for the job. Acquiring the necessary information to do a really big job in this field takes a lifetime, but I think you will find quickly how different the approach of the Europeans is to the problems which concern us all, and I know I can count on you never to forget the American point of view.

Taylor gave further sage advice about how the world was mean and getting meaner, and they shouldn't take risks because another adventure would come along right away. He concluded, "If the above makes me sound like an old man, I would hope that it is only because you are so very young. I would very much like to be along with you."[16]

While NBC was looking to the Jones boys to develop its foreign correspondent corps for television, Secretary of State Dean Acheson hoped their tour would focus the U.S. television audience's attention on Europe rather than Korea. The secretary took immense and unusual interest in their activities, perhaps because *Battle Report – Washington*'s White House connection made it a quasi-official program. He directed the U.S. High Commissioner for Germany to arrange spokesmen to appear on camera and to furnish "liaison services" in other European cities. The High Commission provided the Jones brothers with accommodations and a temporary headquarters in Frankfurt.[17]

In return, the state department orchestrated the Jones boys' reporting. Although embassy and consulate officials often guide and aid reporters in their assigned countries, the directions issued by Acheson and others indicate an unusual level of collaboration. One cable to Germany read, "Objective of the team will be to cover stories and people the State Department considers most important to American audiences." Acheson specified that the film coverage was not to be oriented toward breaking news but rather should be feature treatment, such as would be found in *Life* magazine. He also directed that the Jones boys' footage should not be censored by U.S. officials in Europe, as was the custom when reporters photographed sensitive areas. They were to be restricted only from photographing visiting U.S. congressmen or dignitaries.[18]

Despite all this preparation and groundwork, the Jones boys' European tour turned into a diplomatic fiasco. A series of indignant and puzzled telegrams sent by American officials documents their progress through Europe and the Middle East. The first incident occurred in Yugoslavia. The brothers received explicit directions from the White House to stay away from Yugoslavian politics and confine their coverage to the American aid program and to tame human interest stories. However, their (unspecified) arrogant behavior while photographing Marshall Tito in the Yugoslav Parliament very nearly led to violence at the hands of the legislators.[19] The American ambassador to Yugoslavia, former Assistant Secretary of State for Public Affairs George Allen, lamented that their exploits had damaged press relations in his area; he was relieved that the boys "didn't get roughed up," but the unfortunate impression left by the two young men creates difficulties for other American photographers and journalists. NBC sent a senior correspondent to "lay down the law to the Jones brothers, and although their conduct improved, they were again censured in the British zone of Germany. Acheson cabled the consul at Rabat where they were expected, "Caution that these youngsters are pushy and were involved in two episodes in Europe where they embarrassed our missions by imperious behavior with foreign nationals." The secretary precluded the team from securing any additional audiences with heads of state, and the planned visit to Iran, where the political situation was "delicate," was canceled.[20]

The Jones boys continued to shoot film for *Battle Report – Washington*, but they occasionally faced budget constraints and altogether failed to realize the network's hope that they would mature into seasoned foreign correspondents. More importantly, both NBC and the executive branch learned how problematic it would be to glitz up a program that carried the weight of official diplomatic ties. Neither the White House nor the state department could afford the designation "fabulous."

Bloodthirsty Barbarians and the Future of Civilization

Only one film episode of *Battle Report – Washington* survives, making it difficult to assess the program's content. Most of the scripts have been preserved, but they were sometimes disregarded on the air and often make little sense without the accompanying visuals. From the scripts we can learn, for instance, that John Steelman employed language to describe world communist leaders that ranged from colorful to florid. They were "the fourteen barbarians," "power-drunk atheists," and "bloodthirsty barbarians," full of "diabolical cunning." Such language was not unusual in early Cold War news coverage: Prestige newspapers routinely used the word "Red" to designate communists. Steelman's phrasing went over the top in periods of domestic crisis for the Truman administration. The entry into the war of the People's Republic of China in late 1950 was "the barbarous aggression of the Chinese hoards [*sic*]." President Truman's dismissal of General Douglas MacArthur in April 1951 occasioned unusually graphic statements of the external threat to the United States: "Vast armies are poised to strike. They are like daggers at the heart of the free world – and their ultimate target is the United States."[21]

The scripts do follow the standard pattern that came into focus as the state department's formula for selling the militarization of containment urged by NSC-68. Dire predictions of enemy intentions and capabilities are followed by reassuring profiles of U.S. countermeasures capable of deterring or defeating communist ambitions. The one surviving film, of the program's fiftieth episode (out of eighty-four), follows this pattern closely. The first episode, which did not mention Korea at all, covered a communist youth rally in Berlin. It attempted to frighten its viewers as to the dangers of Soviet propaganda and then to reassure them that American efforts effectively overpowered the Soviet menace. It included recent film of the rally itself, hijacked Soviet footage of children in the eastern zone of Germany, and U.S. government film of American-sponsored programs for German youngsters. This episode was unusual in its variety of film sources and a correspondingly small number of interviews. Henry Byroade, director of the state department's Bureau of German Affairs, appeared in a concluding segment with NBC's Robert McCormick, who always narrated the program.

In his introduction, Steelman soberly editorialized about the meaning of the events portrayed. He pronounced the youth rally "one of the saddest and most frightening spectacles of the postwar world. Youth, innocent and impressionable, youth caught in the web of power politics and shaped to serve the all-too-familiar strings of Soviet Communists. This is one of the most appalling, disgraceful, and potentially dangerous things the Reds have ever undertaken."[22] Steelman and McCormick conveyed both the extreme danger of the Soviet propaganda efforts and supreme confidence that the western powers offered a more compelling lure to German children.

The program drew a blunt parallel between the 1951 communist rally and the Nazi youth movement. "The same place, Berlin, the same kids, German." Film of the rally was intercut with film of Nazi demonstrations and flags. "See any basic difference from the Nazi days?" The film clips mimic one another. "Now in place of Hitler it is Stalin or one of his mouthpieces." An unidentifiable picture of a frenzied man with a mustache flashes across the screen. "As you gaze upon these pictures taken this week in Berlin, will *this* [film of a communist parade] lead again to *this* [film of a waving Nazi flag]?"

McCormick's narration projected sinister implications onto the captured Soviet film showing happy children in the eastern zone. Over film of a girl using a pliers he commented, "girls are trained to a man's job." A sunny picnic suddenly seethes with danger when the audience is told, "Little do the children realize that the thoughts the Communists thrust upon them are like the snake in the grass." Finally, McCormick tells of the Soviet danger lurking in the smiles of happy children. "Look well upon these faces, America. Do you see reluctant youth ground under the heel of Communism? No. For the most part, you see children having the time of their lives, apparently sold, thousands of them, sold on Communism."

To reassure the American public about the competing western efforts to capture the minds of German children, Steelman and McCormick stressed the individualized, voluntary nature of American-sponsored programs, but they also implied that a lack of funds impeded the programs. "With no attempt to gild the lily for our side," Steelman introduced footage that showed "what we are trying to do with the youth who fell under our jurisdiction at war's end." Rather than "burying the individual in the mass" like the Soviets do, "our goal [is] freedom and self-government." The children learned trades, and during vacation they were invited to farms to keep them out of trouble. "Amid the wheat that is the staff of life to learn a new way of life, learn perhaps that one reaps what one sows . . . learn to appreciate the bullfrog and the mushroom rather than the Communist party line." German youth administration centers sponsored boxing, theatricals, music, baseball, and soccer and distributed gift boxes sent from the United States. "A silent doll often speaks louder than the Politburo." McCormick compared film of children marching and singing "in the shadow of a cathedral . . . just for the fun of it" with eastern youth ostensibly compelled to parade for political purposes.

In summary, McCormick asked state department representative Byroade how effective "these commie tactics are going to be?" Byroade replied that although the western efforts were less dramatic and less spectacular, they would be more effective. He believed that the opportunities to come to West Berlin and glance in store windows, voluntarily to participate in whatever programs they wished, to see honest reporting, motion pictures, newspapers, "even TV," would prove more compelling.

McCormick referred to a television demonstration set up by the state department to lure the children at the communist youth rally to the Western zone of Berlin with demonstrations of consumer goods. RCA, CBS, and DuMont each provided the Economic Cooperation Administration with thousands of dollars worth of equipment and the personnel to operate it. Under a page one headline that proclaimed, "Color TV as Western Democracies' 'Secret Weapon' vs. Red Youth Rally," *Variety* reported that "the idea of luring kids over into the Western zone with a 'come-on-a-my-house-and-see-color-TV' as the chief bait was first cooked up by the State Dept. and the Economic Cooperation Administration."[23]

Entertainers from Marshall Plan aid countries performed in a central pavilion at the West Berlin fairgrounds. Thousands of people were able to watch these performances projected on a thirty-foot-square screen supplied by RCA. An adjacent building housed displays of RCA home television sets, CBS phonographs and long-playing records, and a DuMont "See Yourself" exhibit in which one could watch oneself simultaneously on a television screen. CBS broadcast a live show from a third pavilion with color television equipment.[24] Finally, NBC set up several dozen receivers in strategic public locations throughout Berlin, including storefronts and beer gardens, to carry the demonstrations beyond the fairgrounds. The extent of these private contributions to the American counter-rally was not highlighted in the *Battle Report – Washington* episode. Although the Congress and the public generally approved such voluntarism in theory, the Berlin displays juxtaposed private participation in overseas propaganda too closely with *Battle Report – Washington* itself.

The Berlin episode was indeed textbook propaganda. No one involved in its production or in the audience would mistake it for an objective news program. Yet the network remained confident that it would greatly enhance its reputation for public service. Robert McCormick did not worry that cohosting a program with a high-ranking White House advisor would damage his professional reputation. As argued in Chapter Seven, passionate anticommunism became normalized as objective. For television news, *Battle Report – Washington* was business as usual.

Ours Is a Commercial Society

As the war sank into stalemate in late spring of 1951, NBC apparently decided that public relations points aside, *Battle Report – Washington* cost big money. They asked Steelman if the White House would agree to open the program to commercial sponsorship. NBC itself had some reservations about selling the show when it originally billed the program as pure public service, and the President expressed concern that it should not become overcommercialized. But Steelman set the tone for the discussions when he reported that the White House "had decided that ours is a commercial society and sponsorship would be appropriate."[25] With sponsorship, more stations would pick up *Battle Report – Washington*, increasing its audience, an outcome in everyone's interest. The president reserved the right to reject any inappropriate sponsor such as those selling deodorant, laxatives, or beer.

Steelman and Rud Lawrence, NBC's vice-president for news and public affairs, agreed to query large industrial firms tied to the war effort. They discussed Reynolds, Firestone, ALCOA, General Electric, Westinghouse, and AT&T. Steelman reflected that "the commercials could sell a company's contribution to the American way of life and perhaps its contribution to the war effort." He anticipated commercial breaks at the opening and closing of the program, and even one in the middle if necessary. Lawrence asked about trade unions and other noncorporate associations, but the only one they thought might be interested was the Association of American Railroads. Given that the White House supplied most of the show to NBC for free, it would be comparatively inexpensive for the sponsor, and Lawrence concluded that NBC had an excellent chance of selling *Battle Report – Washington*. They set the price at $4,500 per episode, plus the costs of making the commercial announcements.[26] (see Figure 6.)

The NBC sales staff was directed to hype the show's important news breaks. In July, they saw an imminent sale and frantically sought guarantees from Steelman that he would line up very high-ranking officials for the first three sponsored programs. A month later, when the Johns Manville company bought half an hour on Sunday afternoons, they still had no sponsor and fretted that "our commitments to the White House are such that we must at least go through the motions of trying to sell BATTLE REPORT to Johns Manville." NBC also worried how to tell the White House about the sale before it leaked into the trade press. NBC ran advertisements in *Broadcasting* that *Battle Report – Washington* was "unquestionably the most outstanding public service show on television – and an unusual opportunity for institutional advertising."[27] But NBC was learning that corporations bypassed such close association with the increasingly stigmatized Truman administration.

By October, NBC despaired of finding a single national sponsor and broached the question of opening the program to "co-op" sales with Steel-

BATTLE REPORT
WASHINGTON

MAKES NEWS IN

BROADCASTING
TELECASTING

═══RADIO DAILY—TELEVISION DAILY═══

Now, "BATTLE REPORT--WASHINGTON"
can make news for YOU as an advertiser.

Seen since August of 1950 over the NBC
Television Network, "BATTLE REPORT--
WASHINGTON" for the first time will be
available for sale by WNBW, effective with
the program of Sunday, November 4 (at the
new time of 2 p. m.).

Featuring John R. Steelman, the Assistant
to the President, as Master of Ceremonies,
"BATTLE REPORT--WASHINGTON" is a
weekly report to the nation by our nation's
leaders on the progress of Democracy's
struggle against Soviet Communism.

"BATTLE REPORT--WASHINGTON" is
unquestionably the most outstanding public
service show on television -- and an unusual
opportunity for institutional advertising.

Take advantage of this opportunity by
calling your nearest NBC Spot Sales
Office or the WNBW Sales Department
at REpublic 4000 NOW!

WNBW

Channel **4** Washington

Figure 6. The White House drew up a list of acceptable corporations to sponsor
Battle Report – Washington, and NBC attempted to sell the program but met
with little success. This ad appeared in *Broadcasting-Telecasting* magazine on October 24, 1951.

man, which meant that each local station could sell the program to a different local sponsor. Steelman approved, "provided, of course, the same care is exercised in selecting the sponsors on the local level as would be on the national." They worried about hard-sell techniques used by local advertisers, and again reserved the right to yank undignified products, but no one expected such companies to be interested. Steelman provided a list of twenty-four appropriate industries, including automobiles, hardware, jewelry, real estate, soft drinks, and music stores. Although the NBC Washington, D.C. affiliate appears to have sold the program to the Fairchild Aviation Company, there is not much evidence that it sold well on a co-op basis.[28] NBC canceled *Battle Report – Washington* within six months, as we shall see, for reasons including its costs.

Despite its failure to gain a commercial sponsor, *Battle Report – Washington* consistently advertised the bounty of American life. Perhaps Steelman was self-conscious about acting as a promoter on television. He tried to turn his embrace of television into an American virtue with an unapologetic celebration of consumer goods. On December 31, 1950, the last day of the first half of the twentieth century, Steelman reflected on the "electrical gadgets [that] have made life fuller and happier. . . . The fact that [in the United States] more than thirty million people own motor cars and more than forty-two million homes have radios gives proof that our way of life, even though it has imperfections, provides a way for all men to possess material things to make their lives happier." Returning to this theme six months later, he admitted that "we are frequently accused of being 'too materialistic.' Maybe we are. Maybe the material possessions should not be essential to our happiness. The Founding Fathers put much emphasis on both the material and spiritual aspects of life."[29]

Most importantly for his purposes on *Battle Report – Washington*, Steelman routinely linked American material goods with the struggle against totalitarian communism:

> If we have any worldly possessions at all – a television set – an automobile – or even one savings bond, we are considered "enemies of the people" and tools of Wall Street. Every one of us would be marked – to be robbed, enslaved, or slaughtered if the day ever came when the Soviet hoards [*sic*] overran our country. With God's help that will never happen.[30]

American consumption was defined in defiant opposition to a demonized communist enemy as a way to make the threat immediate and rally the public.

Not everyone in the government information community thought such commercial effusion was appropriate. Francis Russell, the state department's director of public affairs, consistently resisted sponsorship for collaboratively produced programs. The White House turned out to be far more willing to open itself to commercial sponsorship than Russell anticipated, and it was corporate advertisers' allergy to controversy that spared the executive branch from being sold like Coke.

Outside the Realm of Political Controversy

At the height of public discontent with the administration's prosecution of the war, Steelman used *Battle Report – Washington* to chide the public for maligning its leadership. "This nation was built by men with courage. Mumblers and grumblers did not deter the men who made this nation great." He portrayed the administration's unpopularity as blaming the messenger and called for renewed determination and unity. "It is fundamental here in the United States that every citizen has the right to know the truth. Sometimes the truth is bad news, but we can take it."[31]

Such blatant appeals for support of the administration brought NBC repeated charges of partisanship. Inasmuch as the administration's unpopularity was a partisan political issue, the charge had merit. As the din about MacArthur's dismissal rang in Truman's ears, an NBC vice-president made Truman an extraordinarily generous offer, beyond what they were already providing with *Battle Report – Washington,* of two hours of prime time for a "Report to the Nation." It began, "We have the feeling here in RCA and NBC that if you and your principal aides could talk face to face to the American people and explain to them as individual citizens the problems we face as a nation and the steps which must be taken to meet them and secure our freedom, most of the apathy and divided counsel which now hamper our government would be swept away at once." Presumably, *Battle Report – Washington* itself was not high profile enough for the president. NBC also included the assurance, "In every respect we would strive for objectivity; not for any party or political purpose, but for our government."[32]

But such distinctions were mere sophistry to many Republicans. In March 1951, a citizen of Nebraska asked his senator to put a stop to *Battle Report – Washington*'s "Democratic propaganda." NBC had anticipated such objections and offered several reasons why the show was actually objective. First, it was presented in cooperation with the Advertising

Council, a "nonpartisan organization." Guests on the program came from administrative and military departments of the government, and the film came from official government releases or NBC. "We can only feel, therefore, that NBC has done its best to present an objective picture of what our Government in Washington is doing."[33]

This is plainly dishonest. Network reporters on both *Battle Report – Washington* and CBS's *The Facts We Face* had their questions written for them in the White House. This was part of the quid pro quo for White House participation. The networks did not set out to cast their lot with one party. They sought access and prestige through proximity to the big war story being written by the Democratic executive branch and, as such, spotlighted Democrats. Likewise, when covering the administration's critics in more oppositional forums, the balance swung to the Republicans.

But television certainly cultivated reverence for authority. In the midst of serious calls for impeachment of the president, Hugh Downs of CBS tossed questions at John Steelman like, "What is the most important domestic fact now facing the American people?" Because it was his own question, Steelman could assuredly answer, "the threat of annihilation by power-drunk despots,"[34] his usual gambit to quiet partisan critics. *Battle Report – Washington*'s producers were less concerned with charges of partisanship, which they felt sure they could fend off with appeals to the national interest, than they were with creating the illusion that the fully rehearsed and security cleared program could "avoid the deleterious impression that the program had been worked out in advance."[35]

NBC further developed its "unbiased good-of-the-country" argument in June 1951 when the Republican National Committee asked for equal time under the provisions of FCC regulations. The entire pantheon of NBC executives passed on the network's reply, as did Steelman. The letter they sent with the signature of William Brooks, NBC's vice-president for news and public affairs, is a masterpiece of public relations hairsplitting, and worth quoting at length:

> I am surprised at your interpretation of the program BATTLE REPORT WASHING-TON, because it seems to us in the public interest to have a weekly television program which reports on the activities of the Federal Administration on behalf of the people of the United States. . . . This series is a result of NBC Television's offer to the United States Government to make available the network facilities for the dissemination of information on military and civilian developments occasioned by the Korean War and the worldwide fight against Communism.
>
> We have a dozen or so members of the Republican Party who were performing official tasks for the Federal Administration as participants on this pro-

gram. They did not appear in their partisan capacities, any more than the Federal Administrators who appear on the program are there as Democrats. . . . It would be unrealistic to think that members of the administration can divorce themselves completely from their political allegiances and opinions. Such opinions color even the most objective news report. Nonetheless, we feel sure that, just as the intention of this program is to be fair and factual, so this is also the intention of the participants. . . .

In the case of BATTLE REPORT WASHINGTON we feel again that the program in both intention and accomplishment serves a useful function which falls outside the realm of political controversy.[36]

This statement contains a rare acknowledgment by someone of Paley's stature in the news industry that opinions color the most objective report. Apparently, it placated the Republican National Committee because there were no further developments.

By spring of 1952, when the presidential primary season got underway, NBC executives anticipated renewed objections from Republicans. The news division began looking for air time to set aside for unpaid political speeches by the major candidates. They decided to cancel *Battle Report – Washington* and use its time for this purpose, citing two principal reasons: "As we get deeper into the political year, any and all Administration shows are more vulnerable to attack as being political," and to save money.[37]

NBC and the White House exchanged letters of thanks and congratulations. Steelman averred, "I have considerable evidence that the program has done a great deal of good."[38] *Battle Report – Washington* unquestionably brought credit to both the network and the administration for their roles in keeping information about the government's mobilization before the public. The lessons that the program taught information specialists both in and out of government stemmed from its need to compete with more lucrative entertainment broadcasting. NBC was happy to donate air time for the cause of war, until the threat receded enough for profit making to once again take precedence. Questions about propaganda could be brushed aside far more easily than the program's mounting costs or the declining value of its public service contribution.

CHAPTER SIX

A MORE VIVID PICTURE OF WAR: THE DEFENSE DEPARTMENT'S DOMESTIC INFORMATION PROGRAMS, 1948–1960

The U.S. government reorganized its military establishment in the late 1940s to meet the changing threats to U.S. security. The National Security Act of 1947 created the Department of Defense, the National Security Council, and the Central Intelligence Agency. The culture of this new national security apparatus, far more than that of the foreign service, regarded all information as military information. Information officials stressed the label "psychological warfare" to wrest money for their programs out of Congress.[1]

James Forrestal, the first secretary of defense, urged that all overt and covert psychological warfare and all domestic and overseas information should be coordinated at the national policy level to prevent damaging foreign use of domestic stories. In a series of reports on "Domestic Activities and Foreign Relations" delivered to NSC in summer of 1948, Forrestal advised "that we develop as quickly as possible some means whereby domestic events . . . are, whenever possible, weighed in light of the international situation at any given time." NSC approved his recommendation and urged the president to tell his cabinet to coordinate the release of domestic information with international affairs. If they were unsure of overseas repercussions, they should consult the secretary of state.[2] To these tacticians, the requirements of domestic information followed from those of overseas information, which were themselves dictated by foreign policy and military strategy.

Although Forrestal advocated precise policy control over domestic information, he also quickly recognized the need for cooperation with private media companies and individual journalists. When his initial appointees to his press staff, career military officers, failed to help solidify his rocky position over the military services and generate good publicity, he took advice from three journalists (Elmer Davis of ABC, William

Matthews of the *Arizona Star*, and Frank Kluckhohn of the *New York Times*) to appoint a civilian with credibility before the Washington press corps. His next three appointees to the office of assistant secretary of defense for administrative and public affairs came from the *New York Times*, the *New York Herald-Tribune*, and the Associated Press.[3]

The defense department's management of domestic information both as prudent foreign policy and sound public relations never occasioned the attacks leveled at similar efforts in the state department, at least not until the watershed 1971 CBS documentary *The Selling of the Pentagon*. In the early 1950s, the state department became the scapegoat for the seeming failures of American foreign policy, and the military establishment seemed to offer the solution. Just as psychological warfare enjoyed more popularity than the OWI's strategy of truth during World War II, postwar information programs attained more legitimacy when attached to the military.

More than any other government agency, the new Department of Defense also adapted its public information campaigns to the changing demands of commercial television. Military activities lent themselves more easily than policy questions to the dramatization that television required. For the networks, popular programming genres like comedies and game shows became too lucrative, as the 1950s progressed, to broadcast little-watched informational series in prime time. Early, experimental public affairs programs highlighting unification of the new DOD and civil defense never attracted large audiences and, with one notable exception, disappeared from the air by 1953. During the mid-1950s, the networks moved into historical compilation documentaries, which did earn high ratings with their monumental scale, symphonic scores, and epic stories. These series drew on DOD film archives and advisory personnel and were subject to official approval. Late in the decade, when the majority of American homes contained television sets, providing competitive entertainment programming overrode educational purpose in the government as well as at the networks. The networks then asked for DOD assistance in producing various dramas based on military records. DOD responded enthusiastically, with hopes of increasing enlistment in the armed forces. Although the formats differed, each of these series promoted American military supremacy and reinforced the axiomatic need to arm the national security state.

This chapter describes the organizational structure of DOD's radio-TV branch within the new Department of Defense and then follows the progression of its programs through increasingly popular forms. The shift in final control from DOD to the networks presented few difficulties for DOD.[4] Private industry performed an official function with no expense to the taxpayer and no threat of controversy over spending tax dollars to influence the public. DOD's cooperation with private broadcasters was increasingly obscured in historically based "entertainment" forms.

Unification Battles

The National Security Act, which established the Department of Defense in 1947, centralized the three armed services' public affairs staffs for the first time in the new office of the secretary of defense. A series of appointments to the post of assistant secretary of defense for administrative and public affairs (ASDPA) geared more to politics than to information experience rendered incomplete the unified DOD's efforts to take over the functions of army and navy information offices until well into the 1950s.[5] Disruptive competition between the services persisted for decades. In addition to his Press Advisory Council, Forrestal appointed a Public Information Coordinating Council and a Public Relations Advisory Council made up of the public affairs chiefs from each service to try to unify information policy.

   In his drive to coordinate information, Forrestal stepped on the toes of the voluntarist media industries. In March 1948, he called a high-level meeting of twenty-two news executives, including representatives of all the networks and the NAB, to consider security measures, or, in his words, "to prevent information which might endanger the United States from being given to a potential enemy." Forrestal's proposed round-the-clock Information Advisory Unit to answer questions on information security met with a mixed response. Whereas "Pat" Morin, the Washington, D.C., bureau chief of the Associated Press, thought that the American public would approve of this "form of voluntary peacetime censorship," Lyle Wilson, his competitor at the United Press, stated, "I don't think any mechanized system involving free censorship will work."[6] After the meeting, the news community buzzed with concern. NBC vice-president Davidson Taylor privately reported to the editor of the *Washington Star*:

> On the basis of the facts presented, it is our feeling that the communications industries of the United States should not be asked to ask for censorship. It does not seem to me that censorship, which is none the less unattractive because it is now labeled "voluntary," is required at this time. There appears to be no question that more censorship at the source is required, and I was encouraged

to hear that the military establishment is taking firm steps to tighten up on security.[7]

Forrestal's proposal died after he determined that if security risks could be averted by tightening control at the source, reporters worked better without censorship proscriptions. A month later, all twenty-two participants in the meeting signed a statement saying, "We do not believe that any type of censorship in peacetime is workable or desirable in the public interest. If any exists, we would not be sympathetic with an intent, on the part of the Military Establishment, to propose peacetime censorship."[8] Executives told Forrestal that media voluntarism would suffice to secure information in peacetime.

The public affairs operation finally gained some administrative order in 1949. William Frye, a former Associated Press reporter and the third ASDPA in three years, formed the Office of Public Information with five branches: press, magazine and book, pictorial, public relations, and radio and television. The OPI also consolidated security review and public opinion analysis operations. The radio-TV branch's official mission was "to assist radio and television networks and independent stations in keeping the public informed of the activities of the National Military Establishment." All the services under the ASDPA suffered a series of massive budget cuts through the mid-1950s due to demobilization after Korea and Eisenhower administration belt-tightening. The ASDPA budget went from a high of $14 million during Korea to a low of $3.2 million in 1956. The OPI received $971,445 in 1952 and $500,000 in 1954.[9]

The radio-TV branch measured its success by estimating the value of the free air time that networks and stations donated to DOD programming. In 1950 for television alone, radio-TV branch chief Charles Dillon estimated that figure to be more than $1.7 million (a high estimate because in 1950 many programs aired without sponsors, or on a "sustaining" basis). On the memo he prepared for his superiors reporting these figures, he included the following explanation of his branch's work:

> The four radio networks, four television networks, and 2700 individual radio and TV stations, reach some 100 million Americans daily with information concerning the Defense Department. Networks commentators alone reach about 40 million persons daily. The way the information is presented has a profound effect upon the attitude of the public toward national defense – particularly from the standpoint of the *complete* story, told without bias, picturing interservice teamwork in action. The Radio-TV Branch, through its multitude of contacts in the Radio-TV industry, and through its own official Department of

Defense programs, week in and week out, makes a major contribution to the telling of the complete story. It "makes friends and influences people" among the groups controlling what goes on the air. There is no way of putting an accurate dollar sign on the value of this service, because the figures shown on the attached page represent only the commercial time value. The general impact on the public is immeasurable.[10]

Dillon's phrase, "the *complete* story, told without bias," does not refer to a standard of journalistic objectivity, as his later reference to influencing journalists in the interests of DOD makes clear. He refers to the jealousies between the newly united services. Thus he highlights "interservice teamwork."

In return for the substantial value in air time donated by the networks, Dillon's staff provided a wide variety of services: free programming produced by the Army Signal Corps, public affairs announcements, personnel to appear on discussion programs, archival footage. They even arranged for naval maneuvers to be performed for network cameras. In a typical month, the OPI released six films for network use, provided thirty or forty newsreel-type clips, and sent a speaker to a broadcasters' convention. During the Korean War, the public affairs units attached to command posts in the Far East took over the majority of film work. In one month in 1953, the information office of the Army's Far East Command fulfilled 269 requests for sound-on-film interviews from ten television stations. Their staff even shot film supplied by domestic television stations that could not afford to send their own camera crews. In a typical month, seven stations sent raw film.[11]

Dillon also censored film releases and briefed Pentagon officials who were scheduled to appear on network programs. In 1950, he prevented the release of a film showing "the murder of a German civilian by an American soldier." When air surgeon Brigadier General Hall was invited to discuss brainwashing on Kate Smith's radio program, Dillon told him to discuss evacuation procedures instead and to "stay away from controversial issues."[12]

The variety of services provided by the public affairs staff caused confusion as to its primary purpose within the huge Pentagon bureaucracy and at the networks, particularly when its budget shrank. The radio-TV branch continuously received directives concerning the order of its priorities from DOD's Public Relations Advisory Council, chaired by the ASDPA. In October 1952, budget cuts forced the cancellation of two programs produced by the radio-TV branch: *Time for Defense* on radio, and the mixed film and interview program *Pentagon – Washington* on television. ASDPA Andrew Berding (whose past positions included Associated Press correspondent in Rome, deputy director of information for the Economic Cooperation Administration, and director of information for the Office of Defense Mobilization and the Mutual Security Agency) instructed Dillon to "concentrate on getting defense material on existing [network-produced] programs." Dillon suggested that his staff try *Report from the Pentagon* and *Headline Edition* on radio and Richard Harkness's NBC television interview program, *Story of the Week*.[13]

Ted Koop, Washington, D.C. bureau chief for CBS news, complained to Dillon that while he imagined that DOD's own shows had to be the radio-TV branch's "principal duty and interest," CBS perceived a lack of cooperation on other projects. Dillon wished "emphatically to deny" that their own shows came first. "It is our mission, by directive, to provide the best possible service we can to the network industry, within the limits of our staff and resources." To placate Koop, Dillon prepared a list of all the instances of service that the branch had provided to CBS A.M. radio and television in the first six months of 1951; the list numbered more than 100. He further gushed, "The cooperation and goodwill of CBS, and of you personally, are vital to the success of our mission. One of the real pleasures has been the association with you and the other members of the CBS organization. You can count on our doing our best to give you what you want."[14]

Dillon courted his industry contacts far more aggressively than did his counterpart at the state department. In April 1950, Dillon asked twenty-two industry contacts for "unreservedly frank" evaluations of DOD information operations before and after consolidation, explaining, "The only reason we have for being here is to perform satisfactorily for the industry." Speaking to an American Television Society luncheon at the Hotel Roosevelt in New York in 1951, he told members that "full cooperation between his department and the TV industry was essential both for the medium and for the taxpayers of this country who want to know what is being done with their money during this national emergency [the Korean War]."[15]

The same respect for industry experience among government information officers that made the state department recruit individuals from private organizations operated in the defense department. Career military officers were seen as even less sensitive to the needs of the press than career diplomats. In addition to appointing journalists as his assistant secretary for public affairs, Forrestal also appointed a *Washington Times-Herald* reporter as his staff publicist and met regularly with a committee of news executives that he called his Press Advisory Council. The OPI's pictorial branch, which handled newsreel services for the networks, consulted NBC executive Ted Ayers about the content, quality, and timing of release for DOD material, but it discontinued this practice when competing networks objected.[16]

Cooperation between the Department of Defense and the general business community was solidified in a series of "Joint Civilian Orientation Conferences" held four times annually where the secretaries of defense, army, navy, and air force briefed business, labor, and civic leaders on the military situation. The civilians toured army, navy, air force, and marine installations. NBC's vice-president Davidson Taylor called it "one of the most rewarding experiences of my life." In turn, NBC hosted a tour of its New York facilities for officers in the U.S. Armed Forces Information School based in Carlisle, Pennsylvania.[17]

Conflicts did arise between the networks and DOD over security information, especially overseas. Where censorship was more formal, reporters often felt manipulated. In 1955, CBS Far East bureau chief Robert Pierpont complained to the director of the OPI that information officers were "very cooperative when they want propaganda stories put out. But whenever we want coverage of breaking hard news, or are looking for television features that may not be necessarily flattering to the military, we receive somewhat less than enthusiastic cooperation." He continued:

> While understanding the necessity for security on vital military information, it seems to me that this necessity has been frequently abused. Often Public Information Officers, and other military personnel as well, hide behind the security requirements in attempts to avoid controversial issues or to play down stories which might in some way put the military in an awkward light. In all fairness I suppose this is a problem in the relationship between reporters and officers which will never be entirely solved. It is in the nature of the beast. But as I am sure you will agree, the job of the newsman is to keep the public fully informed. An informed public is a basic requirement of a functioning democracy. Sometimes, however, it appears that our American military officials lose sight of this.

The OPI held the opposite view of who wielded ultimate power over official information; OPI believed that the networks could do whatever they wanted with information after it was released. Osgood Roberts, the OPI's acting director, wrote: "Basically, there are no government controls over how the free press and radio use our materials, once in their hands." Although Roberts noted that cooperation was the overwhelming rule, he stressed that the OPI exerted no prior restraint on breaking news stories. "The networks are usually scrupulously careful and responsible. If an individual station wants to subvert one of our film releases for any purpose, we can only call the attention of the station to the Act. The same is true of a newspaper and our press releases."[18]

The OPI raised its biggest objections when the networks highlighted interservice rivalry. When General Lemnitzer filled in for General Gavin at the last minute on the CBS interview program *Background*, hosted by Joseph Harsch, neither a script nor a set of questions and answers was submitted to the OPI in advance. Harsch opened the program by using charts to compare the services' strengths and budgets, which, according to the OPI, "gave the intimation that the three Services were going to argue their budgets." The ASDPA's Public Information Coordinating Committee "discussed this type of program and the difficulty of controlling the method of presentation which the commentator might choose to make, also that pre-filmings are cut and edited as desired by the station with no opportunity for review by the Services."[19]

Both sides felt occasional frustration with the other – the networks over the timely release of newsworthy information, and the government over appropriate use of information or scheduling. As time went on, the balance of power shifted more decisively to the networks who, although they remained dependent on the government for the release of information, increasingly controlled what, when, and how information went on the air. Their surfeit of resources and growing technical sophistication became overriding.

Boring Filler

The radio-TV branch's efforts to make friends at the networks evolved between 1948 and 1960 as television audiences and revenues grew. The earliest television programs and series collaboratively produced by the networks and the Department of Defense took the form of public affairs programs about military operations, with occasional diversions like military band performances. These programs were modeled on radio coproductions from the World War II era, particularly NBC's *Army Hour*. NBC and the army information service considered reviving that program for radio and television during the early months of the Korean War. OPI took over its development, but NBC ultimately deemed it too costly.[20]

Diverse film, discussion, and narration were drawn together into overtly educational programs. A 1952 catalogue of films cleared for television broadcast by federal agencies shows that DOD offered most of the 528 titles. The most sensational of these programs concerned imminent nuclear war. Between 1950 and 1952, the public had many opportunities to learn from television "what the average person should do in the event of an atom bomb attack." Walter Cronkite of CBS narrated a documentary based on the National Resources Security Board's 1950 civilian defense report. The navy and local New York station WOR produced *Drill Call*, which told viewers what to do "before, during, and after" such an attack. NBC's 1951 summer series *Survival* was later used by the Federal Civilian Defense Agency for use in training its volunteers. CBS also aired *Command Post*, an army experiment in at-home instruction for its reservists in planning attacks, self-defense, and combat techniques.[21] Many other one-time or local programs reinforced the message that atomic attack could come at any time and that preparedness would make the difference in survival.

In April 1952, the networks learned for the first time in advance of the scheduled test date for an atomic bomb to be exploded at Yucca Flat. Network engineers worked feverishly on the Atomic Energy Commission's firing range near Las Vegas to secure their equipment.[22] Four cameras filmed from eleven miles away, and two filmed from a mountaintop forty miles away. Motion pictures were also shot in case the blast interfered with the direct relay.

The second televised atomic bomb blast took place about a year later. The thirty-third test at Yucca Flat was designed to measure the effects on two buildings and several U.S. Army soldiers placed within a mile of ground zero. The Advertising Council sponsored the program. *Broadcasting* surmised, "The 'sales message' was preparedness. It is a vast understatement to say that a more effective means could not have been found to 'move' this particular product."[23] The magazine used the sales idiom ironically, but the army's psychological warriors studied advertising techniques carefully.

Between 1949 and 1951, NBC and then DuMont carried the DOD-produced program, *The Armed Forces Hour*. Unlike programs produced for other purposes by the military, which were aired as "filler" in broadcast scheduling, *The Armed Forces Hour* was produced each week specifically for television. It reached twenty-nine NBC stations on Sundays in 1949 and 1950, and fifty-six DuMont stations in 1951. Dillon estimated the value of each donated half-hour on NBC to be $144,000.[24] Titles of individual episodes included "Student Nurses of America," "Up Periscope," "Invisible Rampart," and "Normandy Revisited."

DOD described the program's purpose as demonstrating the "increased efficiency and financial economy" resulting from unification of the armed forces. In an appearance on the program, Secretary of Defense Louis John-son pronounced that the armed forces had "weathered the storm of the creation of the Department of Defense." NBC network board chairman Niles Trammell praised the network's public service, saying, "Every citi-zen wishes to know as much as possible about the services which will defend his country if it is ever again attacked. NBC's part in this informa-tional undertaking is to provide its facilities for the Armed Forces mes-sage. It cheerfully does so."[25]

The content of the program varied from performances by the army band to old training and recruiting films to discussion. NBC complained that unlike radio's *Army Hour* during World War II, DOD refrained from breaking important news on the program. After two months on the air, NBC threatened to remove it, at least from prime time. OPI person-nel promised to deliver "more brass" and a "smash" story about once a month.[26]

Osgood Roberts, acting director of OPI, dismissed the possibility of adding a network commentator to host the program because "other net-works would complain if all of the resources of the Department of De-fense were put behind one group of men from one network on an official show." Roberts thought that the assignment would ruin the journalist's reputation. "He couldn't help but tell a very favorable story for us one day and go on his own show the next day to ostensibly present a more inde-pendent and conceivably unfavorable attitude."[27] Yet Roberts shows more concern on this score than did Robert McCormick, the NBC correspon-dent who hosted *Battle Report – Washington* every week during the early 1950s. From this very first collaboratively produced series, both network and DOD staff recognized that the network as a whole eluded any stigma attached to broadcasting official information. Institutional cooperation was legitimate as public service, which NBC "cheerfully" performed.

DOD required that the questions journalists asked on the *Armed Forces Hour* be scripted in advance. NBC's New York director of TV news and special events, Frank McCall, wondered why the program secured fewer appearances from top military brass than NBC's independently produced *Meet the Press*. OPI's Roberts recorded: "This brought up the problem, in comparison to MEET THE PRESS, where the individual does not have prob-lems of news, lines to remember, or a set formula to follow – he merely an-swers questions. This could not be handled on ARMED FORCES HOUR be-cause we would be imitating MEET THE PRESS to some extent and would leave the individual and ourselves vulnerable."[28] An official DOD pro-gram could afford no spontaneity.

Two months later, Dillon ventured another suggestion to McCall that would solve the dual problem of compromising network journalists and embarrassing unrehearsed officials. NBC commentators would submit, on a rotating basis, a "defense question of the week." Submitting the question in advance would allow the guest time to prepare a politic answer while preserving the journalist's integrity. The two figures would then be filmed together. "We could work out a list of commentators and guests to their joint satisfaction and ours,"[29] wrote Dillon.

At the same time, Dillon hoped to stop producing the program during the summer of 1950 to provide his staff with overdue vacation and to get an advance on programming for the fall season. NBC granted the hiatus until the fall, but even with addition of a film editor to the radio-TV branch staff, they could not guarantee a popular show, and the program never reappeared on NBC. DuMont inquired about its renewal the following September,[30] and it ran on that network in the summer of 1951.

Another series produced by the U.S. Army Pictorial Center, entitled *The Big Picture*, was "probably the most widely televised public service program in history." During the Korean War, a former commercial broadcaster by the name of Lt. Carl Bruton conceived the program to use documentary footage accumulated by the Signal Corps. Originally it ran for thirteen weeks on CBS beginning in late 1951, with each broadcast devoted to the Korean War. Later syndicated by the army with an expanded scope, the program eventually aired on 366 television stations, on the CBS, ABC, and DuMont networks, and on many independent stations; 823 episodes were produced, and continued to air in syndication until 1971. Army information units around the world initiated ideas for segments and organized them, and Signal Corps camera crews filmed them. The Far East command produced two or three features each week during the Korean War.[31]

Topics varied from the organization of the army to the occupation of Berlin, to rocket weaponry, to West Point, to historical reenactments of moments in military history. There was no hiding the official sanction; *New York Times* television critic Jack Gould complained that some participants sounded "like an Army publicity release." The lead narration each week proclaimed, "From Korea to Germany, from Alaska to Puerto Rico, all over the world the United States Army is alert to defend our country – you, the American people – against aggression. This is *The Big Picture*, an official television report to the nation from the United States Army."[32] The program may have been bad television, but its message and its public service utility were unassailable.

One incident in 1954 focused Congressional attention on DOD's control over the release of news film to television. *The Big Picture* planned to broadcast film of communist atrocities in Korea, including pictures of mass graves and evidence of starvation and torture. Deputy Secretary of Defense Roger M. Keyes and Under Secretary of State General Walter Bedell Smith together decided that the release of the film was ill timed because a Big Four Conference was forthcoming. Members of Congress criticized any such restriction, which had not prevented some stations outside New York and Washington from airing the program anyway. The "histrionic" episode finally aired in New York a month later.[33]

While *The Big Picture* continued to air for many years in unsold portions of the broadcast schedule, the major networks experimented with other forms of public affairs programming that would draw larger audiences. They began collaborating with OPI to produce programs specifically for television.

Pictures Against Appeasement

Capitalizing on the heroic reputation of General Dwight Eisenhower, the March of Time documentary unit produced a film version of the general's book, *Crusade in Europe*. The twenty-six-episode series aired on ABC in 1949, sponsored by Time, Inc., for $400,000. The pictorial branch of OPI provided the same services to the March of Time that the radio-TV branch provided directly to the networks.[34]

The editors screened millions of feet of film in American, British, and French archives. When footage of an important event was not available, they hired actors and staged it. Most of the archival footage lacked audio, so March of Time recorded a lengthy shell and explosion track. Critics praised the series for its tight camera work, which was better suited to television than long cinematic shots. Although Eisenhower personally disliked television, his advisors recognized its political uses. The general also preferred television to film for *Crusade in Europe*, because he felt that the big screen would render history too theatrical. The series won a Peabody Award in 1950 for "Television's Major Contribution to Education."[35]

In 1951, the March of Time produced a sequel to *Crusade in Europe* for syndication called *Crusade in the Pacific*. Because no book provided an outline, the pictorial branch oversaw the scripting and editing of the Pacific series more carefully than it had for the earlier series. One memo from Major Horton of the pictorial branch to a March of Time vice-president specified:

Inasmuch as the narrative and plan of each of the films in the series will have to be written by you without the guidance of such a volume as "Crusade in Europe," it will be necessary that the scripts be reviewed by the National Military Establishment. This review will not be in any way an imposition of censorship but will give us the opportunity to advise you with reference to technical information, historical records and policy of the National Military Establishment.

The pictorial branch's involvement extended well beyond advising. Horton spent many hours in the naval photo center reviewing footage as possible material for the series. In addition, each statement made on film by military personnel was approved in advance at the Pentagon. The relationship between the pictorial branch and March of Time was close enough for censorship to be unnecessary. The *New York Times* called the series "an editorial in pictures against the consequences of appeasement and lack of preparedness."[36]

Apparently the air force protested that it received shorter treatment in the *Crusade in Europe* series than did the army and navy. Steps were taken to prevent a recurrence for the Pacific series. Lt. Colonel Lindley of the air force brought a man named Norcross from the March of Time to his office for a "general, unofficial discussion" on air force cooperation in the making of the series. He showed Norcross index cards indicating the footage in his possession and "also advised him that we would endeavor to see that all branches of the service were given fair treatment in the scripts." When the chief of the pictorial branch, J. A. Yovin, reviewed a prospectus and some sample scripts for the series, his main criticism was that the first proposed title, *Victory in the Pacific*, was "not considered apropos" because it implied victory was achieved by the navy alone.[37]

However, two years later, Yovin's objection did not apply when NBC produced the popular and acclaimed series *Victory at Sea*, chronicling naval warfare during World War II. Also consisting of twenty-six thirty-minute episodes, the series launched NBC's honored documentary team, Project XX. Henry Salomon, who had assisted Samuel Eliot Morison in researching the navy's official history of its World War II operations, suggested to Robert Sarnoff (son of RCA chairman David Sarnoff) in late 1949 that NBC produce a film version of Morison's epic. Sarnoff was promoted to head the network's film division, and he allocated $500,000 for the series, which included start-up costs for a documentary unit.[38]

When Salomon initially proposed the series to OPI, he envisioned fifty-two episodes. NBC surmised that the navy would have to provide 9,000 feet of negative and film per episode according to Salomon's scripts, as well as use of its photographic center and personnel. Osgood Roberts, director of the OPI, at first rejected the series as "too big and too costly."[39] The final *Victory at Sea* was half that length and cost the taxpayers $65,000.

The Korean War began while the series was in active development, and in late 1950 Salomon proposed integrating contemporary issues "in light of the international situation." The series would combine breaking news with documentary precedent. "The principal military news themes each week would be edited for television and the historical precedent would be shown at the same time, tying present events in with the past." He suggested that the other military services and the state department could also participate in broadening the show's scope. Executives higher up at NBC rejected these suggestions and signed on for a straightforward history of naval warfare during World War II.[40]

NBC would edit, write, and produce the series, providing the initial air time and retaining rights to subsequent syndication. Sarnoff estimated the costs to NBC at $123,150, and the return from the initial syndication at $208,000. In pitching the idea to the network, Sarnoff emphasized the intangible returns in good will generated by the public service nature of the project:

> Such a venture would be of use to NBC because, first, it would be the premier showing of a television historical series produced by NBC with the unique cooperation and contribution of the U.S. Navy. Second, it would create a permanent NBC property, available for commercial reshowing, both network and syndication, plus many other subsidiary uses, such as schools, homes, etc., for all of which NBC would receive credit. Third, it would represent a remarkable public relations project, certain to accumulate favorable press comments. In addition, the U.S. Navy proposed to use the series as a major instrument in their recruiting and education program.

Victory at Sea indeed became a major event in documentary history, winning a special Peabody Award. The navy awarded Distinguished Public Service awards to Sarnoff, Salomon, and Richard Rodgers, who composed the score. Secretary of the Navy Francis Matthews called the series "the finest act of public service any corporation had ever done for the Navy." It was also a landmark in documentary film-making technique. A. William Bluem, author of the pioneering 1965 book, *Documentary in American Television: Form, Function, Method*, praised Salomon for giving the compilation form its "greatest encouragement by the work of a single man."[41]

Salomon had proposed to the OPI that *Victory at Sea*'s initial run would not have commercial sponsorship and that navy recruiting and public service announcements would accompany it. Even though the sustaining feature had been "its principle [*sic*] selling point" for the public service esteem it would generate for both NBC and the navy, Sarnoff later convinced the navy to allow NBC to sell time on the first run. Once the navy allowed sponsorship, NBC abandoned plans to ask the state department's radio-TV branch to participate. Commercial sponsorship offered a greater return than association with the state department. Salomon wrote to Sarnoff:

> In view of the Navy's new agreement [to allow commercial sponsorship], it would be very undignified for NBC to press this point further with the DOS or any other government agency at this time. Any amount of money we might get now would be peanuts and the prestige we would lose might be enormous. I also feel that if we do the type of job we plan and if we keep in close contact with [DOS International Motion Pictures Group Chief Herbert] Edwards, [Edwards' assistant Grant] Leenhouts, and [DOS domestic Radio-TV Chief Bill] Wood, the DOS will eventually come to NBC with an offer for use of some of our material.[42]

The program became much more profitable than Salomon ever dreamed, playing in syndication for more than forty years, repaying NBC's investment in public service hundreds of times over.

Salomon, indeed, held an entrepreneurial view of the network's public service obligations. Someone from DOD suggested that he take a trip to the naval installation at Key West, also the home of the "Winter White House," to meet with the future head of the navy's photographic operations. He mused that "two or three days on Truman Beach or out fishing certainly offer us unheard of cultural advantages and might even be construed as an extenuation of NBC's avowed policy in the Navy Project of rendering a public service."[43]

Following the success of *Victory at Sea*, the television networks produced hundreds of documentaries. The Project XX unit worked into the early 1960s. ABC launched a similar unit to produce its *Close-Up!* series. CBS's premier documentary unit was associated with Edward R. Murrow's *See It Now* series, which later evolved into *CBS Reports*. These series probed contemporary rather than historical topics. Two more major compilation series were produced before the end of the decade with heavy reliance on Pentagon resources.

Widely regarded as CBS's answer to *Victory at Sea*, *Air Power* first aired during the 1956–1957 season and repeated in 1957–1958. Secretary of the Air Force Harold E. Talbott and CBS Television Network president L. J. Volkenburg jointly announced their intention to produce the series for the 1955–1956 season, but apparently it took an extra year to complete the extensive editing required. CBS spent $500,000 on the series, originally entitled *Conquest of the Air*.

Producer Perry Wolff's experience came from producing radio documentaries at CBS station WBBM in Chicago. His co-producer Jim Faichney, formerly head of the USIA's motion picture section, facilitated close cooperation with the air force. Footage was culled from the air force archive at Wright-Patterson Air Force Base and featured German film captured during World War II.

Wolff bridled at the need to receive official sanction for the series outline. In a memo to CBS executives Sig Mickelson and Irving Gitlin, he proposed a unifying premise that would "permit us to work with the Air Force on our terms rather than theirs and will extract maximum dramatic interest from the hundred million feet of film available to us." The premise was the growth of air power during the twentieth century, "inextricably allied with technocratic and scientific advances; with diplomatic conditions; with military tactics." Wolff's resistance stemmed from his objections to those strategists who promoted air power as the means to American world domination analogous to the British navy's control of the seas in the early twentieth century. Unlike extreme proponents of air power, Wolff believed that it had "limitations." He also disliked the air force association with "special pleading from military interests."[44]

In a *Time* interview, Wolff stated that the air force "wanted a flag-waving show at first. We wanted objective reporting." Wolff finally demanded the permanent removal from the project of air force liaison Colonel Wilson when Wilson "insisted that the tone of the programs be compromised more in favor of the Air Force." Yet Wolff clearly subscribed to the basic premise that military superiority equals greatness, that American air power reflects American commercial and political superiority.[45] Although he resisted a simplistically positive rendition of the history of military flight, he structured his history of flight around military innovations and accomplishments.

The series certainly began in sensationally militaristic fashion. The very first episode was a simulation entitled "The Day North America Is Attacked." Broadcast on Armistice Day and narrated by Walter Cronkite from inside the Continental Air Defense Command, the program established "the limits to which the military establishment would go for favorable publicity in entertainment."[46] Generals played themselves in a mock attack, while across the screen a superimposed image read, "AN ATTACK IS NOT TAKING PLACE. THIS IS A MILITARY EXERCISE."

Air Power drew criticism from all sides. Edward R. Murrow complained to the news division president Sig Mickelson that two episodes in particular distorted history "in order to gratify the 'fly boys' in the Pentagon." Yet the one-time director of the Office of Information Service for the air force, General Scott, complained to Mickelson that the same two episodes that irked Murrow for being too blindly supportive were anti-American, "If the Russians were to do a show on the United States Air Force, they couldn't subvert it any better than you have done." While the particulars of certain battles were disputed, *Air Power*, like *Crusade in Europe* and *Victory at Sea*, promoted military might as the answer to the rivalry between nations. An episode entitled "The New Doctrine" concluded, "Air power has made peace no longer a dream, but a hope and a possibility."[47]

Despite Wolff's early recommendation that in order to maintain the Pentagon's respect the program should not utilize Hollywood actors, the series employed guest narrators from the entertainment world including Fred Allen, Art Carney, and Michael Redgrave. Each episode featured dramatic structure and upbeat endings, and *Air Power* won much larger audiences than most straightforward public affairs programs did. It earned CBS tremendous profits from subsequent syndication.

Even more pitched to win large audiences than the epic military documentaries, CBS's series *The Twentieth Century* also relied heavily on the Pentagon for support and advice. Shortly after the series premiere in 1957, a *TV Guide* headline proclaimed, "'The Twentieth Century' turns to reality to thrill and entertain the viewer." In 1960, the magazine's shocked editors asked, "Guess what program came in 69th among 131 evening programs in the last Nielsen ratings, had an average audience of 8,814,000 homes and a higher rating than the average half-hour mystery, adventure or audience-participation quiz show?"[48] Like *Air Power*, the program was narrated by Walter Cronkite and sponsored by Prudential Life Insurance Company. But unlike other compilation documentaries, the series then moved into contemporary biography and current affairs, and it lasted thirteen years.

Bluem points out *The Twentieth Century* producer Burton Benjamin's innovation of using an "eyewitness" point of view in the compilation doc-

umentary. Because the form's freshness had been eroded by its prede-
cessors, Benjamin moved it into a "different, more personal, concentration . . . into the small stories of recent history, seeking the incidents that
reflected the mood and character of a place or an era with greater attention to theme and artistic interpretation."[49]

Despite the networks' increased resources and experience, they continued to seek and receive official approval for content of Cold War programming. The creation of a new form of documentary film for television
began with great, dramatic military stories celebrating American consensus, and this new form gained approval by both government and corporate sponsors.

Dramatic License

Following this same arc toward popularization, network collaboration
with the Pentagon to produce programs entered one more genre before the
end of the 1950s. CBS, ABC, and NBC produced half a dozen dramas
based on military records. Following a network trend toward more outside procurement, independent producers made many more that aired na-
tionally.

DOD had long recruited Hollywood talent to incorporate Cold War
propaganda into its entertainment products, as it had during World War
II. In 1956, the Subsidiary Activities Division of the Joint Chiefs of Staff
undertook cooperation with motion picture and television producers and
directors to weave the themes of the navy's "Militant Liberty" program
into Hollywood productions. "Militant Liberty" was a secret domestic
psychological warfare campaign created in 1955 to "explain the true conditions existing under Communism in simple terms" and to "generate a
motivation to combat this threat." Its creators worked with director John
Ford, actor John Wayne (who started the Motion Picture Alliance to combat communist subversion in the motion picture industry), and producers
Merion Cooper, Charles Schnee, and Cornelius Vanderbilt Whitney to utilize elements of "Militant Liberty" in several forthcoming films. They
agreed to do so for Whitney's "American Film Series" and for two forthcoming MGM films produced by Schnee and directed by Ford, *Eagles
Wings* and *Seabees*. Merian Cooper volunteered to study the possibilities
for "advantageous" use of "Militant Liberty" elements in television programs.[50]

Producers and information officials alike believed that dramatic stories
often conveyed their messages more effectively than documentary presen-

tations. Faced with the tremendous excess of naval film left over after *Victory at Sea*, Henry Salomon had proposed using it to tell fictional stories. He noted that "a fictional treatment of some small aspects of the war gives a more vivid picture of the war, Navy, etc. than the actual facts themselves. . . . We might have a good thing here with commercial value either as single shots or a series for some sponsor, 'Tales of the Sea,' or some other gimmick."[51] Despite Robert Sarnoff's enthusiasm, this series never developed.

The Pentagon policy for cooperation on dramatic series was "not only advance submission of script, but subsequent review of the product." CBS tried to get OPI to drop the requirement for review of the final product for *The Phil Silvers Show*, a satire of military life at the mythical Fort Baxter, Kansas, which ran on CBS from 1955 to 1959. OPI stuck to its own ground rules, despite the OPI director's rating of Silvers's ability "on a par with NBC's great ad libber, Bob Hope." To OPI's chagrin, CBS struck a separate deal with the army for the show's first season. OPI also refused cooperation on a Beetle Bailey series that it deemed "could not possibly be of benefit to the Army."[52]

The California-based defense contractor Aero-jet Corporation pioneered the military anthology series in 1952–1954 with its production, *On Guard*. The series mixed sensational but poorly made episodes about the Anti-submarine Warfare Group, the Continental Air Defense Command, and the Tactical Air Command, with such ho-hum subjects as the Army Language School. Few ABC affiliates bothered picking it up.[53]

The first successful dramatic network series based on DOD records was *Navy Log*, which aired on CBS and then ABC from 1955 until 1958 in prime-time slots on Tuesday, Wednesday, and Thursday. (See Figure 7.) Producer Sam Gallu, a "ninety-day wonder" from Columbia University, served two years aboard an aircraft carrier before transferring to an admiral's staff on Formosa during World War II. Gallu conceived the series "one night in a Pullman berth between Minneapolis and Kansas City – about as far as you can get from either ocean." Each episode focused on a highly dramatic or spectacular incident based on fact, often embellished. Rescues, sacrifices, technological feats, and unlikely heroes ended happily week after week. J. P. Shanley of the *New York Times* observed that it "lacks the authenticity of 'Victory at Sea,'" and *TV Guide* surmised that unlike *Crusade in Europe* and *Victory at Sea*, "'Navy Log' deals with people. And it does a fine job."[54]

The navy provided Gallu with far more than footage. The first episode concerned two navy frogmen whose mission is to dismantle secret equip-

Figure 7. *Navy Log* received tremendous assistance from the navy, including the use of planes and aircraft carriers. This still is from the episode entitled "Helldivers Over Greece." Photograph courtesy of Photofest.

ment in two sunken submarines. Real frogmen performed the underwater scenes (two of whom nearly drowned while a third was attacked by a shark). Navy planes ferried Gallu, his crew, and film from San Diego to the Virgin Islands, from Hawaii to the Pentagon. Navy planes crashed and performed strafing runs for the *Navy Log* cameras, and once Gallu "had a ship pulled out from under him to be sent on a mission."[55]

Senator John F. Kennedy spent two days in San Diego during the filming of an episode on the rescue of PT-109. An episode entitled "The Bishop of Bayfield" dramatized the naval evacuation of Vietnamese Christians from Haiphong harbor in North Vietnam. Using authentic footage of

Figure 8. *West Point Story* was based on U.S. Military Academy files, and exteriors were filmed there, featuring real-life cadets. Photograph courtesy of Photofest.

the evacuation mixed with reenactments, the story was laden with "classic Cold War imagery: protective and paternal military men helping frightened, wretched refugees from the Reds. The story blatantly blended Christian symbols and Cold War propaganda."[56] Gallu produced more than 100 episodes.

The West Point Story aired on CBS and ABC between 1956 and 1958. (See Figure 8.) Based on stories from the files of the U.S. Military Academy with the names and dates changed, the series featured performers such as Clint Eastwood, and two as-yet unknowns, Barbara Eden and Leonard Nimoy.[57] A retired Office of Strategic Services officer, Colonel William Eliscu, produced a series called *O.S.S.* based on that organization's files for ABC's 1957–1958 season.

In 1958, Milton Caniff's famous comic strip *Steve Canyon* was turned into an NBC television series. The fictional air force command pilot became commanding officer of "Big Thunder Air Force Base" in California during the first season, and he traveled around troubleshooting. Authentic footage of the Atlas ICBM missile, zero elevation jet launches, and test detonation of a hydrogen bomb appeared on the program. The air force considered the series a recruiting aid:

> Whether on film or newsprint, the value of Steve Canyon to the Air Force has a measurable public service quotient, second only to its entrance standard. The daily reading of the strip by the young prospect for tomorrow's Air Force now takes on a "wired-for-sound" aspect, which definitely should enhance the effectiveness of the United States Air Force Recruiting Service.[58]

Dean Fredericks, an air force officer with video experience, played Commander Canyon.

The counterespionage files of Rear Admiral Ellis M. Zacharias (retired) provided the raw material for NBC's *Behind Closed Doors*, which ran during the 1958–1959 season. During World War II, Zacharias served as deputy chief of U.S. Naval Intelligence and as the official government spokesman on radio in the Pacific. He summarized his political world view in 1958: "There are three courses open to us in dealing with the world's problems. First, appeasement. That gets us nowhere. Second, law and order. They're words not in the Communist vocabulary. So what's left? Power politics, and that's what we've got to play whether we like it or not."[59]

The October 1957 launch of the Soviet satellite *Sputnik* created a wave of hysteria in the United States that communist science had surpassed American science. Although it was too late to capitalize on interest in the space race for the next television season, CBS presented *Men in Space* during the 1959–1960 season. The Department of Defense retained script approval, ruling out anything that was not in the realm of scientific possibility, such as "little green men from Mercury or insects with tractors for feet." Personnel from the army, navy, and air force supervised filming at Edwards Air Force Base, Cape Canaveral, the navy testing ground at Point Meyer near Santa Barbara, the Space Medicine Center at Randolph Field, Texas, and Wright Patterson Air Force Base. The series aimed at "authenticity," so for an episode about travel to the planet Venus, an air force "space expert" calculated the probable date of humans traveling to Venus to be 1980.[60]

Syndicated dramas from the later 1950s based on military records included the titles, *Pentagon, U.S.A.*; *The Man Called X*; *Citizen Soldier*, also known as *The Big Attack*; *The Silent Service*; *Men of Annapolis*; and *The Blue Angels*.

The programs produced cooperatively by the networks and the Department of Defense evolved according to the growing demand for popular and lucrative entertainment programming. The ideological control exerted by the military appeared quite commendable when presented as fidelity to historical facts found in official records. Cold War propaganda grew increasingly naturalized – first as news, and more effectively as entertainment as the 1950s progressed.

CHAPTER SEVEN

THE MOST VIGOROUS ANTICOMMUNIST CAMPAIGN: OBJECTIVITY AND CONSENSUS JOURNALISM

The previous four chapters complicate news broadcasters' most basic self-portrait. Their claim to professionalism was (and is) their disciplined objectivity – the refusal to inject their boss's, their sponsor's, or their own biases into the news. This objectivity is realized through a set of identifiable procedures and routines for news gathering. As discussed in Chapter Two, journalism historians have charted how these routines change over time, according to the market strategies of media industries and prevailing political orthodoxies. In the mid-twentieth century, the political economy of the mass media was intimately tied up with the articulation of Cold War policies, and objectivity became grounded in a fervent anticommunism. The purpose of this chapter is to explore how such a hotly felt ideology became fully naturalized, or normalized, as objective.

It takes as its principal case the anticommunist campaigns of Senator Joseph McCarthy, his attacks on unfriendly journalists, and the approving portrayal of those attacks by their colleagues on the preeminent public affairs program of the era, NBC's *Meet the Press*. It foregrounds that discussion in a review of the considerable literature on McCarthy and the press, and it argues that this literature does not account for the objectivity practices of early television news broadcasters. Like McCarthy himself, broadcasters paid great heed to the gestures that signaled objectivity, but anticommunism underpinned their broadcasts as surely as did electricity. This historical variant of the journalist's professional code of objectivity manifests a broader phenomenon in postwar intellectual history, the embrace of a determinedly cold realism that denied its own passionate basis in hatred and fear of totalitarianism.

The Literature on McCarthy and Objectivity in Print Journalism

Previous literature analyzing the performance of journalists in the early Cold War focuses exclusively on print journalists. Television before 1963 is dismissed as an immature medium, produced by people with little news experience.

A strict separation of facts and values is supposed to have prevailed in print journalism during the early Cold War. As quoted in Chapter Two, Daniel Hallin calls the period from the end of World War II until the early 1960s "the heyday of straight journalism" when "the ordinary reporter was to tell 'who, what, when, where' and leave it at that."[1] Former news-papermen initially advanced this concept of "detached" objectivity in the late 1950s to explain the press's failures in covering Senator McCarthy. They contended that the routines of objective reporting, including a focus on officials, attention to breaking stories, and prohibitions against inter-pretation and analysis, served to trumpet McCarthy's allegations, often against reporters' wishes. These writers do not ask when or why these routines of objective reporting came into practice: They have the timeless quality of proud professionalism.

Richard Rovere, Washington correspondent for the *New Yorker* and an early McCarthy biographer, mused that the senator had a talent for simu-lating just the kind of facts that the prevailing routines of objective jour-nalism spotlighted. The senator's enterprise was

> a great satire, a gigantic spoof on the kind of scholarship in which the "fact" enjoys its ultimate triumph. . . . Documents, documents, documents – he was always loaded with them. The bulging briefcase – the scholar's toolbox – be-came to him what snapping red galluses and a stream of tobacco juice were to the older southern demagogues. He saw the possibilities of coming before the people with the dust of the archives clinging to him, and he was right.[2]

Because McCarthy mastered the props and gestures of objectivity, Rovere argued, journalists had little choice but to report the senator's allegations.

Douglass Cater of *The Reporter* pinpointed the thorny problem that "all the elaborate reporting mechanisms of the press seemed unable to de-tect and to communicate the basic fact of McCarthy's lies." Professional prohibitions against interpreting official statements disallowed journalists from injecting correctives. McCarthy knew news deadlines and timed his public statements to forestall journalists from checking his allegations or from getting oppositional responses. Although his targets might issue denials, "the answers never did catch up with the charges in the headlines." In 1954, the *New York Times* lamely pleaded that "it is difficult, if not impossible, to ignore charges by Senator McCarthy just because they are usually proved exaggerated or false. The remedy lies with the reader."[3] Journalists were thus held captive by overly restrictive, but presumably apolitical, professional codes. This argument entails a striking and unlikely paradox: Just as anticommunist ideology became hegemonic, journalism became nonideological.

More politically attuned critics have argued that this detached objectivity reflected journalists' acquiescence in anticommunist ideology rather than timeless professional standards. James Aronson, a veteran reporter for both mainstream and left-wing newspapers, argued that the mainstream press became a "voluntary arm of established power" in the 1950s. Michael Schudson contends that like most members of U.S. government and society, journalists agreed with the basic assumptions and strategies of the Cold War. In explaining the collapse of critical distance in the coverage of McCarthy, he explains, "The press, like the Congress, sympathized with Cold War ideology and rarely questioned the presuppositions of national security doctrine." Indeed, to do so was to commit political suicide. Schudson adds the procedural argument that the growth of centralized news management in the executive branch made it increasingly difficult for journalists to find alternative sources of information.[4]

This scholarship addresses a very selected segment of the press. Aronson's sources are the prestige newspapers published in New York and Washington, and Schudson draws mostly on elite journalists' accounts (including Rovere's) and professional journals. More ranging scholarship has shown that only the most elite segment of the print press practiced such highly detached objectivity. In his book-length study of McCarthy and the press, Edwin Bayley, formerly of the *Milwaukee Journal*, found a wide variety of coverage of McCarthy among different newspapers. He contends that most papers took sides and did not pretend to be objective, that "partisanship among newspapers was at its peak." He argues that the restraint from contextualizing official statements "applied only to the wire services and the papers that sought to avoid criticism at all costs."[5]

Bayley suggests that the wire services had economic incentives to remain neutral because they served clients of all political stripes. Prestige papers, which based their authority on their political neutrality, likewise had compelling economic reasons to avoid commentary. Detached objectivity served as a corporate strategy to protect these specialized news outlets from blacklisters. Bayley thus explains the varieties of opinion and objectivity as commercial strategies to sell papers to different readerships. Less highbrow papers, notably those owned by the Hearst and McCormick-Patterson families, targeted working-class audiences with tabloid-style revelations of spies, plots, and betrayal, which fanned the flames of McCarthyism. [6]

The view that journalists retreated into a highly detached objectivity thus describes a relatively small but highly influential number of prestigious print news outlets.[7] This picture is not incorrect, just incomplete, and it leaves out television entirely. Bayley's evaluation of journalistic performance actually reflects a more diverse marketplace of ideas than was generally reckoned to exist, but it also highlights the variability and subservience to sales of the journalist's professional code.

Television and Objectivity

Television's performance regarding the professional ideal of objectivity during the early Cold War varies as widely as that of print outlets. From station to station, from network to network, and indeed from program to program, the standards for objectivity and achievement on that scale varied. This section briefly treats two ends of that spectrum, and the rest of the chapter presents a case study of the NBC program *Meet the Press*, whose panels of reporters represented a spectrum of American journalism.

We can certainly find examples of Hearst-like anticommunist hysteria in early television news. In January 1951, just past the midpoint of the twentieth century, the NBC News and Special Events Department produced a series of six special reports entitled *America at Mid-Century*. The third broadcast addressed "the meaning and menace of communism" ("We urge you not to switch your dial – you can't escape it"). The scripts of these broadcasts reveal an extraordinary tension between the network's purposes of arming the public against communism and retaining claims to professional objectivity. The episode opened with starkly fearful warnings. Communism "is a creeping, sinuous ideology that destroys man's soul – makes impotent his will to resist – and degrades the very dignity of Creation itself." Radcliffe Hall, writer and narrator, then immediately began making claims for the program's factuality and objectivity. "The contents of this program represent no editorial opinion – they are a compilation of existing facts, brought together for your information, as a public service."

Although not billed as an editorial, the program engaged in outright and slightly veiled advocacy on almost every major issue in U.S. foreign policy. For example, Hall states as fact, "The only hope for Siam is full military aid from the United States and Britain." He repeatedly signals what issues are important and which are not, and he concludes with a menacing list of Soviet military capabilities. At the very end, he holds out tentative hope of survival. "Yet, armed with facts, aware of the danger, fortified with courage and conviction, America can take its destined place in the long, unending course of life."[8]

Throughout, Hall makes much of the unassailability of his sources and the objectivity of his report. The presented facts "have been compiled from official and private intelligence sources – the reports of thoroughly reliable observers throughout the world – as well as from the press wire services which are available to everyone." Yet a bibliography for the program lists three principal sources, all of which any reasonably sophisticated political reporter would recognize as politically infused. It cites several publications of the ultraconservative U.S. Chamber of Commerce, and the magazine *Plain Talk* (assuredly "under competent editorial direction"), which was published by the equally ultraright anticommunist Alfred Kohlberg. Finally, it lists the pamphlet "100 Things You Should Know About Communism," put out by the House Committee on Un-American Activities.

Hall's defense of his facts, coupled with the highly inflammatory language of the broadcast, suggested a strategy to ward off charges of political bias. The following week's broadcast, on domestic communist subversion, showed similar sophistication when it advertised, "This is no witch-hunt . . . this is a factual report of Communism in America, and how it is working to achieve its avowed purpose of bringing the United States completely under the Soviet orbit" [ellipsis in original].[9] Like McCarthy, this NBC reporter mastered the gestures and props of objectivity but presented a highly selected and emotionally charged series of broadcasts.

By contrast, a systematic and sincere attempt to evaluate television's capacity for and track record in objectivity occurred at the CBS network in 1954. In the wake of the famous *See It Now* broadcast on McCarthy, during which Edward R. Murrow issued a forceful editorial on the climate of unreasoning fear in the nation, the network felt compelled to evaluate its policy on airing political opinion. This "corporate soul-searching"[10] resulted in a major speech by network chairman William S. Paley to the National Association of Radio and Television Broadcasters in Chicago on May 25, 1954.

The speech, entitled "The Road to Responsibility," read like a call to arms against those who assailed television as a dangerous political force. In news and public affairs, Paley averred, broadcasters faced two principal threats. On the one hand, commercial pressures pushed broadcasters toward "self-sterilization." They were "so frightened or nervous of the powerful impact of the medium that opinions are required to die before utterance." Despite his own role in implementing loyalty oaths and otherwise bowing to blacklisters at CBS, Paley pronounced such cowardice unacceptable. "As has been said so often, it is essential, in order to maintain a vital democracy, to assure a free market for the exchange of ideas." On the other hand, government officials who "look upon the broadcasting organization as an instrument created to serve their own purposes, whatever these may be," also threatened the marketplace of ideas. Paley judged that timidity here too had spurred a self-perpetuating cycle of pressures that threatened to crush broadcasters' "independence and stature." The speech was widely acclaimed, but it does not square with CBS's record in news and public affairs, as detailed in previous chapters, where Paley seemed to define the network's stature more on its closeness to the national security state than on its independence from it.

Paley's solution rested with the "will and the intent" of the individual broadcaster to be fair and objective. In a rare philosophical moment, he acknowledged the limitations of subjective consciousness, "I think we all recognize that human nature is such that no newsman is entirely free from his own personal prejudice, experience, and opinions and that, accordingly, 100 percent objectivity may not always be possible." But if the telecaster's goal is to enable the viewer to make up his own mind, the purposes of fairness would be well served. This method for ensuring fairness and objectivity, like the networks' defense of their cave-in to blacklisters (as detailed in Chapter Two), draws attention away from the institutional power and alignments of network broadcasting to the political allegiances of individual broadcasters. The struggle for responsible broadcasting would, according to Paley, be fought between the individual broadcaster and an individual advertiser or official – and not over the structural relationships between media corporations, their advertisers, and the government.

One passage in the speech seems to contradict the reassuring message of the rest of it. Lest anyone think that at the height of the Cold War all points of view would be fairly treated, or that fairness was the same thing as a thoroughgoing relativity, Paley also exclaimed, "And it must be recognized that there *is* a difference between men, ideas and institutions:

some are good and some are bad, and it is up to us to know the difference – to know what will uphold democracy and what will undermine it – and then not to do the latter!" At the same time that he argued for broadcasters to codify procedures to ensure fairness, he also told broadcasters that they individually bore the responsibility to judge which ideas served democracy and which did not. This was a plain enjoinder to demonstrate the industry's anticommunism.

In the wake of Paley's self-assessment of CBS's performance in public affairs, CBS News contracted with a group of professors at the University of Wisconsin School of Journalism to conduct a study of the network's performance in living up to its own objectivity policies. The scholars performed a content analysis of the radio programs of Allen Jackson and Edward R. Murrow, and of the television program, *CBS Evening News with Douglas Edwards*. Each sentence in a series of randomly selected broadcasts was coded by three people into one of six categories: straight news, background, significance, consequence, valuation, and advocacy. Only the first two categories complied with a strict interpretation of the network's news policy.

On the whole, the newscasters performed remarkably well. They engaged in almost no advocacy and rarely attributed significance to reported events, although one could well argue that inclusion in a news broadcast, or the power of selection, confers some significance. A tendency to add valuation and to forecast consequences was slightly more problematic. Valuations would include telling phrases such as "businesslike and pleasant" pickets or "meaningless formality." Attributions of consequence could point to ordinary sequence or causality ("the antagonists will probably face each other across a conference table in the next few days") or make proscribed predictions ("but the will to fight is always diminished when compromises or peace settlements are in prospect"). The most striking difference came between the first and second halves of the Murrow program, between straight news and commentary, but the latter was billed as such.[11] Certainly *America at Mid-Century* would have failed this test miserably.

Both the *America at Mid-Century* series and the CBS evaluations demonstrate that broadcasters in the early to mid-1950s gave tremendous thought to their own objectivity. In the case of *America at Mid-Century*, a great deal of effort was expended to simulate the routines of objectivity. The CBS News Division, directed from the highest corporate level, wanted very much to understand its own performance. In both cases, however, anticommunism served as a bottom line to the need for objectivity. On *Mid-*

Century, the props of objectivity served to support an explicitly anticommunist agenda. In Paley's speech, communism was the one issue not subject to fairness or balance. This incorporation of anticommunism into the professional routines of objective journalism can be seen most clearly in the most honored public affairs program of the period, NBC's *Meet the Press*.

Meet the Press and the Normative Objectification of Anticommunism

Meet the Press provides an important case study of political discourse in the early Cold War because it claimed to represent the entire political spectrum on its panel of reporters. They came largely from prestige papers, and they questioned the leading political newsmakers of the day. In 1951–1952, about thirteen percent of the American population, or thirty-four percent of the television audience, watched any given episode, a far larger percentage than in its subsequent forty years.[12]

The program began in 1945 as a promotional stunt to advertise the *American Mercury* magazine on the Mutual radio network. Founded by H. L. Mencken in 1924, the *American Mercury* voiced his skepticism and iconoclasm. Lawrence Spivak, its Harvard-educated business manager, bought the publication in 1939 but never secured enough readers or advertisers to turn a profit. Spivak added *Ellery Queen's Mystery Magazine* and a series of science fiction magazines and paperback books to Mercury Publications to keep it afloat. When Spivak filled in for a panelist on the radio show, his testy style of questioning vitalized it. General Foods took *Meet the Press* to NBC television in 1947, and television proved far more profitable than the magazines. Spivak sold his publishing ventures in 1950, bought his co-producer Martha Rountree's interest in *Meet the Press* in 1953 for $117,000, and then sold it to NBC in 1955 for a reputed $1,100,000.[13]

The program seemed to fulfill television's democratic promise of bringing government into the home, of making representatives more accessible to citizens. On December 23, 1951, the president of its sponsor, the Revere Copper and Brass Corporation, praised the program's contribution to the American political process. He exulted, "Programs such as this help shape the American way of life, to bring truths out into the open, to give us a better understanding about what the leaders of this country are striving to accomplish, how they are serving our country."[14]

Erik Barnouw argues that the main value of Sunday morning "cultural ghetto" press panel programs was their ability to generate newspaper stories and thereby to bring the network free publicity. Broadcaster Ray Scherer wrote of the shows' importance: "I wonder occasionally how the Monday morning dailies ever filled up page one before television." Twenty-seven out of fifty-two episodes of *Meet the Press* in 1955 made the first page of the *New York Times* the following day.[15] Crucially, the guests, rather than the program's producers, generated the headlines. NBC received publicity without responsibility for any subsequent controversy. The program seemed to promote accountability in government.

Meet the Press thus supported the government by providing a forum for officials to go before the public. During the 1950s, eighty-three percent of the guest appearances on the program were made by government officials, whether appointed or elected. United States senators made thirty percent of the appearances. Guests always appeared voluntarily, presumably when they had something to gain by going before the public. Many used *Meet the Press* to break major news during the late 1940s and 1950s. For example, Whittaker Chambers first made public the allegations that led to the conviction of Alger Hiss; General Walter Bedell Smith first hinted that the Soviet Union had exploded an atomic bomb; and Governor Thomas E. Dewey announced that he would not run against Eisenhower for the 1952 Republican nomination. Senator Walter George called for "a meeting at the summit" that led to the Big Four Conference in Geneva in 1955.[16]

Guests chose to appear only when confident of a positive outcome. Records show many officials declining to go on *Meet the Press* at risky times. For instance, the assistant secretary of state for public affairs recommended that Secretary of State Dean Acheson decline Spivak's July 1951 invitation but recommended "that your reply indicate to Mr. Spivak that an invitation to you when circumstances were favorable for such an appearance would receive serious consideration in the Department." As we saw in Chapter Three, the state department prohibited its officials from discussing major policy questions on unscripted television programs.[17] Guests always appeared on *Meet the Press* voluntarily, when they had something to gain.

At the same time that it performed this supportive function for the government, *Meet the Press* purported to serve an oppositional or investigative function. Indeed, it had a reputation for putting its guests on the "hot seat." In later years, *TV Guide* entitled articles about it, "Ten Minutes on That Show Can Age You Ten Years" and "The Program That Likes It

Hot." Spivak kept his reputation as a combative, obstinate questioner un-til his retirement in 1976, when he explained that he was "pretty much the same son of a bitch off camera as on. This is the way I've always ques-tioned. I've always challenged people." He searched the public record for contradictory statements and came armed with notoriously damning note cards. When friends of his appeared on the program, Spivak cautioned them that he would pull no punches, and said that, "If your position is a strong one, the tougher the question, the better you're going to do."[18] One widely reprinted *New Yorker* cartoon showed a middle-aged woman re-marking to her husband, "Lawrence Spivak would take that tone with *me* just once." The *Washingtonian* entitled a 1970 profile, "This Is Lawrence Spivak and I'm Not Afraid of Anybody." After appearing with him on a panel interrogating an avowed communist, I. F. Stone wondered if Spivak had been a grand inquisitor in some other existence.[19]

How did the program reconcile its supportive and oppositional func-tions? Guests always consented, and sometimes asked, to go on, so they must have felt that they had something to gain from facing the questions they would receive. Many of them realized they could give evasive or re-hearsed answers to the toughest questions, and they always got the last word. Robert Kennedy later quipped, "I don't know what the first question is going to be, but I know what the first answer is going to be." Marquis Childs found the format's weakness was "the difficulty of catching a lie."[20]

Many people, even participants, pointed to the format's limitations for exposing hidden information. The moderator, often controlled by Spivak from the press panel, critically curtailed the program's spontaneity by lim-iting the number of follow-up questions that each reporter was allowed. Arthur Krock, chief of the *New York Times* Washington bureau, parodied the format's niceties. "Under the TV panel system each questioner must have his inning: hence each line of inquiry is broken off before the subject can be pinned down to the spot he really is on." When Krock's Senator Slick hears that one panelist, Mr. Gimlet, will speak for all four panelists, he tries to beat a hasty retreat. When pressed about his own statements, he utters nonsensical truisms about necessary exceptions and inherent ambi-guities. Slick's parting line is, "Gimlet, you lay off me or I won't help this pitiless probe for the truth any more." Guests know they can always evade uncomfortable questions. One New Left critic, citing effusive accolades that the program received from Richard Nixon, John Kennedy, Hubert Humphrey, and Barry Goldwater, wrote in the early 1970s: "No news program which draws such praise from the men they question can be all that good."[21]

In reconciling the program's supportive and oppositional functions, a more deeply normative argument can be made. Sociologist Alvin Gouldner coined the term "normative objectification" to denote the process by which the practices and ideologies of objectivity incorporate prevailing social and political norms, but retain and even strengthen their claims to objectivity.[22] Spivak was terribly feisty in defense of deeply held norms, so he appeared to be oppositional but ultimately played a supportive role. Specifically, he provides striking evidence for the normative objectification of anticommunism. Anticommunism did not register in his world view as an ideology and therefore did not seem to violate his concept of objectivity. Nor did his personal conceptions of right and wrong register as value judgments. In an extraordinarily revealing description, Spivak even points to the vigor of his anticommunism as evidence for his neutrality:

> [T]he thing that we've always tried to do in television is that we've never taken a political point of view in terms of left and right or middle, but always in terms of, in my judgment, what I considered right and wrong. . . . So ideologically, I really never took a position. I never was identified with any party so that didn't trouble me. So we punctured, or thought we did, Republicans and Democrats, labor and capital, and of course we carried on probably the most vigorous anticommunist campaign from the very beginning.[23]

Vigorous anticommunism became consistent with objectivity through the bipolar world view of the Cold War. The market-driven American media was cast as free and pluralistic in opposition to the ideological rigidity of state-controlled communist media. For Spivak, anticommunism did not violate professional standards of objectivity; rather, it was necessary to them. The program's aggressiveness satisfies the requirements of professional objectivity by policing prevailing orthodoxies rather than challenging them. It provides support for orthodoxies while taking an oppositional tone; thus, it appropriates the legitimacy of tough journalism.

By defining objectivity as balance, Spivak suggested that he subscribed to cultural, moral, or epistemological relativism, yet he repeatedly expressed intolerance of ambiguity or dissent. As many commentators have observed, the American alternative to communism became itself a dogmatic ideology, often confusing prescriptive and descriptive visions of the United States.[24] As we shall see, even those few journalists who acknowledged the suppression of unorthodox views by the mainstream media still defended their ultimate orthodoxy – that corporate ownership was the only desirable alternative to communistic state control.

Spivak's oppositionalism was not predicated on disapproval of Truman or Eisenhower administration policies but on the insufficiency of their efforts to fulfill those policies of containment abroad and vigilance at home. He actively contested the major critiques of anticommunism in each administration: the defense of civil liberties under Truman, and fiscal prudence under Eisenhower. He held public officials accountable to more extreme anticommunist standards than those of either administration, particularly over the threat of domestic subversion. The program generated a lot of heat because of the vehemence with which panelists policed anticommunism, not because the range of contention that it offered was very broad.

Other authors have noted the anticommunist basis for journalists' oppositionalism in this period. Michael Parenti observes that liberal editors and commentators opposed McCarthy on "Cold War anticommunist grounds" and indicts them for cowardice. He judges them for failing to defend the rights of communists as well as the rights of the unjustly accused. David Caute likewise sums up the position of the *New York Times* as "sensitive to the rights and liberties of certified anti-Communist liberals, insensitive to the rights and liberties of the left, of those who questioned the Truman Doctrine." Caute judges that journalists' "double standards reflected, and presumably intensified, the temporary moral collapse of American liberalism."[25]

Rather than spawning reticence, this collapse formed the basis for aggressive objectivity practices. On *Meet the Press*, reporters challenged McCarthy directly, but not on his violations of civil liberties, and not because they disapproved of his goals. Their central question about the senator's campaign was not, as Parenti and Caute would have it, whether it was just or fair, but whether it was effective. They often perpetuated McCarthyite injustice, but they were not passive. *Meet the Press* legitimated public officials in sync with prevailing anticommunist orthodoxy and denounced those guests and the occasional panelist who did not conform to that orthodoxy. Although the room for dissent was very narrow, the program's combativeness suggested the free play of democratic debate and sufficed as professional objectivity.

Standards of Anticommunism

Joseph McCarthy appeared seven times on *Meet the Press* between 1950 and 1954.[26] No kinescopes survive of his first appearance, on March 19,

1950. On each remaining broadcast, the senator was rigorously challenged to defend his record and his honesty. But the panelists' combativeness was explicitly premised on their advocacy of an anticommunist agenda.

On July 2, 1950, several of the panelists pressed McCarthy about the flimsy facts he marshaled in his accusations against alleged communists in government. Spivak asked if the senator thought that he "helped clarify the situation by the way you have made accusations against these people? Do you think you have submitted enough proof so that you, for example, who was once a judge, would be satisfied with that proof?" Frank Mac-Naughton of *Time* asked, "Senator, do you think that you have proved one case yet, of all the cases that you submitted?" Spivak and Mac-Naughton highlighted the insufficiency of McCarthy's evidence but did not press the senator to verify the basis of specific charges or question his motives in light of his unsuccessful record in making accusations stick. They seemed to presume that adequate evidence existed and effectively urged the senator to be more thorough in producing it.

Moderator Martha Rountree made explicit the anticommunist sensibility behind criticisms of McCarthy's methods. She both chided and prompted him: "People say, Senator, that they hope you win out and they're on your side but they're against your tactics. This has been said by a lot of Republicans, too. If you had this to do all over again, would you have changed any of your tactics?" The panels always endorsed McCarthy's intentions.

By 1953, journalists had learned to anticipate McCarthy's evasion of specific questions. On the December 13, 1953 broadcast, John Madigan of the pro-McCarthy Hearst chain attempted to clarify the senator's fast and easy use of numbers about communists in government. I quote this exchange at length because it demonstrates both the appearance of oppositionalism and the ultimate endorsement of McCarthy's agenda. Spivak, serving as moderator, also jumped in to pin down the senator.

MADIGAN The type of specific complaints that they make is this instance of some fifteen hundred people in the government being fired for security reasons in the Eisenhower administration. You've used that figure, have you not?

MCCARTHY One thousand four hundred and twenty-seven up until about two months ago.

MADIGAN Do you know how many of those were actually loyalty risks and how much involved human frailty?

MCCARTHY   I can't give you that exact number.

MADIGAN   Do you know the figure, Senator?

MCCARTHY   I have an estimate from various people in government as to the percentage. It varies, the number who are discharged on the ground of communist connections.

MADIGAN   What is that number? Do you mind telling us what that estimate is?

MCCARTHY   It varies but it is extremely high, discharged for communist connection and perversion. Add the two together, it runs over ninety percent.

SPIVAK   Ninety percent of what?

MCCARTHY   Ninety percent of the total of 1,427.

SPIVAK   Ninety percent for perversion or ninety percent for loyalty?

MCCARTHY   A combination of communist activities and perversion.

SPIVAK   What of that is communist acts?

MCCARTHY   I couldn't break that down for you, Larry.

MADIGAN   Do you think they should be made public by the administration as protection against those who maybe just had bad companions?

MCCARTHY   Should the administration tell those who are discharged because he had bad companions?

MADIGAN   And those who are loyalty risks because of treasonable potentiality.

MCCARTHY   I doubt anything would be gained by it.

McCarthy evaded Madigan's original question five different ways before admitting he did not want to answer it. The panelists astutely reframed the question to frustrate each evasion. McCarthy never said that he didn't know the answer to the question but averred instead that he "couldn't" break down the difference.

Madigan finally alluded to the motivation behind the senator's obfuscation, asking if McCarthy thought the distinction was important to protect the rights of dismissed noncommunists. McCarthy's brief answer, "I doubt anything would be gained by it," ended the exchange, but no one asked why such a distinction should not be made in fairness to the accused or to prevent inflation of the domestic communist threat.

That the panelists pushed McCarthy this far but no farther on a civil liberties critique signaled the illegitimacy of such ostensibly leftist opposition. Recognizing the rights of accused communists tread dangerously close to defending them. Likewise, Madigan's pressure to determine the actual number of alleged communists confirmed the legitimacy of more "responsible" anticommunism. Seeking accurate numbers of traitors in government conformed to the journalist's role as government watchdog. This respectful treatment of the senator probably served to sanitize his irresponsible campaigns.

Policing Anticommunism

Two *Meet the Press* broadcasts concerning the effects of McCarthyism on the press reveal more directly journalists' own conception of their role in this period, and the astonishing tenacity of the notion that passionate anticommunism did not lead to a distortion of information but only served the truth. McCarthy called *New York Post* editor James Wechsler before closed sessions of his committee twice in the spring of 1953. Wechsler insisted that the senator release transcripts of the hearings. As a college student in the 1930s, Wechsler had been a member of the Young Communist League, had long since resigned, was open about his past affiliation, and, as a founding member of Americans for Democratic Action, was an active liberal anticommunist. The *Post* regularly editorialized against the threat of communism from abroad *and* against the threat of McCarthy at home. Controversy raged over why McCarthy called Wechsler. The senator and his principal investigator Roy Cohn alleged that a book Wechsler had written when he was a communist was found in an overseas state department library, but they would not name the book. Wechsler claimed that the senator was attempting to intimidate the press, and he asked the American Society of Newspaper Editors to investigate this possibility.

Cohn appeared on *Meet the Press* on May 3, 1953. He had just returned from the famous whirlwind trip to Europe where he and his colleague G. David Schine investigated the contents of U.S. Information Service libraries. Spivak broached the subject of Wechsler with Cohn, asking, "What was the purpose of calling James Wechsler, the editor of the *New York Post*, to your hearing? Was his testimony of sufficient importance for you to take the risk of being accused of interfering with the free press?" Spivak seemed to chide Cohn for interfering with the press, but he actually asked about the risk of being accused of such interference, which might have diverted attention and credibility away from the anticommunist fight. When Cohn implied that Wechsler was still a communist, Spivak defended the editor, saying, "He hasn't been active recently." But two weeks later when Wechsler appeared on the program, Spivak alleged that the editor still served the party.

When Wechsler appeared on May 17, 1953, the panelists were Spivak, the liberal columnist Marquis Childs, Frank Waldrop of the *Washington Times-Herald*, and Bert Andrews of the *New York Herald-Tribune* (see

Figure 9. *New York Post* editor James Wechsler appeared on *Meet the Press* on May 17, 1953, and was grilled by (left to right) Marquis Childs, Frank Waldrop, Bert Andrews, Lawrence Spivak, and moderator Martha Rountree. Printed with permission of NBC.

Figure 9). The anticommunist allegiances of the latter two journalists were revealed later: Waldrop authored HUAC's inflammatory pamphlet "100 Things You Should Know About Communism," and Andrews advised Richard Nixon in the Alger Hiss case.[27] Spivak, Waldrop, and Andrews completely denied that McCarthy menaced freedom of the press, and they defended McCarthy's promiscuous use of his committee's investigatory prerogative. These three journalists began by attempting to defend the McCarthy committee's actions and soon turned to trying to prove that Wechsler was still an active communist. Childs asked more neutral questions about the relationship between Senator McCarthy and the press, but he also sanctioned the senator's agenda.

Childs began the questioning by trying to determine whether McCarthy's alleged attempts to intimidate the *Post* had been successful. He asked if the paper's circulation or advertising had suffered since Wechsler's appearance before the committee. Childs then observed that since Eisenhower's inauguration, the press seemed to be tougher on McCarthy. Wechsler answered that McCarthy's failure to silence his critics did not mean that the senator was not trying to do so.

From the beginning of the Wechsler broadcast, Spivak took an extremely adversarial position. While maintaining the question-and-answer format, he tried to establish that McCarthy's intention was not to interfere with the press:

> SPIVAK   When you appeared, you said, "I regard this inquiry as a clear invasion of what used to be a newspaper's right to function independently." It may have been unpleasant to you, but just how was it an infringement of the free press?
>
> WECHSLER   Mr. Spivak, I can only answer that I was called ostensibly because a book I'd written was located in an embassy overseas. In the course of two hearings neither Senator McCarthy nor his staff could ever agree on which book it was or where it was found. I submit this was a perfectly pointless inquiry inspired by the fact that the *Post*, I'm proud to say, has been fighting Senator McCarthy pretty vigorously for a long time. Fighting him I may add as vigorously as we fought a man named Joe Stalin.
>
> SPIVAK   But Mr. Wechsler, freedom of the press as I understand it means freedom to print news and opinion. But does it also mean immunity from Congressional investigation, from criticism, or even from abuse?
>
> WECHSLER   I made very clear in the hearing: first, I was not subpoenaed, I went voluntarily. There were many questions I considered improper, but I answered them fully. I do not stand on any immunity. I say only in light of the transcript it seems to me that I had been there only as a newspaperman since there was no other legitimate reason for having me there.
>
> SPIVAK   But the Senate might have called you, any committee might have called you. They have such broad powers. Do you say a newspaper man ought never to be questioned by a Senate committee lest he be intimidated?
>
> WECHSLER   I certainly do not say that. I say only that the inquiry should be relevant to some particular business and there should be some showing of relevance in the course of the hearing. I submit that there was not in this proceeding.
>
> SPIVAK   Because it wasn't relevant, you think freedom of the press was involved?
>
> WECHSLER   Since it was not relevant, since the *Post*'s record with regard to Senator McCarthy is known, it seems that there was another purpose. I think it was harassment and an attempt at intimidation.

Spivak became feistier and more combative throughout this exchange. He gradually gave up the pretense of playing devil's advocate and began openly arguing his position. Greatly agitated, he finally pronounced:

Your major problem then is why you were called. That doesn't really involve freedom of the press. Now did Senator McCarthy do anything to you that he couldn't have said on the Senate floor with immunity, with no answer from you? Would that have been better?

By any standard, Spivak entered the realm of advocacy. Not only did he dismiss the question of freedom of the press in favor of McCarthy's mysterious agenda; he defended McCarthy's behavior by stating that the senator could have done even worse damage to Wechsler's rights. Spivak violated his own ideal of objectivity defined as balance, and he verged on harassment. The only other guests who were treated with equal hostility in more than 100 *Meet the Press* broadcasts that I screened were the pacifist, socialist British philosopher Bertrand Russell and the Soviet Premier Anastos Mikoyan.

Waldrop deliberately conflated and confused the nature of Wechsler's objections to being called before McCarthy. Although the committee would be well beyond its mandate in investigating the *New York Post*, Waldrop found it unreasonable that Wechsler should object. He repeatedly interrupted Wechsler, charging that Wechsler's communist associations were the real reason for his objections. Granting no validity whatsoever to Wechsler's concerns about intimidation of the press, Waldrop stated that if Wechsler were truly anticommunist he would defend the committee's right to investigate anything.

Andrews asked Wechsler if he had a personal conflict with McCarthy. When Wechsler denied any personal history with the senator, Andrews brought up a series of critical articles that ran in the *Post*, as if to catch Wechsler in a lie. "That was sort of 50–50, Mr. Wechsler, wasn't it? You attacked the Senator and he was turning around and attacking you." Andrews thus sanctioned McCarthy's use of his Senate committee to attack his political opponents.

Then the panelists turned to maligning Wechsler. Andrews asked if he was willing to take a lie detector test on his statement that he had broken with the communist ideal. Waldrop asked, "Mr. Wechsler, why is it if you're such a strong anticommunist you manage to wind up against people who are anticommunists?" The example Waldrop repeatedly cited was a series of articles published in the *Post* critical of the anticommunist columnist and radio personality Walter Winchell.

Then Spivak asked why, when Wechsler was opposed to the McCarthy committee's investigations, he did not also speak out against a Senate investigation of McCarthy that made serious allegations about McCarthy's financial activities but never formally charged him. Wechsler pointed out that unlike himself, McCarthy had refused to appear before the committee investigating him, so the only course of action open to the committee was to publish the allegations. Spivak also implied that Wechsler's failure to criticize the Tydings committee report, which had called McCarthy a "fraud" and his allegations a "hoax,"[28] was evidence of his procommunism, ostensibly because all anticommunists had condemned it.

Only Childs assumed Wechsler's integrity. An eloquent critic of McCarthy and defender of civil liberties, Childs tried to give Wechsler a chance to endorse responsible anticommunism. He asked, "In the course of the hearing, as the record shows, Mr. Wechsler, Senator McCarthy accused you of constantly attacking him and others who are fighting communism. I'd like to ask you if you think there is a communist danger in this country." Wechsler said he believed that the military threat posed by the Soviet Union far outweighed the threat of domestic subversion. Childs then asked a question that reaffirmed the necessity of domestic vigilance, "In the course of your editorial policy, do you feel McCarthy and the others have made no contribution?" In trying to help Wechsler, even Childs characterized McCarthy's abuses as secondary to his leadership on domestic anticommunism.

Co-producer and moderator Martha Rountree stated this position explicitly during the Wechsler broadcast. A soft-spoken young woman with a southern accent, Rountree did not raise her voice or become hostile as other panelists did. She rarely interjected questions at all. When she did, she asked her questions rhetorically, with phrases such as, "don't you think" and "I would say, wouldn't you," implying that to disagree with these obvious claims was to violate basic shared beliefs. In this case, Rountree made explicit her belief that civil liberties were less important than effective surveillance, asking, "Don't you think the dangers of communism as a threat to this country and its freedoms, don't you think that's a more important issue than an individual?"

The Wechsler broadcast illustrates the power of the normative objectification of anticommunism. The panelists dismissed Wechsler's charges that McCarthy was attempting to intimidate the press and defended the senator's prerogative to question anyone for any reason. The program's contentiousness suggested the free play of democratic debate, but its range of debate was tightly circumscribed by political fear. Forty years later, it reads like an inquisition, but no one, including Wechsler, voiced surprise or outrage at his treatment on the program. *Meet the Press* continued to garner awards for its outstanding news reporting and its service to democracy. The program actively advocated anticommunism yet retained and embellished its reputation for objectivity. Its claim to serving democracy was predicated not on pluralism or openness but on the vigor with which it guarded a narrowly defined consensus.

Historicizing Objectivity: The Narrative of Chastened Liberalism

Many intellectual and literary historians have argued that the norms for objectivity and experience shifted in the early Cold War. They observe that a "hardheaded realism" supplanted naive optimism among intellectuals and writers in the wake of the Nazi-Soviet Pact and the horrors of totalitarianism. In order to prevent repeating the British failure to stop the Nazis at Munich, Americans assumed that the Soviet aggressive design was as limitless and irrational as Hitler's proved to be. Spivak's *American Mercury* said that the differences between fascist and communist totalitarianism "were like the differences between the poisons arsenic and strychnine." The most influential political treatise of the era, Hannah Arendt's *The Origins of Totalitarianism*, argued that the systems shared a necessary expansionism. Peter Novick writes that totalitarianism

> was a slogan which succeeded in justifying continuous mobilization of consciousness from the forties through the sixties: promoting currents of thought which furthered a militant posture and underwrote the belief in a dichotomized world; disparaging those currents, and their spokesmen, which did the opposite.[29]

This dichotomized, zero-sum world view allowed easy exaggeration of the communist threat and changed the standards of facticity.

The Truman administration's deliberate overstatements of the communist military threat to Western Europe compounded this tendency. Such exaggerations came back to haunt the Democrats in the domestic sphere as McCarthy used every failure to contain communism as a partisan bludgeon. The clandestine nature of the domestic communist threat also contributed to its magnification. Alleged subversion became effectively irrefutable: No evidence could simply mean that the enemy had succeeded. Likewise, Soviet reasonability could be a trick. As Andrews told Wechsler, leaving the Communist Party was a ruse for more successful infiltration of American institutions. The presumption of secret subversion negated facts, such as Soviet military exhaustion or the discreditation of communism among the American left, which supported alternative scenarios to inexorable communist expansionism. The criteria for evidence, for what was admissible as fact, became politicized. Edward Herman and Noam Chomsky have written, "When anti-Communist fervor is aroused, the demand for serious evidence in support of claims of 'communist' abuses is suspended, and charlatans can thrive as evidentiary sources."[30]

This new normative objectivity was closely related to the increasingly powerful construct of realism. The lesson of Munich was distrust, doubt, suspicion, and cynicism. "Thus, prepare for the worst, get tough, and avoid compromise." Realism became synonymous with alarmism. Thomas G. Paterson argues that, ironically, the "realism" of the red-fascist analogy "substituted emotion for intellect, and it particularly distorted the American perception of reality, ballooning the Soviet threat."[31]

Thomas Hill Schaub similarly argues that the central narrative in Cold War fiction was the movement from innocence to experience, from the "myopia of the utopian to the twenty-twenty vision of the realist," or the "narrative of chastened liberalism." The shocks and disappointments of the Nazi-Soviet Pact, Stalin's show trials, and the horrors of Nazism, all led American intellectuals to disdain idealism and to embrace "tough-mindedness." In the same vein, the historian Richard Kirkendall wrote in 1955 that among his colleagues at Wesleyan, liberalism "connotes first of all naivete – tender mindedness – a failure to recognize the 'sinfulness' of men."[32] Opposition to this alarmist objectivity was thus cast as a dangerously credulous simplicity.

Professional practices incorporated these norms and kept journalists (and others) safe from the suspicions that ruined careers. It was much more prudent to overestimate the threat to the United States than to underestimate it.

In television news, the pressure to please government officials, network brass, and corporate sponsors had no forceful countertraditions. William Paley stressed in his 1954 "Road to Responsibility" speech that although over the centuries print journalists and their editors had learned "how to keep a manageable degree of freedom against the pressures of readers, advertisers, and powerful critics in government and other high places," broadcasters were very new at that art. In addition, they performed a wide and bewildering variety of social functions. Radio and television

partake of the newspaper, of the magazine, of the stage, the movies, the concert hall, the lecture platform, the museum, the medical center, the university, and the battlefield. To say nothing of the town meeting, the Senate committee room, the whistle stops of political campaigns, and the auditoriums for great debate. . . . No wonder we are a little confused.[33]

Yet this is a poor excuse. The same principles would guard free speech traditions no matter what the news medium, if those traditions were highly valued.

Amid these puzzling challenges, Paley placed faith in the wisdom of the democratic free market of ideas, defined as corporate control, particularly against the alternative of government control:

> But I for one have enough faith in the vitality of the democratic process, in the intelligence of the American people and in the freshness of the competitive climate to believe that the good will and determined intent of broadcasters to be fair, coupled with the powerful voice of the people, will provide far better protection against abuse than any other form of control. And let me remind you that those who would take this control away from the broadcaster are the ones who would put it in the hands of Government.[34]

Rovere too made the defense of corporate control explicit when he endorsed detached objectivity as the press's best alternative in covering domestic anticommunism. He prized objectivity as the only alternative to communistic state control of information. "I suspect there is no surer way to a corrupt and worthless press than to authorize reporters to tell the readers which 'facts' are really 'facts' and which are not. Certainly in those countries where this is the practice, the press serves the public less well than ours does."[35] Rovere defended the free press's failure to check official lies as preferable to lies disseminated by the state, and he could see no ground between these alternatives. Although this may echo McCarthy's obfuscations, Rovere considered himself and was perceived among McCarthy's bitterest opponents. A comparative liberal, he nevertheless believed that anticommunists alone could treat information responsibly. The left found this a maddening hypocrisy, but to Rovere, corporate control of the media seemed the only viable alternative to communistic state control. Like Paley, Rovere found the dangers of commercial ownership and sponsorship, caution and docility, to be far preferable than the pitfalls of the alternative. For this position, James Aronson dubbed him "the upholder of the canon of objectivity."[36]

Anticommunism became normatively objective in the early 1950s in the particular idiom of corporate superiority to communist abuses of information. To most practicing journalists, this was an obvious and unproblematic choice. Only a few wondered aloud whether the choice was fairly drawn.

In his work on the television documentary, Michael Curtin suggests that the discourse that normalized anticommunism underwent a shift in the late 1950s. The prestigious network documentaries of the early 1960s based their authority in an idiom that Curtin terms "scientific anticommunism." He argues that

> the concept of objectivity played an important role in a discursive struggle whereby a transnational elite sought to reconfigure public attitudes toward the Cold War. . . . The rhetoric of this group valorized the notion of American leadership in an active struggle against the forces of monolithic communism throughout the globe. But just as importantly, it celebrated expertise, science, and professionalism as weapons in the American arsenal. Thus, the dispassionate language of scientific method was married to the political rhetoric of the superpower struggle.[37]

We have here the beginning of a chronology of the broad cultural norms underlying journalistic objectivity. It is well past time to dispense with that concept as a working standard for journalists[38] and to see it as a historical construct related to the shape of news markets and to prevailing economic and political orthodoxies.

SELLING AMERICA: CORPORATE PREROGATIVES AND THE NATIONAL INTEREST

Assessing the import or legacy of the journalism described in the previous chapters is an interpretive rather than a scientific exercise. We are left with an emblematic set of cultural equations and oppositions, which are themselves in part the product of deliberate campaigns such as those documented here. But because these associations and negations result *not only* from such campaigns, we are left asking thorny questions about the construction of culture.

The Blurred Line Between Culture and Conspiracy

Assertions about the misuse of corporate power are often dismissed as irrational conspiracy theories. Although there is no shortage of lunatic theory on media control, corporate apologists stereotype writers who rationally document adverse effects of corporate control on public information as blind ideologues who have no appreciation for the freedoms we do enjoy. Pointing to the social costs of capitalism is still mistaken for disloyalty, or for psychosis.

Conspiracy theory is unacceptable as serious scholarship. Indeed, arguments that show how contradictions within a culture justify unsatisfactory conditions are much more interesting and plausible than assertions of tyranny or intrigue. This is the notion at the heart of the concept of hegemony: Disadvantageous social relations need to be legitimated.

But in the case of people whose job it is to persuade the public of one proposition or another, the line between culture and conspiracy seems rather blurred. What is the difference between, for instance, advertising, public relations, and propaganda? Its source? Intention? Scope? Success? If a campaign to sway public opinion succeeds, is that because its claims had merit, or because the public was brainwashed? If such a campaign fails, is that because its claims were false, or because the campaign was badly designed? Just because the purveyors of mass-mediated messages say they believe in the free will of the public does not mean that the public can discriminate between fact and fiction, or between news and advertising. And just because large sections of the public choose the silliest entertainments does not mean the public always has poor judgment.

In joining forces to sell the Cold War to the American people, government and industry professionals clearly knew they violated precepts of a free and independent press, but they justified it to themselves as a necessary patriotic duty in a fearsome age. As their patterns of news sourcing became institutionalized and indelible, their work achieved amazing feats of rationalization.

When you look at some of their language, it is tempting to attribute to them some conspiratorial mindedness, but these campaigns do not amount to a thoroughgoing conspiracy. Although these people designed public information campaigns to promote particular public attitudes on everything from the role of organized labor in the economy to the Korean War, there was no central plot or direction beyond a system of institutional interests and shared beliefs. The networks, for all their similarities, were also fierce competitors, and there were strict limits to the cooperation between government and the corporations. Sometimes making profits and stopping the Soviets demanded the same approach, but not always. The limits to cooperation were not set by the dictates of truth. Rather, the institutional self-interests of defense agencies and corporations stood as an accidental bulwark between culture and conspiracy.

Americans in the early Cold War wanted to have it both ways: They wanted to use information effectively in their fight against communism, but they also wanted to be the champions of truth. If it is true that, as columnist Joseph Alsop said, "the notion that a newspaperman doesn't have a duty to his country is perfect balls,"[1] it is still crucial to remember that there is a difference between truth and a more strategic conception of the national interest. In the early Cold War, as always, truth itself was a contested area. We can observe patterns of argumentation about what constituted admissible facts, real facts, and important facts. The available evidence regarding information professionals shows both confusion about, and a willingness to blur, the difference between truth and the national interest.

How does this happen? How does a sense of national righteousness come to overwhelm simple facts? The answer is: the requirements of sustaining vast military, political, and economic power. The first testing ground of U.S. policy in the Cold War was the civil war in Greece, during which the community of high-profile U.S. foreign policy journalists sided fully with the requirements of national security.

Whitewash in Greece

CBS News entered the Cold War era of U.S. policy making in Europe with a tragedy, the political murder of one of its youngest and most respected foreign correspondents. When the most basic principles of truth and freedom jeopardized U.S. policy, CBS and a distinguished group of American journalists who claimed to represent the rights of a free press sided unanimously with the needs of U.S. policy rather than pursue the truth about who killed one of their own.

As the network's chief correspondent in the Middle East, George Polk gained wide admiration during the 1940s for fair and vigorous reporting. In covering the Greek civil war in 1948, he did not curb his reports on the "corruption and venality of the unrepresentative Greek government, and refused to take its side against the communist guerillas,"[2] despite U.S. support of the Royalist regime. In May 1948, he was preparing to return home after many years abroad. He planned to take a leave of absence from CBS and write a book about the Middle East as a Nieman Fellow at Harvard. He had recently married a Greek woman.

In the last days before his planned departure from Greece, Polk traveled to Salonika to meet with members of the communist opposition, including its leader, General Markos. Just before this last trip, Polk received an unsolicited letter from an employee of the Chase Manhattan Bank in New York. It concerned Constantine Tsaldaris, the head of the Royalist Party and the Greek foreign minister, who had played an important role in securing massive American aid to the Royalist government. At a time when it was a criminal act to send money outside Greece, Tsaldaris had just deposited $25,000 ($325,000 in 1990 dollars) into a personal account at the New York bank. Clark Clifford, assistant to President Truman, noted forty years later, "It would have been extremely difficult for us to go back to Congress and ask for more money for Greece had this information come to light."[3]

Polk intended to make the information public once he returned to the United States. As a conscientious but perhaps naive or overconfident reporter, he asked for an appointment with Tsaldaris to get a comment on this revelation. Polk's wife Rea later said, "I am surprised he lived for three days after that interview."[4] Polk's willingness to cover the insurgency as a credible political movement and to interview communist leaders would in itself have been enough for many Royalist Greeks to kill him. Polk was shot in a boat on Salonika Bay on the night of Saturday, May 8, 1948. His body washed ashore on the morning of Sunday, May 16.

Secretary of State George Marshall appointed two CIA agents based in Athens, Robert Driscoll and Christian Freer, to coordinate the Greek and American investigations. The state department also dispatched special FBI investigator Frederick Ayer. To supplement the official investigations, a group of American journalists formed the "Overseas Writers' Special Committee to Inquire into the Murder of George Polk." Chaired by Walter Lippmann, the committee included William Paley, James Reston of the *Times*, columnist Marquis Childs, Joseph Harsch of CBS, Eugene Meyer, publisher of the *Washington Post*, Ernest Lindley of *Newsweek*, and others. Justin Miller of NAB sat on a separate finance committee. The stated reason for the formation of the committee was the protection of journalists and the free press: "It was evident that the American press and radio, and all others interested in a free press and in the safety of American correspondents overseas, should do everything within their power to see that the murderers of George Polk were arrested, brought to trial, and convicted."[5]

Members of the committee met with Secretary Marshall as early as May 24, eight days after the body surfaced in Salonika Bay. Lippmann appointed Washington attorney and former Office of Strategic Services director William "Wild Bill" Donovan to conduct the committee's investigation. Over lunch at Washington's Metropolitan Club, Lippmann and Donovan "agreed that the Polk case was charged with troublesome implications for both Lippmann's profession and one of the linchpins of America's Cold War foreign policy: unlimited support for Greece."[6] How deliberately they conspired to conceal the Royalist motives for the murder remains unknown.

Howard K. Smith and Eric Sevareid also volunteered to conduct an investigation on behalf of CBS but were denied permission on the grounds of their friendship with Polk. Instead, CBS sent Rome correspondents Peter Tompkins and Winston Burdett to Greece. Tompkins, a former OSS agent, was taken off the case after suggesting that he try to find the communists whom Polk had been trying to meet. (The distinguished reporter Homer Bigart of the *New York Herald-Tribune* interviewed Markos later that summer, but his paper initially found the articles too controversial to print.) CBS replaced Tompkins with John Secondari, son of a prominent right-wing Italian politician. Among other correspondents, "Secondari was better known for his ultra-rightist views than for his reporting skills."[7]

Burdett revealed his own personal baggage in the case before the Senate Internal Security Subcommittee in 1955, where he admitted that he had been a Communist Party member from 1937 until 1942. His wife, Italian party member Leah Schiavi, had accidentally discovered a Soviet training camp for communist guerillas in northern Iran and been assassinated by Soviet agents.[8]

Despite these anticommunist predilections, when Burdett and Secondari arrived in Athens, they told Frederick Ayer, the FBI investigator appointed by the state department, that they believed Polk was murdered by right-wing Greek agents. Ayer quickly persuaded them to believe that the communists had more to gain from Polk's murder by discrediting the Royalist regime. The CBS correspondents then spent most of their energies turning suspicion on Polk's wife Rea, his brother Bill, and Kosta Hadjiargyris, George Polk's friend, assistant, and a *Christian Science Monitor* correspondent, who protested the official investigation's exclusive focus on communist suspects. Hadji, as he was known, was also the stepson of the only Liberal in the Royalist ruling coalition, Prime Minister Themistocles Sophoulis.[9]

Whether Burdett and Secondari conspired with officials, or whether it was, as Elias Vlanton contends, "journalism-as-usual," where lack of investigative initiative and overreliance on government information shrouded the inconvenient truth, remains unknown. As one longtime investigator of the case wrote of Lippmann, one would like to think that they were "merely naive in [their] 1948 assumption that . . . working hand in hand with the State Department and their official representatives in Greece – Rankin, Gibson, and Ayer in particular – would help the American press get to the truth."[10] It strains credibility to think they were so naive, when the basis for U.S. foreign policy was at stake. U.S. government officials certainly participated in the cover-up, and CBS correspondents had intimate access to the official investigation.

Donovan looked around for a crack investigator and hired Lieutenant Colonel James Kellis, an OSS war hero trained in infiltration and guerilla warfare. Kellis knew Greece and Greek, unlike most of the investigators on the case, and he enjoyed a reputation for fairness. By July, Kellis discovered the Tsaldaris bank deposit, providing a motive for the murder, something lacking in the lagging official investigations, which he told to a gathering of officials that included Karl Rankin, the chief of British police, Sir Charles Wickham, Driscoll and Freer of the CIA, and Fred Ayer of the FBI, all of whom dismissed it. Rankin said, "I don't see why you're breaking your back trying to uncover who killed this correspondent. . . . If you as a military officer, or I as a diplomat were killed, none of these people would give a damn."[11] Kellis recognized the cover-up and was promptly recalled to the States.

The final report of the Lippmann committee condemned Kellis's recall, particularly because, "at that time, he was, to the best knowledge of this committee, the only investigator who was testing a [right-wing] theory of the crime," but the committee never pursued the theory. If one were to look for an explanation of why, the report says, "the committee knew very well that even in an American community, far more than a foreign country, the odds are against private solution of a mysterious crime." The presence of so many American reporters and lawyers, concerned that one of their own had been murdered for political reasons, did apparently spur the lagging official Greek investigation,[12] but in retrospect, it spurred a forced confession to put the matter to rest.

Late in July, the Royalists affixed blame on the marginally communist, mostly opportunist, reporter Gregory Staktopoulos and his elderly mother. They advanced no particular motive. After weeks of imprisonment and torture, Staktopoulos signed a fabricated confession saying that he had set up Polk's meeting with two gunmen who later disappeared into the communist-held mountains. Lippmann's committee of overseas writers asked Professor E. M. Morgan of Harvard Law School to review and comment on the text of Staktopoulos's confessions. Morgan found them weak and unpersuasive – that "indeed the whole performance cries aloud for cross-examination," an uncommon practice in Greek jurisprudence. Still, the committee lodged no complaints with Greek or American authorities. Staktopolous spent twelve years of a life sentence in prison before his conviction was overturned. He later named Frederick Ayer of the FBI as one of the torturers who had extracted his confession.[13] Most subsequent investigators agree that Royalists murdered Polk, but no one has ever been indicted.

Only one American journalist protested the whole performance. I. F. Stone, in a series of five articles in the *Daily Compass* under the title "I. F. Stone Exposes Polk Murder Case Whitewash," attacked Lippmann's committee and General Donovan for allowing "the Greek and American authorities to pull the wool over the eyes of the American public, and that it was willing to hold back vital information rather than go to bat with these authorities on behalf of justice for their dead colleague." He singled out Donovan because, as an "experienced and able courtroom lawyer," he should have seen the duplicity in the Salonika court.[14]

Although this outcome certainly suited U.S. officials, and perhaps Donovan, who was plainly more concerned with U.S. policy than with broadcasting the truth, what of the special committee of distinguished newsmen? Cold Warriors would later say that truth and principles were luxuries that the United States could not afford in the fight against communism. The Polk case was an early and definitive case of Cold War journalists' confusion about truth and patriotism. It also foreshadowed ensuing systematic collaboration between CBS and the Central Intelligence Agency.

The "Mighty Wurlitzer"

The paradoxes of claiming truth on the side of national interest are revealed most baldly in some of the few stories that have come to light about network involvement with the intelligence community once the Cold War was underway. Like most investigators of this relationship, Daniel Schorr argues that "the most active period of CIA–media cooperation had been in the cold war days of the 1950s."[15] Because both corporate and national security secrecy cloak these operations, we may presume that the public record represents only a portion of the collaboration that occurred.

To the CIA, journalists and news executives constitute "an intelligence asset of the first magnitude." At a 1977 Congressional hearing to investigate the relationship between the CIA and the news media, former Director of Central Intelligence Stansfield Turner observed that the CIA and journalists "are in the same business. Both the Agency and the journalists are out looking for information and both of them have something that the other one wants." Frank Wisner, head of the CIA's covert operations in the 1950s, reputedly boasted to play the press as part of his "mighty Wurlitzer" of private organizations loyal to the agency, implying that he relied on the cooperation of top management. According to CIA officials, the most active and rewarding relationships with media outlets were with the *New York Times, Time,* and CBS.[16]

Information gathering naturally constituted the bulk of these activities, because it was so vital to the goals of both agents and journalists. During the 1950s, they exchanged and confirmed information; agents prebriefed journalists traveling abroad and "tasked" them to look for certain information; agents debriefed journalists after they returned from abroad; and journalists provided agents with access to their notes, files, and film. Most journalists found nothing objectionable about such "reporting." Many described it as desirable or routine. CBS News president Sig Mickelson said "anyone news gathering abroad who *didn't* check in with a station chief as part of his rounds would have been remiss in the performance of his duty." Others noted that debriefing "got to be so routine you felt a little miffed if you weren't asked."[17]

But journalists also undertook roles in covert operations. They hosted parties, provided safe houses, and acted as couriers for agents abroad. They spotted, assessed, and recruited potential agents and "handled" them once recruited. They also propagandized in their news reporting.[18] Most journalists strenuously object to these activities. Participation in covert operations often entailed payments of money or gifts, which intrinsically compromised the journalist's ability to report honestly.

The associations most inimical to a first amendment sensibility did not involve professional journalists but rather professional agents, who used media credentials as "covers" for their operations. The ability to investigate and ask questions without appearing suspicious was indispensable to covert agents. Top-level media executives often arranged for these credentials. Sketchy evidence for at least three such cases came to light in the Congressional investigations of the mid-1970s. During the 1950s, the CIA even ran a formal school to train agents to act as journalists. But these cases seem to have been fairly rare. The majority of CIA–media personnel began as professional journalists and then voluntarily performed intelligence tasks.[19]

The Czechoslovakian police noted the similarity of reporting and espionage in 1951 when they arrested the AP bureau chief in Prague for espionage. William Oatis spent two years in Pankrac Prison after confessing to gathering information that the government had not released, with the intention of sending it out of the country. As *Time* put it, "The crime was accuracy." Ironically, while the Western journalism community protested such treatment for routine news gathering practices, ABC radio aired a series called *American Agent*, where a newspaper reporter covering world trouble spots doubled as a secret government operative. In the context of the Oatis case, it made the collective hair of the Overseas Press Club stand on end, but ABC president Robert Kintner shrugged it off as "just an adventure story with no political or social significance." The program's producer also defended it with the fine point that "the show is very clean. Barclay's editor in the show *knows* that he's a secret agent."[20]

Chairman William S. Paley of CBS admitted that he personally helped the CIA at the agency's request when the political climate allowed him few options, but he (falsely) denied that the network organization participated in any way. Paley also denied that the relationship went through Wisner, whose wife Paley knew well. Indeed, formal agreements about the nature or secrecy of the relationship between the agency and media executives would have been unnecessary because social contacts, "the P and Q Street axis in Georgetown," provided familiarity and trust based on common assumptions and values. The explanation offered by the few executives who have admitted their participation is that at the height of the Cold War, collaboration with the CIA seemed a natural and necessary thing to do. NBC News president in the 1970s, Richard Wald, expressed the unquestioned nature of the service: "It was a thing people did then."

Paley admitted little. He told former CBS reporter Daniel Schorr in 1977:

> I cooperated with them – was helpful to them a few times on a very personal basis, and nothing whatsoever to do with CBS. . . . I was approached as someone who could cooperate with them to their advantage. And this was back in the early fifties, when the cold war was at its height and where I didn't hesitate for a second to say, "Okay, it's reasonable, I'll do it."

Paley most likely referred to a service rendered by his personal nonprofit corporation, the William S. Paley Foundation, which laundered a donation the CIA made to a research project that could not be publicly identified with the agency.[21]

He sanctioned intelligence operations involving the news staff ranging from the nearly comical, as when he arranged for CIA agents to use the CBS broadcast booth at the United Nations to lip-read the whispered conversations of the Soviet delegation during Premier Nikita Khruschev's visit in 1959, to far more systematic arrangements involving CBS News journalists that, when made public in 1976, jeopardized the reputation of even CBS paragon Walter Cronkite. Sig Mickelson, News president from 1954 to 1961, directed most of the activities. He grew so tired of using a pay telephone to call the agency that he finally installed a private phone line that bypassed the CBS switchboard.[22]

The relationship between CBS and the CIA in the 1950s was so friendly that Allen Dulles, CIA director from 1953 until 1961, hosted annual New Year's parties for CBS News staff at his home or at his private club, the

Alibi, in Washington, D.C. They were, as Mickelson told Murrow biographer Ann Sperber,

> part of the long history of good relations between the CIA and the news media in those years, particularly with CBS, marked by annual briefing sessions. These were freewheeling discussions with the correspondents, delightful evenings – the Director set a good table – top newsmen, top agency men, good talk and cigars, each side out for what it could get but then, said one who was there, they were all adults; you took the point of view into consideration as you would anybody else's. And the fact was, some of these guys had the best information going and you were free to check it out.

William Bundy, Dulles's chief aide, similarly described the exchange of information at these dinners as mutually beneficial and enjoyable:

> It was a terribly nice party. There would be about twenty-five of us all told, about fifteen of them from CBS. We had a CIA man next to each CBS, and there was general table conversation, very useful in giving the feeling of Allen's thinking without giving them secret material, and at the same time extracting their views and thoughts – he was particularly good at this. Later critics like David Schoenbrun and Eric Sevareid would be there, and it was a very warm and relaxed occasion.[23]

Clearly, at the time, no one who participated felt that their gatherings violated professional ethics: To be invited to share such prominent company indicated that one had reached the pinnacle of professional esteem. The correspondents trusted themselves to recognize disinformation and to analyze competently the information they received. These intimate gatherings were based on mutual respect, and they celebrated the journalism of insider access.

Does this intimate relationship signal the disappearance of the ostensible line separating news and government, or does it represent reasonable service to country on the part of the broadcasters? Is it conspiracy, or is it culture? When the culture of reporting is so proudly and unapologetically intimate with the government, that line is rather hard to draw. The lingering question is how such an access-proud news establishment maintains a public image of oppositionalism.

A Certain Price

No matter how successful or how superior to the alternatives, commercial control of the news media exacts a certain price from American democracy. The rhetoric of corporate voluntarism masks the degree to which federal officials have been able to control the flow of news. In the early Cold War, the safe course for the networks was to focus persistently on high-ranking federal officials and to refrain from analyzing or contextualizing their statements. The operations described in this book promoted individual policies and praised federal institutions. They fostered an image of the government that was competent, responsible, and modestly heroic in an inescapable struggle with world communism. Television helped to create a political culture where political authority and legitimacy derived from proximity to federal power. It was so successful a blend that a substantial feat of imagination was required to realize that this was not the only possible understanding of the government's role in the Cold War.

The first price that commercial control of the news media extracts from democracy is dissent. In the early Cold War, that meant principally the exclusion of leftists from mainstream news outlets. Airing dissent would have jeopardized future network access to the great majority of federal officials who did not challenge Cold War orthodoxy. It could have given extreme anticommunists ammunition for their charges that the networks harbored subversives. More fundamentally, the networks approved of the government's Cold War policies in securing stable democratic allies and access to overseas markets, and of its rhetoric in inscribing private corporations as the most desirable form of social organization. By concentrating the sources of political discourse, network television news marginalized alternative voices and helped to create and sustain Cold War orthodoxy.

The second price that commercial control of the news media places on democracy is less tangible. Before the mid-nineteenth century in the United States, and in most democratic nations today, news outlets unabashedly proclaimed and embraced partisanship. Their audiences recognized the interests and positions they represented. In contrast, American television networks seek the widest possible audience and present the political lowest common denominator. Government regulation to guarantee diversity or to preserve minority voices has always precipitated revulsion and dismissal as patently un-American elitist claptrap.

The networks have always justified their programming practices in the language of populist democracy: "We give the people what they want." This blanket excuse is crudely majoritarian for an ostensibly advanced democratic system. The greatness of the American political tradition stems not from its responsiveness to the majority but from its protection of the minority and in this, television news had failed utterly.

The networks make implicit as well as explicit claims to comprehensiveness and objectivity. Even though political information must pass through several institutional, ideological, and procedural filters, it pretends to be value-free. This denial that information is politicized by the structure of the news industry has serious consequences for the democratic process.

Above all, it fosters a confusion of the prerogatives of capitalism with the processes of democracy. The art of political argumentation differs fundamentally from the art of salesmanship. There is a sense of the common good and long-term advisedness in, for instance, the paradigmatic town meeting, and this sense is lacking in a consumer-choice or even a plebiscite or instant political poll. Consumers do not pause to consider community and group interests when making their picks. Corporate capitalism breeds a politics of selfishness and isolation.[24]

The most common notion of television news bias construes liberal broadcasters injecting their own personal biases into their reporting. With the striking horizontal and vertical integration of media industries over the last several decades, and the encroachments of tabloid-style journalism into even the sacred precincts of the flagship network news shows, a reflexive disappointment with the news media has also become part of common parlance. Yet this has not translated into an anticommercial critique, leaving the residual but contradictory impression that all media failures are the fault of powerful individual liberals. Voluntary industry solutions fail to stem the seeming descent of public discourse, but public disgust with overcommercialism does not manifest itself as dissatisfaction with corporate ownership and sponsorship. This amazing failure may represent a calculation that the system, warts and all, works best. But certainly it stems from the great power of media corporations in policy and culture and of their success in selling corporate benevolence.

Difficult and unpopular as it is to overcome resistance to the idea that markets sometimes fail to foster democracy, it is nonetheless easier to assess the legacy of collaboration between the national security state and the television networks on the history of news gathering than it is to gauge its legacy for the history of the Cold War. The "victory" of the United States in the Cold War has made a critique of U.S. aims and methods even less acceptable in mainstream political discourse than it was when the outcome was not yet written. As stated in the Introduction, it does not diminish the horror of totalitarianism to say that U.S. performance in the Cold War was not perfect, or that it acted reprehensibly, or even that it mimicked its totalitarian adversary. One would hope that the end of the Cold War would make it easier rather than harder to say these things. An unquestioning and self-satisfied faith in American virtue has pushed the United States over the line between defending security and subverting freedom more than once. Americans claimed to champion freedom in the early Cold War, but the effort actually to protect it fell far short. We need a much fuller tally of the domestic costs to the United States in its war against Soviet communism.

NOTES

Introduction: The Marketplace of Ideas

1. Daniel Yergin defines the national security state as the "unified pattern of attitudes, policies, and institutions . . . derived from the two commanding ideas of American postwar foreign policy – anticommunism and a new doctrine of national security. The policies included containment, confrontation, and intervention, the methods by which U.S. leaders have sought to make the world safe for America." Daniel Yergin, *Shattered Peace: The Origins of the Cold War and the National Security State* (Boston: Houghton Mifflin, 1978), 5–6.

2. Cobbett Steinberg, *TV Facts* (New York: Facts on File, 1985), 85, 86, 401, 418.

3. James Reston, *Deadline* (New York: Times Books, 1991), 278.

4. My students have cited the presence of news cameras on the beach during the 1992 marine landing in Somalia as evidence of network power to control military events. When I respond that the cameras were there only because the U.S. military wanted them there, the nearly universal response is a confused surprise.

5. Quoted in Elmer Davis, "War Information," in Elmer Davis and Byron Price, *War Information and Censorship* (Washington, D.C.: American Council on Public Affairs, 1943).

6. Robert M. Hutchins et al., "A Free and Responsible Press," supplement to *Fortune*, April 1947.

7. Simpson reports, for instance, that the state department illegally financed studies by the respected National Opinion Research Center (NORC) as part of a Cold War Congressional lobbying effort, "making NORC's ostensibly private, independent surveys financially viable for the first time." Christopher Simpson, *Science of Coercion: Communication Research and Psychological Warfare, 1945–60* (New York: Oxford University Press, 1994), 4, Chapter 4, and passim. Bernard C. Cohen, *The Public's Impact on Foreign Policy* (Boston: Little, Brown and Company, 1973), 58–72.

8. See also Jerry W. Sanders, *Peddlers of Crisis: The Committee on the Present Danger and the Politics of Containment* (Boston: South End Press, 1983); Alan Wolfe, *The Rise and Fall of the Soviet Threat: Domestic Sources of the*

Cold War Consensus (Boston: South End Press, 1984); Thomas G. Paterson, *Meeting the Communist Threat* (New York: Oxford University Press, 1988); and Frank Kofsky, *Harry S Truman and the War Scare of 1948: A Successful Campaign to Deceive the Nation* (New York: St. Martin's Press, 1993).

9. Robert Griffith laid the groundwork for this literature. His articles are cited throughout. See also works cited by Elizabeth Fones-Wolf, Kim McQuaid, and, on radio in an earlier period, Robert McChesney.

10. As E. Bruce Geelhoed has noted, the misquotation, "What's good for General Motors is good for the country," has a slightly different meaning. Geelhoed contends that by "vice versa," Wilson meant that what was bad for the country was bad for General Motors, rather than what was good for General Motors was good for the country. The quotation is still emblematic of the equation between corporate and public interests. See Geelhoed's *Charles E. Wilson and Controversy at the Pentagon, 1953 to 1957* (Detroit: Wayne State Press, 1979), 46.

11. A useful discussion of this controversy appeared in the *American Historical Review* 97:2 (December 1992). Jackson Lears's "Making Fun of Popular Culture," 1417–26, a response to Lawrence Levine's "The Folklore of Industrial Society: Popular Culture and Its Audiences," 1369–99, sets out a most appropriate approach for the particular institutions in this study. It restates many of the arguments Lears advanced in his seminal "The Concept of Cultural Hegemony: Problems and Possibilities," *American Historical Review* 90:3 (June 1985), 567–93.

12. Robert Griffith, "The Selling of America: The Advertising Council and American Politics, 1942–1960," *Business History Review* (Autumn 1983), 412.

13. Quoted in Peter Novick, *That Noble Dream: The "Objectivity Question" and the American Historical Profession* (Cambridge: Cambridge University Press, 1988), 7.

14. On MacLeish, see Brett Gary, *Nervous Liberals: Scholars, Lawyers, and the War on Propaganda, 1919–1948* (New York: Columbia University Press, forthcoming); and Allen M. Winkler, *The Politics of Propaganda: The Office of War Information, 1942–45* (New Haven: Yale University Press, 1978). On Jackson, see Chapter 6, "C. D. Jackson: Psychological Warriors Never Die," in H. W. Brands, Jr., *Cold Warriors: Eisenhower's Generation and American Foreign Policy* (New York: Columbia University Press, 1988), 117–37; and Blanche Wiesen Cook, "First Comes the Lie: C. D. Jackson and Political Warfare," *Radical History Review* 31 (1984), 42–70. For dualisms, see John Lewis Gaddis, "Morality and the American Experience of the Cold War," in *The United States and the End of the Cold War: Implications, Reconsiderations, Provocations* (New York: Oxford University Press, 1992), 47–58; and Arthur M. Schlesinger, Jr., "National Interests and Moral Absolutes," in *The Cycles of American History* (Boston: Houghton Mifflin, 1986), 69–86.

15. Oral history interview, Lawrence Spivak, 1976, Louis G. Cowan Broadcasting Collection, William E. Wiener Oral History Library, New York Public Library.

Chapter One: Market Failure

1. Gary, *Nervous Liberals.*
2. Elmer Davis, "War Information" in Elmer Davis and Byron Price, *War Information and Censorship* (Washington, D.C.: American Council on Public Affairs, 1943), 7, 14, 8.
3. Sherwood quoted in Elmer Davis, "Report to the President," *Journalism Monographs* 7 (August 1968), 9; Eisenhower quoted in Blanche Wiesen Cook, *The Declassified Eisenhower: A Startling Reappraisal of the Eisenhower Presidency* (New York: Penguin, 1984), 15; Stout quoted in Davis, "War Information," 28.
4. Davis, "War Information," 30; Byron Price, "War Censorship," in Davis and Price, *War Information and Censorship*, 78; Davis, "War Information," 50.
5. Sydney Weinberg, "The Writers' Quarrel in the Office of War Information," *Journal of American History* 55:1 (June 1968), 83.
6. Winkler, *The Politics of Propaganda*, 42–47.
7. Winkler, *The Politics of Propaganda*, 64–65; and Weinberg, "The Writers' Quarrel," 84–86.
8. Quoted in Jackson Lears, *Fables of Abundance: A Cultural History of Advertising in America* (New York: Basic Books, 1994), 249.
9. *Fortune*, February 1944, 88, quoted in Fox, *Madison Avenue*, 69.
10. J. A. R. Pimlott, "Public Service Advertising: The Advertising Council," *Public Opinion Quarterly* 12:2 (Summer 1948), 210; quoted in Robert Griffith, "The Selling of America: The Advertising Council and American Politics, 1942–1960," *Business History Review* (Autumn 1983), 390.
11. Fox, *Madison Avenue*, Chapters 2 and 3; Griffith, "The Selling of America," 391; and Pimlott, "Public Service Advertising," 211.
12. Erik Barnouw, *The Sponsor* (New York: Oxford University Press, 1978), 39; Fox, *Madison Avenue Goes to War*, 28–29; Davis, "War Information," 26.
13. Winkler, *Politics of Propaganda*, 71; Repplier, "Advertising Dons Long Pants," 274–75.
14. Fox, *Madison Avenue Goes to War*, 72–73; Griffith, *The Selling of America*, 388; Jackson Lears, *Fables of Abundance*, 249.
15. Lary May's influential volume of essays on the political culture of the Cold War couples the disintegration of a longstanding critique of capitalism with the postwar Red Scare in explaining the final legitimation of the corporate order following 1945. Lary May, ed., *Recasting America: Culture and Politics in the Age of Cold War* (Chicago: University of Chicago, 1989), 10–11. See especially essays by May, Lears, and Noble.
16. See, for instance, Stephanie Coontz, *The Way We Never Were: American Families and the Nostalgia Trap* (New York: Basic Books, 1992).
17. Kim McQuaid, *Big Business and Presidential Power: From FDR to Reagan* (New York: William Morrow, 1982), 118–21; Alan Brinkley, "The New Deal and the Idea of the State," in Steve Fraser and Gary Gerstle, eds., *The Rise and Fall of the New Deal Order, 1930–1980* (Princeton: Princeton University

Press, 1989), 85–112. The business leader was Paul Hoffman, whose career is detailed later in the text. Elizabeth A. Fones-Wolf, *Selling Free Enterprise: The Business Assault on Labor and Liberalism, 1945–60* (Urbana: University of Illinois Press, 1995), 23; Kim McQuaid, *Uneasy Partners: Big Business in American Politics, 1945–1990* (Baltimore: Johns Hopkins, 1994), 20.

18. Young quoted in Griffith, "The Selling of America," 394; Theodore S. Repplier, "Advertising Dons Long Pants," 272.

19. McQuaid, *Uneasy Partners*, 61.

20. Griffith, "Selling of America," 388.

21. Fones-Wolf, *Selling Free Enterprise*, passim.

22. McQuaid, *Big Business*, 149–50.

23. Kim McQuaid, *Uneasy Partners: Big Business in American Politics* (Baltimore: Johns Hopkins University Press, 1994), 45; McQuaid, *Big Business*, 156–58; Michael Wala, "Selling the Marshall Plan at Home: The Committee for the Marshall Plan to Aid European Recovery," *Diplomatic History* 10:3 (Summer 1986), 247–65.

24. Oral history interview, William Benton, p. 166, July 12, 1968, Columbia University.

25. Sydney Hyman, *The Lives of William Benton* (Chicago: The University of Chicago Press, 1969), 294–318.

26. See Robert W. McChesney, *Telecommunications, Mass Media, and Democracy: The Battle for the Control of U.S. Broadcasting, 1928–1935* (New York: Oxford, 1993); and Susan Smulyan, *Selling Radio: The Commercialization of American Broadcasting, 1920–1934* (Washington, D.C.: Smithsonian Institution Press, 1994).

27. Hyman, *William Benton*, 329.

28. Margaret Blanchard, "Americans First, Newspapermen Second?: The Conflict Between Patriotism and Freedom of the Press During the Cold War, 1946–1952," Ph.D. dissertation, University of North Carolina, 1981. The quote, "American newspapermen are Americans first and newspapermen second," is from an editorial in *Editor and Publisher*, April 3, 1948, quoted on page 313 of Blanchard's dissertation.

29. Department of State press release, January 18, 1946, No. 46, Folder O.F. 136, Official File 571, Harry S Truman Papers, Harry S Truman Library.

30. Quoted in Walter Hixson, *Parting the Curtain: Propaganda, Culture, and the Cold War, 1945–1961* (New York: St. Martin's Press, 1997), 5.

31. We can distinguish between three types of countries receiving U.S. information. The "free" zone of countries like Canada or Mexico could be fully supplied by private companies. The "Iron Curtain" countries virtually excluded private companies and thus had to be supplied by the state department. "Mixed" countries such as France and Italy presented the biggest dilemma. Although private firms very much wanted to expand their services there, they faced a problem in the nonconvertibility of currency. A dollar shortage in these countries meant American companies were being "starved out" for lack of currency to pay for their services and would be forced to withdraw without government intervention. Nichols to Sargeant, October 18, 1947, Folder: William I. Nichols, *This Week Magazine*, Box 10, ASSPA 45–50. Macy re-

called that *Time* magazine led the agitation for a currency exception over its operations in France, but he found that *Time* did not even need this exception because it was spending all of its francs plus some dollars in France. Oral history interview, Noel Macy, 44–49, Harry S Truman Library.

32. Oral history interview, Noel Macy, 44–49, Harry S Truman Library; C. D. Jackson, "Private Media and Public Policy," in Lester Markel, ed., *Public Opinion and Foreign Policy* (New York: Harper and Row for the Council on Foreign Relations, 1949), reprinted in Daniel Lerner, ed., *Propaganda in War and Crisis* (New York: George W. Stewart, 1951), 329.

33. Public Statement by the Associated Press Board of Directors, January 14, 1946, F: O.F. 136, Official File 571, Harry S Truman Papers, see also, Folder: William I. Nichols, Box 10, ASSPA 45–50.

34. Hyman, *William Benton*, 347. The three men were Wilbur Forrest of the *New York Herald-Tribune*, Ralph McGill of the *Atlanta Constitution*, and Carl Ackerman of the Columbia School of Journalism. William Benton to Robert McLean, January 16, 1946, Associated Press #1, Box 7, ASSPA 45–50; there is also a copy in WHCF:OF 571, Truman Papers.

35. Elmer Davis Broadcast (ABC), January 15, 1946, WHCF:OF 571, Truman Papers.

36. Cooper to Allen, May 27, 1948, Associated Press #1, Box 7, ASSPA 45–50.

37. Howard to Benton, January 17, 1946, Associated Press #2, Box 7, ASSPA 45–50. See also, Margaret Blanchard, *Exporting the First Amendment: The Press–Government Crusade of 1945-1952* (New York: Longman, 1985), 107–8; Benton, "American News Abroad," speech to ASNE April 18, 1946, cited in draft of Hixson, *Parting the Curtain*.

38. Benton to McLean, April 24, 1946, Associated Press #1, Box 7, ASSPA 45–50.

39. C. D. Jackson, "Private Media and Public Policy," 330.

40. Quoted in Blanchard, *Exporting the First Amendment*, 117.

41. Ibid., 120.

42. Robert William Pirsein, *The Voice of America: A History of the International Broadcasting Activities of the U.S. Government, 1940-1962* (New York: Arno Press, 1979), 115.

43. John W. Henderson, *The U.S. Information Agency* (New York: Praeger, 1969), 38; Oral history interview, Gordon Gray, 55, June 18, 1973, Harry S Truman Library; Oral history interview, Edward W. Barrett, 34, July 9, 1974, Harry S Truman Library; Edward P. Lilly, "The Development of American Psychological Operations, 1945-1951," December 19, 1951, U.S. DDRS 1991, 2302, 22.

44. Sally Bedell Smith, *In All His Glory: The Life of William S. Paley, the Legendary Tycoon and His Brilliant Circle* (New York: Simon and Schuster, 1990), 207-25; Paley to Benton, October 16, 1946, IBD Radio Foundation, Box 1, ASSPA 45–50.

45. Benton to Acheson, February 7, 1947, Under Secretary Acheson, 1947, Box 4, ASSPA 45–50.

46. Even model CBS broadcaster Edward R. Murrow, who sat on the state department's Advisory Committee on Overseas Information and the NAB's In-

ternational Affairs Committee, and was thus twice committed to cooperation, thought that to make the chairman of the foundation board a political
appointee doomed it to failure, and he refused to support it. Murrow to
Cohen, April 9, 1947, IBD 1947, Box 1, ASSPA 45–50.

47. McDonald to McMahon, March 10, 1947, Radio Foundation, Box 8, ASSPA
45–50. Ironically, Zenith's plan to launch a domestic television network was
about to fall prey to the "acid spur" of NBC and CBS's market dominance.
See Chapter Two, this volume.

48. Blanchard, *Exporting the First Amendment*, 115; Miller to Benton, March
11, 1947, Committee on International Affairs, 1946–48, Box 100, Miller
Papers.

49. Pirsein, *The Voice of America*, 131; Benton reported his conversation with
Trammell in a memo to Acheson, May 15, 1947, Under Secretary Acheson,
1947, Box 4, ASSPA 45–50.

50. Lilly, "The Development of Psychological Operations," 93; Pirsein, *The
Voice of America*, 136–39.

51. Mark Ethridge of the *Louisville Courier-Journal* and Erwin D. Canham of
the *Christian Science Monitor* chaired it in the late 1940s. Other members
were G.E. Chairman Philip Reed, Mark May of Yale, and Justin Miller of the
National Association of Broadcasters. An array of industry advisory boards
monitored the state department's overseas information operations, and this
seemed to ensure their quality and professionalism. Boards set up by Congress (the US Advisory Commission on Information), the National Association of Broadcasters (its International Affairs Committee), and the state department (the Advisory Committee on International Broadcasting) shared
several members in 1948: Walter Lemmon of World Wide Broadcasting,
Frank Stanton and Edmund Chester of CBS, Charles Denney of RCA, and
James Lawrence Fly of Associated Broadcasters, Inc.

52. PL 402, Section 502 and Title 5, quoted in Pirsein, *The Voice of America*,
139–41; Brooks to Mullen, January 8, 1948, State Department, Box 285,
Brooks Papers.

53. Fry to Stone, June 2, 1947, Radio Foundation-IBD, Box 8, ASSPA 45–50.

54. Fry to Stone, August 19, 1947, IBD, Box 8, ASSPA 45–50; Hunt to Stone,
August 22, 1947, IMP 1950, Box 2, ASSPA 45–50.

55. Benton to Stanton and Trammell, September 30, 1947, Radio, Subject Box 8,
Russell Papers.

56. Stanton to Sargent, October 8, 1947, IBD 1947, Box 1, ASSPA 45–50;
MacKnight to Allen et al., April 5, 1948, Associated Press, Box 7, ASSPA
45–50.

57. Brooks to Trammell, February 7, 1948, State Department, Box 285, Brooks
Papers.

58. Benton to Mansfield, February 9, 1948, Congressional Miscellaneous, Box 7,
ASSPA 45–50; Oral history interview, Edward W. Barrett, 66, July 19, 1974,
Harry S Truman Library; Richardson to Brooks (reporting about Delgado of
the VOA), June 15, 1948, State Department, Box 285, Brooks Papers.

59. Oral history interview, Noel Macy, 24, Harry S Truman Library; Richardson
to Brooks, June 15, 1948, State Department, Box 285, Brooks Papers; Re-

port of the Chenoweth State Department Committee (June 1948), State Department, Box 285, Brooks Papers; Ross to Hunt et al., June 10, 1948, Know America Series, Box 7, ASSPA 45–50.

60. Pirsein, *The Voice of America*, 145; Quoted in Hixson, *Parting the Curtain*, 31; Report of the Chenoweth State Department Subcommittee, Committee on Expenditures in the Executive Departments, on its investigation of the Voice of America (June 1948), State Department, Box 285, Brooks Papers.

61. Statement of Charles R. Denny before Joint Senate and House Subcommittees (June 1948), Chenoweth Committee, Box 7, ASSPA 45–50.

62. Brooks to Vice-Presidents, Station Managers, and Department Heads, July 1, 1948, State Department, Box 285, Brooks Papers; Allen to Denny, July 22, 1948, State Department, Box 285, Brooks Papers, NBC Records, SHSW. Hollywood implemented a voluntary system to guard against overseas release of films that could be damaging. The Motion Picture Association of America maintained a selectivity department that reviewed films for suitability for foreign release. They might recommend some re-editing or approve release for some countries but not others. The studios became so adept at self-censorship that in practice virtually no films were judged fully unsuitable. See C. D. Jackson, "Private Media and Public Policy," 335–37.

63. Recommendations of NAB Advisory Committee on International Broadcasting, June 7, 1949, NAB, Box 286, Brooks Papers.

64. Barrett to Rooney, July 25, 1951, "D," Box 1, Barrett Papers; Chester to Sevareid, November 15, 1951, CBS Correspondence, 1946–53, Box 1, Sevareid Papers.

65. Blanchard, *Exporting the First Amendment*, 142.

66. C. D. Jackson, "Private Media and Public Policy," 328.

67. Rankin to Fry, October 9, 1947, Radio Foundation, Box 9, ASSPA 45–50.

68. "Who Needs Propaganda?" editorial reprint from the *New York Daily Mirror*, February 5, 1953, Abbott Washburn, Box 7, Pre-Accession Records, C. D. Jackson Papers.

69. Andrew Berding, "Opening the Door on Foreign Affairs, " in Ray Eldon Hiebert and Carlton E. Spitzer, eds., *The Voice of Government* (New York: John E. Wiley and Sons, 1968), 111–25.

70. Repplier to Russell, July 2, 1948, Advertising Council, 1945–52, Subject Box 1, Russell Papers.

71. Sig Mickelson, *America's Other Voice: The Story of Radio Free Europe and Radio Liberty* (New York: Praeger, 1983), passim; and Christopher Simpson, *Blowback: The First Account of America's Recruitment of Nazis, and Its Disastrous Effect on Our Foreign and Domestic Policy* (New York: Macmillan, 1988), 125–36, 227–29. The quote is from Barnouw, *The Sponsor*, 143.

Chapter Two: A Weapon for Truth

1. Hugh M. Beville, Jr., "The Challenge of the New Media: Television, FM and Facsimile," *Journalism Quarterly* 25:1 (March 1948), 3–4. NBC's own circulation estimates are higher, about 250,000 sets in January 1948. NBC Televi-

sion Circulation Estimates, January 1, 1946–December 1, 1948, Television, Box 288, Brooks Papers.

2. James L. Baughman, "The Promise of American Television," *Prospects* 11 (1986), Vol. 2, 119–34.

3. Richard Campbell, *60 Minutes and the News: A Mythology for Middle America* (Urbana: University of Illinois Press, 1991), 2; and Gary Paul Gates, *Air Time: The Inside Story of CBS News* (New York: Harper and Row, 1978), 60; Desmond Smith, "TV news did not just happen – it had to invent itself," *Smithsonian* 20:3 (June 1989), 76.

4. Sig Mickelson, *From Whistle Stop to Sound Bite: Four Decades of Politics and Television* (New York: Praeger, 1989), 11; Smith, "TV news did not just happen," 78.

5. This figure is culled from *Meet the Press* records at the Motion Picture and Recorded Sound Division at the Library of Congress and *New York Times* television listings. A similar study conducted in the mid-1970s found similar percentages for *Meet the Press*, ABC's *Issues and Answers*, and CBS's *Face the Nation*. See William C. Adams and Paul H. Ferber, "Television Interview Shows: The Politics of Visibility," *Journal of Broadcasting* 21:2 (Spring 1977), 141–49.

6. Gay Talese, *The Kingdom and the Power* (Garden City: Doubleday, 1978), 134; Oral history interview, Leonard Reinsch, March 13–14, 1967, Harry S Truman Library, 49 and 68; A. M. Rosenthal, "TV Antics Can Kill the Press Conference," *International Press Institute Report* (October 1953), 4; "CBS Editorial," August 26, 1954, CBS 2, Post Presidential Files, Truman Papers.

7. A. M. Rosenthal, "TV Antics," 4; Ray Scherer, "Television News in Washington," in Ray Eldon Hiebert, ed., *The Press in Washington* (New York: Dodd Mead and Co., 1966), 98; *Sponsor* quoted in William Boddy, *Fifties Television* (Urbana: University of Illinois Press, 1990), 102.

8. Jack Gould, "Political Leaders Acclaim TV But Warn Against Its Misuse," *New York Times*, June 6, 1951, 1:2.

9. Lynn Spigel, *Make Room for TV: Television and the Family Ideal in Postwar America* (Chicago: University of Chicago Press, 1992), 133–34.

10. Quoted in Harold Lord Varney, "How TV Molds Your Mind," *American Mercury* (April 1954), 52; "The Battling Panelists," *Newsweek* (Jan. 16, 1956), 78; Henry R. Cassirer, "Television News: A Challenge to Imaginative Journalists," *Journalism Quarterly* 26:3 (September 1949), 279.

11. Quoted in Steve M. Barkin, "Eisenhower's Television Planning Board: An Unwritten Chapter in the History of Political Broadcasting," *Journal of Broadcasting* 27:4 (Fall 1983), 319; Sigurd to Eisenhower, July 18, 1952, Folder: Sigurd Larmon, Box 9, Robinson Papers; Jack Gould, "On Television: No Comment," *New York Times*, Nov. 13, 1955, II, 9:1.

12. CBS editorial, August 26, 1954, CBS 2, WHCF:PPF, Truman Papers; "Free Television: How It Serves America" (NAB pamphlet), General File 129-A-2, 1958 (1), Box 1004, White House Central Files, Eisenhower Papers.

13. Quoted in Rosenthal, "TV Antics," 4.

14. Ruth Nathan, "All the World's a Stage, and United Nations Diplomats Are Eager to Prove It on TV," *TV Guide*, March 14, 1959, 9.

15. Barrett to Heller, June 25, 1951, 911.44; Barrett to the Secretary, January 9, 1951, The Secretary, 1951, Box 6, Barrett Papers; "Campaigning on TV (Television edition of 'Is Your Hat in the Ring?')," Folder: NARTB, Box 8, Quick Papers.
16. Boddy, *Fifties Television*, 100.
17. Oral history interview, George Tames, 32, June 1, 1980, Harry S Truman Library.
18. Varney, "How TV Molds Your Mind," *American Mercury* (April 1954), 51; Folsom quoted in Stephen J. Whitfield, *The Culture of the Cold War* (Baltimore: Johns Hopkins University Press, 1991), 154; this was a *Counterattack* publication. Attached to Ross to Kirkpatrick, October 21, 1947, WHCF:OF 572, Truman Papers, Truman Library.
19. Erik Barnouw, *Tube of Plenty: The Evolution of American Television*, revised edition (New York: Oxford University Press, 1982), 112.
20. "Anti-Red Laws: Congress Pressure Mounts," *Broadcasting*, July 10, 1950, 19; Bryce Olivor, "Thought Control – American Style," *New Republic* (January 13, 1947), 12–13.
21. John Cogley, *Report on Blacklisting II: Radio and Television* (New York: The Fund for the Republic, Inc., 1956), 1–2.
22. Erik Barnouw, *The Sponsor: Notes on a Modern Potentate* (New York: Oxford University Press, 1978), 49; Boddy, *Fifties Television*, 99; David Caute, *The Great Fear: The Anti-communist Purge Under Truman and Eisenhower* (New York: Simon and Schuster, 1978), 521–22; Ross to Kirkpatrick, October 21, 1947, WHCF:OF 572, Truman Papers.
23. Whitfield, *The Culture of the Cold War*, 166; Cogley, *Blacklisting*, 23, 68; Robert Metz, *CBS: Reflections in a Bloodshot Eye* (Chicago: Playboy Press Books, 1975), p. 282.
24. Quoted in Caute, *The Great Fear*, 528.
25. Quoted in A. M. Sperber, *Murrow: His Life and Times* (New York: Freundlich Books, 1986), 365.
26. Quoted in Boddy, *Fifties Television*, 100–1.
27. Boddy, *Fifties Television*, 100.
28. Robert W. McChesney, "Off Limits: An Inquiry Into the Lack of Debate over the Ownership, Structure, and Control of the Mass Media in U.S. Political Life," *Communication*, 1992, Vol. 13, 1–19.
29. Robert W. McChesney, *Telecommunications, Mass Media, and Democracy: The Battle for the Control of U.S. Broadcasting, 1928–1935* (New York: Oxford University Press, 1993).
30. Quoted in Boddy, *Fifties Television*, 33.
31. Quoted in Boddy, *Fifties Television*, 45.
32. Quoted in Boddy, *Fifties Television*, 38.
33. Quoted in Boddy, *Fifties Television*, 47.
34. Boddy, *Fifties Television*, 51.
35. Michael Ritchie, *Please Stand By: A Prehistory of Television* (Woodstock, NY: Overlook Press, 1994), 153.
36. Allen B. DuMont, "Summary of National TV Situation" (July 1954), 1954 (2), WHCF:OF 250-D, Truman Papers.

37. Stuart Lewis Long, *The Development of the Network Television Oligopoly* (New York: Arno Press, 1979), 101.
38. Untitled memo, filed by Dawson, November 5, 1952, WHCF:OF 136B, Truman Papers.
39. Quoted in Boddy, *Fifties Television*, 52.
40. Quoted in Boddy, *Fifties Television*, 52.
41. Taylor to Weaver and Wile ["Horizon" memo], September 11, 1951, Operation Frontal Lobes, Box 278, Taylor Papers; "Operation Frontal Lobes," *Time*, January 21, 1952.
42. Edward R. Murrow, RTNDA Speech, October 15, 1958, reprinted in Edward Bliss, Jr., ed., *In Search of Light: The Broadcasts of Edward R. Murrow* (New York: Alfred P. Knopf, 1967), 355.
43. "Free Television: How it Serves America" (NAB pamphlet), General File 129-A-2, 1958 (1), Box 1004, White House Central Files, Eisenhower Papers.
44. Jeffrey B. Abramson, F. Christopher Arterton, and Gary R. Orren, *The Electronic Commonwealth: The Impact of New Media Technologies on Democratic Politics* (New York: Basic Books, 1988), 287.
45. Menachem Blondheim, *News Over the Wires: The Telegraph and the Flow of Public Information in America, 1844–1892* (Cambridge: Harvard University Press, 1994); and Edwin R. Bayley, *Joe McCarthy and the Press* (New York: Pantheon, 1981).
46. See Dan Schiller, *Objectivity and the News: The Public and the Rise of Commercial Journalism* (Philadelphia: University of Pennsylvania Press, 1981); Michael Schudson, *Discovering the News: A Social History of American Newspapers* (New York: Basic Books, 1978); and Schiller, "An Historical Approach to Objectivity and Professionalism in American News Reporting," *Journal of Communication* 29 (August 1979), 46–57.
47. Daniel Hallin, "The American news media: a critical theory perspective," in *We Keep America on Top of the World: Television journalism and the public sphere* (London: Routledge, 1994), 25.
48. Daniel Hallin, *The "Uncensored War": The Media and Vietnam* (New York: Oxford University Press, 1986), 116f.; Hallin, "American News Media," 28.

Chapter Three: Clearer Than Truth

1. Hearings before House Appropriations Subcommittee, 83rd Congress, 1st Session, p. 93. See also William O. Chittick, "The Domestic Information Activities of the Department of State," unpublished Ph.D. dissertation, The Johns Hopkins University, 1964, 51.
2. Benton to Marshall, September 3, 1947, September 1947–January 1953, Benton File Box 20, Sargeant Papers.
3. Oral history interview, William Benton, 166, July 12, 1968, Columbia University; Jackson to Barrett, February 8, 1951, Time, Inc. Box 26, C. D. Jackson Papers; Department's Information Program on the Marshall Plan, August 1, 1947, Publicity/Propaganda 1945–51, Subject Box 8, Russell Papers.

4. Russell to Schwinn, January 4, 1950, Planning Operations, Domestic and Overseas Information Programs, 1949–50, Subject Box 7, Russell Papers.

5. Russell to Sargeant, June 7, 1949, Planning Operations, Domestic and Overseas Information Programs, 1949–50, Subject Box 7, Russell Papers; Russell to Sargeant and Barrett, June 6, 1950, Planning Operations, Domestic and Overseas Information Programs, 1949–50, Subject Box 7, Russell Papers.

6. George F. Kennan, "The Sources of Soviet Conduct," reprinted in *American Diplomacy* (Chicago: University of Chicago Press, 1984), 115; Postscript, Russell to Sargeant, June 7, 1949, Planning Operations, Domestic and Overseas Information Programs, 1949–50, Subject Box 7, Russell Papers; Oral history interview, Francis H. Russell, p. 17, July 13, 1973, Truman Library; Oral history interview, Edward W. Barrett, p. 12, July 9, 1974, Truman Library.

7. Michael Wala, "Selling the Marshall Plan at Home: The Committee for the Marshall Plant to Aid European Recovery," *Diplomatic History* 10:3 (Summer 1986), 248; Jerry Sanders, *Peddlers of Crisis: The Committee on the Present Danger and the Politics of Containment* (Boston: South End Press, 1983); and Sig Mickelson, *America's Other Voice: The Story of Radio Free Europe and Radio Liberty* (New York: Praeger, 1983).

8. Oral history interview, Francis H. Russell, p. 17, July 13, 1973, Truman Library; "How U.S. Tries to Influence You: Government Spends Millions to Tell Its Story," *U.S. News and World Report* (June 15, 1951), 18. The report of Acheson's contact with journalists comes from historian Robert L. Beisner from his work on a biography of Dean Acheson. Television historians argue that because broadcasters targeted the widest possible audience, and were entirely supported by sponsor dollars in the era of the blacklist, they were more politically cautious than even the most prestigious papers claiming objectivity. See Erik Barnouw, *The Sponsor: Notes on a Modern Potentate* (New York: Oxford, 1979); Karen Sue Foley, *The Political Blacklist in the Broadcasting Industry: The Decade of the 1950s* (New York: Arno Press, 1979); and John Cogley, *Report on Blacklisting II: Radio and Television* (The Fund for the Republic, 1956).

9. An Evaluation of Televising of the San Francisco Meetings (Wood to Russell), September 19, (1951), Television, Subject Box 11, Russell Papers; Russell to Barrett, January 21, 1950, Public Relations Working Group, Box 5, ASSPA 47–50.

10. Hulten to Benton, January, 20, 1947, Charles Hulten 1947–48, General Subject File Box 2, ASSPA 47–50.

11. Past and Present Services to Radio and Television by Radio Branch (Russell to Barrett, April 14, 1950), Radio, Subject Box 8, Russell Papers; Memo of Conversation, Gordon Hubell, Wilett Kempton, Bill Wood, and Larry Warwick, September 23, 1948, Television, Subject Box 11, Russell Papers.

12. Russell to Wood, May 6, 1949, Television, Subject Box 11, Russell Papers; Memo of Conversation, Charles Kelly, Gordon Hubble, Bill Wood, February 3, 1949, Television, Subject Box 11, Russell Papers.

13. During August and September 1954, ABC aired various government-produced documentary programs on subjects such as communism and democracy under the title, *This World – 1954*.

14. Edwards and Carter to Russell et al., January 25, 1949, 811.4061, DOS Records.

15. On Pommer's former position, see Lawrence H. Suid, ed., and David Culbert, editor-in-chief, *Film and Propaganda in America: A Documentary History*, Vol. 4, *1945 and After* (New York: Greenwood Press, 1990), 61 ff.; Memo of Conversation between Pommer, Simpson, Mann and Carter, July 15, 1949, 811.4061, DOS Records.

16. Bennett to Leyva, January 5, 1954, 911.44, DOS Records.

17. Russell to Wood, September 21, 1950, Radio, Subject Box 8, Russell Papers.

18. Dulles to Barrett, October 3, 1951, and Edward W. Barrett to Mr. Dulles, October 16, 1951, Special Assistants: Battle, Jessup, Dulles, Box 6, Barrett Papers.

19. This is how Dean Acheson described the Republican assault on his competence and loyalty. Dean Acheson, *Present at the Creation* (New York: Norton, 1969), 354.

20. Memorandum by the Assistant Secretary of State for Public Affairs (Barrett) to the Under Secretary of State (Webb) and Annex, March 6, 1950, *Foreign Relations of the United States, 1950*, Vol. 1 (Washington, D.C.: Government Printing Office, 1966) (hereafter cited as *FRUS*), 185; Player to Barrett, March 9, 1950, Public Relations Working Group, Box 5, ASSPA 47–50.

21. Lehrbas to Webb, April 21, 1950, ARA 1950, Box 1, ASSPA 45–50; Author's transcript, *Meet the Press* broadcast, July 19, 1953, Motion Picture and Recorded Sound Division, Library of Congress, Washington, D.C.

22. Barrett to Crawford, March 14, 1950, Deputy Under Secretary for Administration and Component Parts, Box 1, ASSPA 45–50. The findings of the study were inconclusive. Several commentators seemed to devote more time to foreign affairs, "but of course this tendency may be attributable to other factors besides contact with the Department's 'information' circuit." Lehrbas to Russell, March 14, 1951, and Russell to Lehrbas, March 30, 1951, Radio, Subject Box 7, Russell Papers.

23. Russell to Barrett, March 13, 1950, and attached memos "Department Broadcast Relations," and "Draft of Memo to PIC on Department Broadcast Relations," Radio, Subject Box 8, Russell Papers; Russell to Barrett, March 24, 1950, Television, Subject Box 11, Russell Papers; Barrett to Carter, March 16, 1950, Television, Subject Box 11, Russell Papers.

24. Members of the PRWG in 1950 were Lloyd Lehrbas (special assistant to the under secretary), Francis Russell (director of public affairs), Roger Tubby (press secretary to President Truman), William O. Player, Jr. (public affairs specialist), Edward W. Barrett (assistant secretary of state for public affairs), Bromley Smith (special assistant to the secretary of state), Erasmus H. Kloman (foreign affairs analyst), Walter Wilgus (assistant to the director of the executive secretariat), and Jack McDermott (chief, International Press and Publications Division). Public Relations Working Group 1950, Box 5, ASSPA 47–50; Terms of Reference for Departmental Working Group on Public Relations (undated), Public Relations Working Group, Box 5, ASSPA 47–50; Colcord to Barrett, Notes on Public Relations Working Group Meeting, August

17, 1950, August 18, 1950, Numbered Minutes, 1950–52, PRWG 50–52 Box 1, Russell Papers.

25. Player to Barrett, April 5, 1950, Radio, Subject Box 11, Russell Papers.

26. Russell listed acceptable scripted shows as *Battle Report* (NBC) and *The Facts We Face* (CBS), and unacceptable "ad lib" television shows as *Meet the Press* (NBC), *People's Platform* (CBS), and *American Forum [of the Air]* (NBC). Russell to Barrett, January 22, 1951, Documents 1950–52, Public Relations Working Group Box 1, Russell Papers. The *Meet the Press* figures are culled from NBC records at the Motion Picture and Recorded Sound Division at the Library of Congress and *New York Times* television listings of the guests; Wood to Russell, An Evaluation of the Televising of the San Francisco Meeting, September 19, (1951), Television, Subject Box 11, Russell Papers; Spivak to Russell, February 21, 1950, Radio, Subject Box 11, Russell Papers.

27. Many historians contend that television contributed to McCarthy's downfall. They cite the live coverage of the U.S. Army-McCarthy hearings, and Edward R. Murrow's March 1954 *See It Now* broadcast. Murrow himself said that the mass media made McCarthy by giving "nationwide circulation to his mouthings" but that prolonged exposure on the U.S. Army-McCarthy hearings also contributed to his defeat. Murrow felt that *See It Now* was "bringing up the rear" behind broadcasters Elmer Davis and Drew Pearson on ABC and Eric Sevareid on CBS, who had steadily attacked McCarthy. Only when McCarthy "broke the rules of the club" by attacking members of the Senate was he finished. See Chapter 13 in A. M. Sperber, *Murrow: His Life and Times* (New York: Freundlich, 1986); and Daniel J. Leab, "See It Now: A Legend Reassessed," in John O'Connor, ed., *American History/American Television* (New York: Ungar Books, 1983), 1–32.

28. Russell to Allen, March 4, 1949, Television, Subject Box 11, Russell Papers. A third unsuccessful attempt at such a series was made in 1953.

29. Memorandum by the Assistant Secretary of State for Public Affairs (Barrett) to the Secretary of State, April 6, 1950, *FRUS* 1950, Vol. 1, 225–26; Memorandum by the Director of the Office of Public Affairs (Russell) to the Assistant Secretary of State for Public Affairs (Barrett), March 6, 1950, *FRUS* 1950, Vol. 1, 185–86.

30. Record of the Meeting of the State–Defense Policy Review Group, March 16, 1950, *FRUS* 1950, Vol. 1, 191–92, 196–200; Sanders, *Peddlers of Crisis*, 54 ff.

31. Address on Foreign Policy at a Luncheon of the American Society of Newspaper Editors, April 22, 1950, *Public Papers of the Presidents: Harry S Truman, 1950* (Washington, D.C.: Government Printing Office, 1965), 263.

32. Walter H. Waggoner, "Acheson Declares U.S. Is in Danger as Kremlin Target," *New York Times*, April 23, 1950, 1:8; "Text of Address by Acheson to Society of Newspaper Editors," New York Times, April 23, 1950, 28.

33. Acheson, *Present at the Creation*, 374–75.

34. List of TV Stations and List of Films and Playdates, Marshall Plan in Action, ECA Records.

35. Statement made by Mr. William C. Foster at opening and closing of television program, "The Marshall Plan in Action," The Marshall Plan in Action, ECA Records; Memorandum titled, "13 week TV Series ABC," Marshall Plan in Action, ECA Records.

36. Unsigned memo (probably Robert Mullen, ECA Director of Information) to Roscoe, April 15, 1952, Moving Pictures-Television-ABC File, ASSPA Suitland; Robert Hammel Stewart, "The Development of Network Television Program Types to January 1953," unpublished Ph.D. dissertation, Ohio State University, 1954, 396; Hutchinson to Berding, April 28, 1952, Moving Pictures-Television-ABC, ASSPA Suitland.

37. Ibid.

38. Wood to Russell, March 31, 1950, Television, Subject Box 11, Russell Papers.

39. Swihart to Carter, August 10, 1950, Television, Subject Box 11, Russell Papers. The correspondent's name is Quincy Howe; Byroade to Hay, Prud'homme and Kellerman, August 14, 1950, 911.44/8–1450, DOS Records; Hall to Flynn, October 22, 1950, 911.44/8–1450, DOS Records.

40. PA Staff Meeting Minutes, August 29, 1950, PA Staff Meetings, 1948–50, Subject Box 7, Russell Papers; Barrett to Webb, August 30, 1950, Television, Subject Box 11, Russell Papers; PA Staff Meeting Minutes, August 29, 1950, PA Staff Meetings, 1948–50, Subject Box 7, Russell Papers.

41. Jay Walz, "Acheson Doubts Peiping War Entry," *New York Times*, September 11, 1950, 1:5.

42. "This is background to Murrow 'kill order'" (unsigned and undated, probably Jesse Zousmer or Larry LeSeur, August 1950), CBS Files 343, Murrow Papers; Author's transcript *Battle Report – Washington*, September 10, 1950, Motion Picture and Recorded Sound Division, National Archives, Washington, D.C.

43. Barrett to Members of the Public Relations Working Group, September 11, 1950, PRWG, Box 5, ASSPA 47–50.

44. Gallup poll cited in Ole R. Holsti, "Public Opinion and Containment," in Terry L. Deibel and John Lewis Gaddis, eds., *Containment: Concept and Policy*, Vol. 1 (Washington, D.C.: National Defense University Press, 1986), 77. The figure swung back up to fifty percent in January 1953, the month of Eisenhower's inaugural; Barrett quoted in James Aronson, *The Press and the Cold War* (Indianapolis: Bobbs-Merrill, 1970), 104.

45. Barrett to The Secretary (Acheson) and Webb, December 5, 1950, Under Secretary 1951, Box 5, Barrett Papers; *New York Times*, December 4, 1950, and Sanders, *Peddlers of Crisis*, 55.

46. Jackson to Barrett, September 20, 1950, E. W. Barrett, Box 26, C. D. Jackson Papers; Russell to Sargeant, June 7, 1949, Russell to Schwinn, January 4, 1950, and Russell to Sargeant and Barrett, April 6, 1950, Planning Operations, Domestic and Overseas Information Programs, 1949–50, Subject Box 7, Russell Papers.

47. Minutes of the Public Relations Working Group, September 21, 1950, Box 5, ASSPA 47–50; Barrett to Webb, December 18, 1951, U.S. EC, 1951, Box 5, Barrett Papers.

48. Sargeant to Barrett, September 7, 1951 (Memo entitled, "What Are the Major Priority Jobs for the Assistant Secretary of State for Public Affairs, Looking Ahead from September 1951?"), Correspondence: Deputy Assistant Secretary for Public Affairs, 1951, Box 4, General File, Sargeant Papers, and Sargeant to The Secretary, April 9, 1952, Correspondence, Deputy Assistant Secretary for Public Affairs, 1952, Box 4, Sargeant Papers.
49. National Opinion Research Center, January 19, 1951, (Sheatsley to Russell), correspondence: Deputy Assistant Secretary of State, 1952, Box 4, Sargeant papers.
50. Jackson to Benton, January 2, 1952, William Benton, Box 27, C. D. Jackson Papers; Benton to Cowan, January 24, 1952, C + CARE + D, Subject Box 1, Barrett Papers; Oral history interview, Howland H. Sargeant, December 15, 1970, pp. 4–5, Eisenhower Library.
51. Text of McCardle speech, Conference on U.S. Foreign Policy, June 5, 1953, McCardle speeches, Box 11, Series III, McCardle Papers; C. D. Jackson, "The U.S. Public: A Matter of Orchestration," 62 (confidential source paper for "Psychological Aspects of U.S. Strategy"), November 1955, Nelson Rockefeller (5), Box 61, WHCF:CF, Eisenhower Papers.
52. Deborah Welch Larson, *Origins of Containment: A Psychological Explanation* (Princeton: Princeton University Press, 1985), 21. See also W. Scott Lucas, "Campaigns of Truth: The American Psychological Offensive Against the Soviet Union, 1947–54," forthcoming.

Chapter Four: Ready, Willing, Able

1. "Radio-TV Stock Drops, War Scare Cited," *Broadcasting*, July 17, 1950, 19:2; Folsom to Buck, July 14, 1950, Korean War Impact Reports, Box 287, Brooks Papers.
2. George Rosen, "Radio's Big Second Chance," *Variety*, July 26, 1950, 1:3; Herb Golden, "Show Biz Eyes War Changes," *Variety*, July 19, 1950, 1:3; Wile to Brooks, August 17, 1950, Korean War Impact Reports, Box 287, Brooks Papers.
3. "Truman Speech May Hold Key To Korean War's Effect on TV Industry," *Variety*, July 19, 1950, 25:4; Hitz to Brooks, July 27, 1950, Korean War Impact Reports, Box 287, Brooks Papers; "Norge Cancels Out on 15G TV Show in Korea 'Alert,'" *Variety*, August 2, 1950, 31:4.
4. Frank W. Fox, *Madison Avenue Goes to War: The Strange Military Career of American Advertising, 1941–45* (Provo, UT: Brigham Young University Charles E. Merrill Monograph Series in the Humanities and Social Sciences, 4:1, 1975), 11–12; Wile to Brooks, September 27, 1950, Korean War Impact Reports, Box 287, Brooks Papers.
5. de las Ossa to Brooks, December 20, 1950, Korean War Impact Reports, Box 287, Brooks Papers; "No Purchases by Govt. Yet," *Variety*, August 23, 1950, 31:3; "Production: Civilian Radio-TV Cutbacks Mulled," *Broadcasting*, July 31, 1950, 23.
6. Cobbett Steinberg, *TV Facts* (New York: Facts on File, 1985), 85, 126.

7. Kim McQuaid, *Uneasy Partners: Big Business in American Politics, 1945–1990* (Baltimore: Johns Hopkins University Press, 1994), 61.

8. Erik Barnouw points out that many NAB codes are vague and that the organization does not enforce them. In 1963, forty percent of its member stations exceeded the NAB's prescribed amount of advertising. If charged, the station could lose the right to display the NAB's "seal of good practice," but none did (as if viewers would have noticed). Erik Barnouw, *Tube of Plenty: The Evolution of American Television*, rev. ed. (New York: Oxford University Press, 1982), 355–56.

9. David R. Mackey, "The Development of the National Association of Broadcasters," *Journal of Broadcasting* 1 (Fall 1957), 303. However, historians of regulation have shown that a simple "captive thesis" – that industries captured the New Deal agencies set up to regulate them – oversimplifies the transformations in American business after World War II. In his study of the FCC, James Baughman enumerates factors that weakened the agency from within. Presidents Truman and Eisenhower used the commission as political spoils, and they appointed unqualified commissioners. Several of Eisenhower's appointees were investigated for accepting gifts and loans from license applicants. Congress imposed awkward procedural changes and interfered with the commission's work. Few activist groups complained because "the general public mood favored free enterprise over regulation." Under Newton Minow, the FCC attempted to make the voluntary NAB codes mandatory but failed. James L. Baughman, *Television's Guardians: The FCC and the Politics of Programming* (Knoxville: The University of Tennessee Press, 1985), passim, 19, 117–26.

10. Miller to Steelman, August 3, 1950, WHCF:OF 571, Truman Papers.

11. "RCA Pledges Aid," *Broadcasting*, July 24, 1950, 18:4; Norman Chandler to Louis Johnson, August 10, 1950, 311.25, OPI Records; Louis Johnson to Norman Chandler, August 29, 1950, OPI Records; "Defense Aid: Services, Facilities Offered by Broadcasters," *Broadcasting*, July 24, 1950, 36.

12. "Defense Meet: Radio-TV Talks Underway," *Broadcasting*, July 31, 1950, 20:1; Handwritten notes, "Defense Council of Broadcasters," undated, Broadcasters Advisory Council, 1949–August 1950, Box 98, Miller Papers.

13. Telegram, Ryan to Miller, July 22, 1950, Broadcast Advisory Council, 1949–August 1950, Box 98, Miller Papers; Handwritten notes titled "Broadcasters Advisory Council," Broadcast Advisory Council, 1949–August 1950, Box 98, Miller Papers; Steelman to Hardy, July 21, 1950, WHCF:OF 571, Truman Papers; "News from NAB," July 21, 1951, NAB Library; Assistant Secretary of State for Public Affairs Edward Barrett reported to Secretary of State Dean Acheson that Justin Miller "as spokesman for the broadcasting industry offered to organize a top-level industry council to aid the Government in whatever way possible in the present emergency through the broadcasting medium." Barrett to the Secretary, December 13, 1950, Radio, Subject Box 8, Russell Papers.

14. Telephone interview with the author, March 14, 1989; Steelman to Ewing, August 23, 1950, WHCF:OF 571, Truman Papers.

15. "Broadcasters Defense Council: A Plan Prepared by the National Association of Broadcasters for Radio-Television Assistance in the Current National Emergency," Ryan to Steelman and Jackson, August 1, 1950, Broadcasters' Advisory Council, 1949–August 1950, Box 98, Miller Papers; Jackson to Ryan, August 3, 1950, National Association of Broadcasters, Box 23, Jackson Papers. The panels were military, civilian mobilization, censorship, information, and production. The proposed advisory panel consisted of the chairmen of the NBC, CBS, ABC, and Mutual networks, Justin Miller, four station presidents, two attorneys, and Elmer Davis, ABC commentator and former chief of the OWI. Richards to Ryan, September 29, 1950, Broadcasters Advisory Council, September–December 1950, Box 98, Miller Papers.

16. "News From NAB" press release, August 7, 1950; "Meeting of NAB Board with Mr. John Steelman," August 8, 1950, Broadcasters Advisory Council, 1949–August 1950, Box 98, Miller Papers.

17. Ibid.; see also "News From NAB" press release, August 7, 1950, NAB Library.

18. "News From NAB" press release, October 3, 1950, NAB Library; "News From NAB" press release, November 17, 1950, NAB Library; "News From NAB" press release, November 29, 1950, NAB Library.

19. Reproduced text of letter from Hayes to Steelman, printed in *Broadcasting*, January 1, 1951, 22, Broadcasters Advisory Council, 1951, Box 98, Miller Papers; "Broadcast Council: Expansion Mulled," *Broadcasting*, January 8, 1951; "News From NAB" press release, January 8, 1950.

20. Edward M. Kirby and Jack W. Harris, *Star-Spangled Radio* (Chicago: Ziff-Davis, 1948), 4. The members were Dr. Irwin L. Stewart, president of the University of West Virginia, Dr. Lee A. DuBridge, president of the California Institute of Technology, David H. O'Brien, William L. Everitt, dean of the College of Engineering of the University of Illinois, and Dr. James R. Killian, Jr., president of the Massachusetts Institute of Technology. "Letter to Dr. Irwin L. Stewart on the Establishment of the President's Communications Policy Board," February 17, 1950, *Public Papers of the Presidents of the United States: Harry S Truman, 1950* (Washington, D.C.: U.S. Government Printing Office, 1965), 169–71; "Communications Readied: 'Nerve System of Defense,'" *Broadcasting*, January 15, 1951. See also "Advisory Board Mulled to O'See U.S. Radio Policy," *Variety*, March 14, 1951, 22:3.

21. Dave Berlyn, "America's Sentinels: Radio, TV," *Broadcasting*, September 25, 1950, 19.

22. Quoted in "Civil Defense: Hill Approval Seen," *Broadcasting*, January 1, 1951, 21.

23. "Radio Bill Hearing Set," *New York Times*, February 11, 1951, 40:1. "U.S. Requests Power Over Radio in Crisis," *New York Times*, January 18, 1951, 19:6; "Emergency Role: Radio-TV Vital, Says Pierce," *Broadcasting*, January 1, 1951, 20. Meanwhile, the BAC met to consider an alternative plan put forward by one of its members. A. Frank Katzentine of Miami advocated linking all broadcast stations by telephone lines to a master switch in Washington, D.C. Katzentine acknowledged to Miller that most broadcasters

objected to giving such control over their stations to the president, but he offered his plan "in the belief that business as usual is not the credo of the radio broadcasters of the United States. I hold that the use of our facilities for the Nation's good in this hour of National peril is not only the desire of every broadcaster, but is our duty." The BAC ultimately endorsed a much more limited plan, one that satisfied civil defense officials and anticommunist alarmists but retained station control. Katzentine to Miller, December 21, 1950, Broadcasters Advisory Council, September–December 1950, Box 98, Miller Papers.

24. "News From NAB" press release, February 21, 1951, NAB Library; "News From NAB" press release, February 21, 1951, NAB Library; Miller to Johnson, February 28, 1951, Broadcasters Advisory Council, 1951, Box 98, Miller Papers; "Shutdown Fought By Broadcasters," *New York Times*, February 23, 1951, 38:1.

25. *Digest of General Bills with Index*, 82nd Congress, 1st session (Washington, D.C.: Library of Congress Legislative Reference Section, 1951), p. xii; Executive Order 10312, White House Press Release, December 10, 1951, 250-A-1 Conelrad, WHCF:OF 914, Truman Papers.

26. "Broadcasters to Huddle with FCC on Emergency Operation Setup," *Variety*, March 21, 1951, 24:1; "War Role Outlined: Broadcasters Urge Advisory Unit," *Broadcasting*, April 2, 1951, 27; "Gov't Gives Plans of B'caster Role in Civil Defense," *Variety*, April 18, 1951, 28:4; White House press release, December 1, 1952, 250-A-1 Conelrad, WHCF 914, Truman Papers, Truman Library; "Civil Defense: FCC Alert Plan Outlined at Meet," *Broadcasting*, December 31, 1951; "Radio 'Alert' Plan Going into Effect," *New York Times*, May 15, 1953, 32:3.

27. See McQuaid, *Uneasy Partners*, 60.

28. Quoted in Loch K. Johnson, *America's Secret Power: The CIA in a Democratic Society* (New York: Oxford University Press, 1989), 202. One serious security breach did occur during World War II. *Chicago Tribune* reporter Stanley Johnson wrote an article based on navy dispatches revealing how much Admiral Chester Nimitz knew about the Japanese fleet before the battle of Midway. The Japanese deduced that the United States had broken its naval codes and hence changed them. It was months before the United States broke the new ones. See Frederick S. Voss, *Reporting the War: The Journalistic Coverage of World War II* (Washington, D.C.: Smithsonian Institution Press, 1994), 36–39; quoted in Margaret Blanchard, "Americans First, Newspapermen Second? The Conflict Between Patriotism and Freedom of the Press During the Cold War, 1946–52," Ph.D. dissertation, University of North Carolina at Chapel Hill, 1981, 313.

29. "Army Eases New Rules," *New York Times*, July 28, 1950, 5:2; quoted in Blanchard, "Americans First," 349; *Editor and Publisher*, January 20, 1951, quoted in Mott, 853.

30. Minutes of the Public Relations Working Group, August 1, 1950, Numbered Minutes, 1950–52, Records Relating to the Public Relations Working Group, 1950–52, Russell Papers; Report of meeting with special ASNE Committee and Mr. Stuart Symington, Chairman National Security Resources Boards,

August 15, 1950, Broadcasters Advisory Council, 1949–August 1950, Box 98, Miller Papers; Edward M. Kirby and Jack W. Harris, *Star-Spangled Radio* (Chicago: Ziff-Davis, 1948), 4–9; and Voss, *Reporting the War*, 22–25.

31. Frank Luther Mott, *American Journalism: A History, 1690–1960*, 3rd ed. (New York: Macmillan, 1962), 853. See also Loren B. Thompson, "The Media Versus the Military: A Brief History of War Coverage in the United States," in Loren B. Thompson, ed., *Defense Beat: The Dilemmas of Defense Coverage* (New York: Macmillan, 1991), 33–37.

32. "Broadcasters Defense Council: A Plan Prepared by the National Association of Broadcasters for Radio-Television Assistance in the Current National Emergency," Ryan to Steelman and Jackson, August 1, 1950, Broadcasters Advisory Council, 1949–August 1950, Box 98, Miller Papers.

33. Joseph Persico, *Edward R. Murrow: An American Original* (New York: McGraw-Hill, 1988), 289; *New York Times*, August 6, 1950, 5:1.

34. "Edward R. Murrow with the News," June 27, 1950, CBS Files 342, Murrow Papers; A. M. Sperber, *Murrow: His Life and Times* (New York: Freundlich, 1985), 341, 345.

35. "Edward R. Murrow with the News," August 14, 1950, CBS Files 343, Murrow papers.

36. Undated, unsigned memo marked, "This is background to Murrow 'kill order,'" CBS Files 343, Murrow Papers; Robert Slater, *This . . . Is CBS: A Chronicle of 60 Years* (Englewood Cliffs, NJ: Prentice-Hall, 1988), 141.

37. "Situation Not Normal," *Newsweek*, September 25, 1950.

38. Ibid. and "M'Arthur Sets Up New Security Code," *New York Times*, December 13, 1950, 8:1.

39. Richards to Ryan, September 29, 1950, Broadcasters Advisory Council, September–December 1950, Box 98, Miller Papers.

40. Telegram, Marshall to Miller, December 16, 1950, Broadcasters Advisory Council, September–December 1950, Box 98, Miller Papers; Quoted in Mott, *American Journalism*, 854.

41. "M'Arthur Asserts Press Asked Curb," *New York Times*, January 19, 1951, 6:6.

42. Blanchard, "Americans First," 357–58.

43. "Censorship Considered," *New York Times*, December 19, 1950, 21:2; "Screening of Korea News Announced by MacArthur," *New York Times*, December 20, 1950, 2:4; "Censorship Is Tightened," *New York Times*, December 27, 1950, 4:7.

44. "Korea Censorship Tightened Again," *New York Times*, January 7, 1951, 14:1; "U.S. 8th Army Bars Word 'Retreat' as It Rivets Censorship onto Korea," *New York Times*, January 10, 1951, 1:6.

45. Fox, *Madison Avenue Goes to War*, 16, 51–52; Miller's handwritten notes on BAC, entitled "Concerns," Broadcasters Advisory Council 1949–August 1950, Box 98, Miller Papers.

46. Minutes of Meeting of NAB Board with Dr. John Steelman, August 8, 1950, Broadcast Advisory Council, 1949–August 1950, Box 98, Miller Papers.

47. Ibid.

48. Jackson to Ryan, August 3, 1950, NAB, Box 23, Jackson Papers.

49. *Defense Bulletin*, September 18, 1950, NAB Library.
50. The Crusade for Freedom was the domestic fundraising arm of Radio Free Europe. Both organizations were conceived and secretly funded by the Central Intelligence Agency as a strategy to produce "spontaneous" public anticommunist allegiance; *Defense Bulletin*, September 25, 1950, NAB Library; *Defense Bulletin*, October 9, 1950, and December 18, 1950, NAB Library.
51. Katzentine to Miller, December 21, 1950, Broadcasters Advisory Council, September–December 1950, Box 98, Miller Papers.
52. Memorandum, Material for Sept. 22 Defense Bulletin, NAB. Defense Bulletin, Box 2, 1951 E-W, Quick Papers.
53. "News From NAB" press release, December 13, 1950, NAB Library; Notes on Secretary's Remarks to the Broadcast Advisory Council, December 14, 1950, Radio, Subject Box 8, Russell Papers; "News From NAB" press release, December 14, 1950, NAB Library.
54. "News From NAB" press release, December 14, 1950, NAB Library; State Department Report to Broadcast Advisory Council (Russell to Miller), January 5, 1951, Broadcasters Advisory Council, 1951, Box 98, Miller Papers; Russell to Barrett, January 11, 1951, Documents 50–52, Public Relations Working Group Records, Russell Papers; Barrett to the Secretary, December 26, 1950, The Secretary, 1951, Box 6, Barrett Papers.
55. Minutes of the Meeting of the Broadcast Advisory Council, Broadcasters Advisory Council, September–December 1950, Box 98, Miller Papers.
56. Miller to Marshall, December 5, 1950, Dillon, 1949–53, OSD Records; Minutes of the Meeting of the Broadcast Advisory Council, Broadcasters Advisory Council, September–December 1950, Box 98, Miller Papers.
57. "News From NAB" press release, December 14, 1950, and Minutes of the Meeting of the Broadcast Advisory Council, Broadcasters Advisory Council, September–December 1950, Box 98, Miller Papers.

Chapter Five: Closer to Your Government

1. Burton I. Kaufman, *The Korean War: Challenges in Crisis, Credibility, and Command* (New York: Knopf, 1986), 37.
2. Jerry Walker, "TV Gets its Chance to 'Sell' News Shows," *Editor and Publisher*, July 29, 1950, 38.
3. "'One Nation:' CBS Show Views War Role," *Broadcasting*, August 21, 1950.
4. Stanton to Steelman, December 18, 1950, WHCF:OF 575, Truman Papers; Marvin to Roberts, August 30, 1950, 311.25, DOS Records.
5. McAndrew to Roberts, July 21, 1950, 311.25, DOS Records.
6. Raymond L. Carroll, "Factual Television in America: An Analysis of Network Television Documentary Programs, 1948–1975," unpublished Ph.D. dissertation, University of Wisconsin-Madison, 1978, 100; *Battle Report – Washington* script, August 13, 1950, Jackson Papers.
7. Gibson to Steelman, November 20, 1950, Battle Report 1951, Box 1, Quick Papers, and Meagher to Russell and Sargeant, March 11, 1952, *Battle Re-*

port – Washington, Box 21, Jackson Papers; Lawrence to Network Sales Staff, August 29, 1951, Armed Forces Show, Box 277, Taylor Papers.

8. Telephone interview with the author, March 14, 1989; Dorothy Gilfert, "Battle Report – Washington," *TV Guide* (Washington-Baltimore edition), week ending February 22, 1952, 5.

9. Wile to Brooks, August 17, 1950, Korean War Impact Reports, Box 287, Brooks Papers; Wile to Brooks, September 11, 1950, Korean War Impact Reports, Box 287, Brooks Papers; Congressional Record Clippings of Telecasts of *Battle Report – Washington*, Box 29, Jackson papers.

10. Wile to Steelman, September 5, 1950, WHCF:OF 136B, Truman Papers.

11. Meagher to Russell and Sargeant, March 11, 1952, *Battle Report – Washington*, Box 21, Jackson Papers; Taylor to McCormick, August 17, 1951, Armed Forces Show, Box 277, Taylor Papers.

12. Taylor to Wile and Weaver, May 2, 1951, and McCall to Flynn, May 2, 1951, Armed Forces Show, Box 277, Taylor Papers, Steelman to McCall, May 3, 1951, *Battle Report*, Box 310, McCall Papers.

13. Holton to Acting Director of Public Information (Mullen), July 25, 1950, 311.25, DOS Records; Dillon to Newlon, August 4, 1950, OPI Records.

14. Dillon to Acting Director, August 24, 1950, OPI Records; Jackson to Steelman, December 26, 1950, WHCF:OF 575, Truman Papers; Ayers to McCall, March 1, 1952, Armed Forces Show, Box 277, Taylor Papers.

15. "Korean Coverage," *Newsweek*, September 4, 1950, 48.

16. Taylor to Gene and Charlie Jones, January 30, 1951, Jones Brothers, Box 278, Taylor Papers.

17. Acheson to HICOG (Office of the American High Commissioner for Germany), December 21, 1950, 911.44, DOS Records. These cables went out under Acheson's name but were most likely written by someone on his staff.

18. Acheson to HICOG, January 6, 1951, 911.44, DOS Records.

19. Jackson to Ayers, February 2, 1951, A, Box 18, Charles Jackson Papers; Memorandum for the Files, Office of Greek, Turkish and Iranian Affairs, May 24, 1951, 911.44, DOS Records.

20. Allen to Jackson, March 30, 1951, A, Box 18, Jackson Papers; Memorandum for the Files, May 24, 1951, 911.44, DOS Records; Acheson to Amconsul, Rabat, May 25, 1951, 911.44, DOS Records; Memorandum for the Files, May 24, 1951, 911.44, DOS Records.

21. *Battle Report – Washington* scripts, June 3, 1951; December 16, 1951; May 20, 1951; April 4, 1952; Charles Jackson papers. *Battle Report – Washington* script, December 19, 1950, Charles Jackson Papers. *Battle Report – Washington* script, April 22, 1951, Charles Jackson Papers.

22. All quotations are from the author's transcript, *Battle Report*, August 10, 1951, Motion Picture, Sound and Video Branch, National Archives, Washington, D.C.

23. George Rosen, "Color TV as Western Democracies 'Secret Weapon' vs. Red Youth Rally," *Variety* 183:9 (August 8, 1951), 1:1.

24. Nielsen to Drummond, May 22, 1951, Berlin Television Show folder, ECA Records.

25. Lawrence to Taylor, May 4, 1951, Armed Forces Show, Box 277, Taylor Papers.

26. The letter notes that "Steelman approves all their copy anyway." As far as I can tell, this grew out of negotiations that Steelman conducted with railroad representatives when President Truman threatened to nationalize the railroads to avert a strike in 1950; Lawrence to Taylor, May 4, 1951, Armed Forces Show, Box 277, Taylor Papers; Taylor to McConnell, July 9, 1951, Armed Forces Show, Box 277, Taylor Papers.

27. Lawrence to NBC Network Sales Staff, August 29, 1951, Armed Forces Show, Box 277, Taylor Papers; Taylor to Ayers, July 10, 1951, Armed Forces Show, Box 277, Taylor Papers; Taylor to Fray, August 9, 1951, Armed Forces Show, Box 277, Taylor Papers; advertisement in *Broadcasting*, October 24, 1951, 28.

28. Steelman to McCall, October 8, 1951, Battle Report, Box 310, McCall Papers; McCall to Taylor, October 5, 1951, Armed Forces Show, Box 277, Taylor Papers.

29. *Battle Report – Washington* script, December 31, 1950, Charles Jackson papers; *Battle Report – Washington* script, June 15, 1951, Charles Jackson Papers.

30. *Battle Report – Washington* script, May 20, 1951, Charles Jackson Papers.

31. *Battle Report – Washington* script, January 13, 1951, Charles Jackson Papers; *Battle Report – Washington* script, July 20, 1951, Charles Jackson Papers.

32. Stanley to Truman (draft, mid-May 1951), Report to the Nation, 1951, Box 340, Brooks Papers.

33. Apart from informal ties to Advertising Council personnel, I do not know what *Battle Report* received in this cooperative relationship; McCall to Barnard, March 12, 1951, Battle Report, Box 310, McCall Papers.

34. *The Facts We Face* script, April 22, 1951, Facts We Face, Box 29, Jackson Papers.

35. Numbered Minutes, Public Relations Working Group, October 5, 1951, Russell Papers.

36. Brooks (draft) to Gabrielson, July 3, 1951, Armed Forces Show, Box 277, Taylor Papers.

37. Taylor to McConnell, March 7, 1952, Armed Forces Show, Box 277, Taylor Papers.

38. Steelman to McConnell, April 17, 1952, WHCF:OF 136B, Truman Papers.

Chapter Six: A More Vivid Picture of War

1. Oral history interview, Edward W. Barrett, p. 7, July 9, 1974, Harry S Truman Library.

2. NSC-23 and NSC-23/1, quoted in Edward P. Lilly, "The Development of American Psychological Operations, 1945–1951," U.S. DDRS 1991, 2302, 61–62.

3. James E. Swartz, "The Professionalization of Pentagon Public Affairs: The Evolution of a Role in United States Government, 1947–1967," unpublished Ph.D. dissertation, University of Iowa, 1985, 109–17.

4. This parallels changes in sponsorship patterns of entertainment programs at the networks in the mid-1950s. The networks first took production over from advertising agencies and then farmed it out to independent production companies. See Chapter 9 in William Boddy, *Fifties Television: The Industry and Its Critics* (Urbana: University of Illinois Press, 1990).

5. Swartz, "The Professionalization of Pentagon Public Affairs," Chapter 4.

6. Meeting of Executives of Information Media to Discuss Security Problems, March 3, 1948, Censorship, Defense Department Conference, 1948, Box 100, Miller Papers.

7. Taylor to McKelway, March 11, 1948, Censorship, Defense Department Conference, 1948, Box 100, Miller Papers.

8. Richards to Miller, November 8, 1948, Civil Defense, 1948–51, Box 100, Miller Papers; Office of the Secretary of Defense Press Release No. 39–48, March 29, 1948, U.S. Government, Box 284, Brooks Papers. See also, *NAB Reports* 182, March 8, 1948, NAB Library.

9. Frye to Pritchard et al., Consolidation Memorandum No. 3, April 22, 1949, OSD Records; Schooley to Ross, June 28, 1956, April 1–June 30, 1956 (1), Schooley Papers and Steven L. Reardon, *History of the Office of the Secretary of Defense: The Formative Years, 1947–50* (Washington, D.C.: Historical Office, Office of the Secretary of Defense, 1984), 497; Swartz, "The Professionalization of Pentagon Public Affairs," 130.

10. "TOTAL Radio and TV" memo, April 10, 1950, Dillon folder, OSD Records.

11. See monthly activity reports, Public Affairs Records 1949–1953, OSD Records. The naval maneuvers were reported on May 31, 1955; AFFE/PIO Radio-Television Handbook (May 1953), Radio and Television Miscellaneous Material, Box 6, Rosengren Papers.

12. Charles Dillon to the PMG, March 28, 1950, OPI Records; "Meeting With Radio-TV Liaison Officers," May 11, 1953, OSD Records.

13. Minutes of the Public Relations Advisory Council meeting, October 30, 1952, OSD Records; Meeting with Radio-Television Liaison Officers, February 10, 1953, Staff Meetings (5), Radio-TV Branch, OSD Records.

14. Dillon to Koop, July 9, 1951, Public Affairs Records 1949–1953, OSD Records.

15. Dillon to Brooks (and twenty-two others), April 24, 1950, 311.25, OPI Records; "Defense Official Says Cooperation Needed," unidentified newspaper clipping, April 19, 1951, OSD Records.

16. Swartz, "The Professionalization of Pentagon Public Affairs," 112–15; Memorandum, Kalisch to Yovin, undated, probably March 1952, OSD Records.

17. Advance Program for Joint Civilian Orientation Conference, April 8 to 16, 1951, and attached Typical Opinions Expressed by Former Members of Secretary of Defense Joint Orientation Conferences, Department of Defense 1945–51, Box 100, Miller Papers; NBC Meeting with Officers from U.S. Armed Forces Information School, February 18, 1949, U.S. Government, Box 286, Brooks Papers.

18. Pierpoint to Schooley, September 9, 1955, July 1–September 30, 1955 (2), Box 1, Schooley Papers; Roberts to Leva, September 7, 1950, 311.25, OPI Records.

19. Meeting of the Public Information Coordinating Committee, Minutes of Meetings, July 29, 1954–February 10, 1955, Box 2, DOD Series F, Seaton Papers.

20. Kirby to Trammel, July 24, 1950, Brooks to Kirby, August 1, 1950, U.S. Government, William F. Brooks records, Box 287, and Kirby to Juster, December 6, 1950, and Taylor to McCall, January 22, 1951, Armed Forces Show, Taylor Papers.

21. Seerley Reid and Anita Carpenter, "U.S. Government Films for Television, 5th ed." (produced by the Federal Security Agency's Office of Education), October 1952, National Association of Radio and Television Broadcasters, Box 8, Quick Papers; Sidney Lohman, "CBS to Offer Atom Bomb Documentary," *New York Times*, September 24, 1950, II, 11:4; Jack Gould, "Atomic Defense Described on TV," *New York Times*, February 14, 1951, 42:1; J. Fred MacDonald, *Television and the Red Menace* (New York: Praeger, 1985), 41; Tim Brooks and Earle Marsh, *The Complete Directory to Prime Time TV Shows, 1946–Present*, 3rd ed. (New York: Ballantine Books, 1985), 180.

22. "Televised Atomic Blast Scheduled for Tuesday," *New York Times*, April 19, 1952, 12:8.

23. *Broadcasting*, March 23, 1953, 14–15.

24. For instance, DuMont's *Visit with the Armed Forces*, which aired from 1950–51, or ABC's *On Guard*, which aired from 1952–54; Memo for record, April 25, 1955, OSD Records.

25. *New York Times*, October 13, 1949, 48:2; "Johnson Says Forces Accept Unification," *New York Times*, January 16, 1950, 3:5; "Defense Video: 'Armed Forces Hour' on NBC," *Broadcasting*, November 14, 1949, 63.

26. Memorandum for the Files by Osgood Roberts, February 27, 1950, Armed Forces Hour, OPI Records.

27. Roberts to Early, February 14, 1950, Dillon, OSD Records.

28. Memorandum for the Files by Osgood Roberts, February 27, 1950, Armed Forces Hour, OPI Records.

29. Dillon to McCall, April 26, 1950, Armed Forces Hour, OPI Records.

30. Roberts to Rosten, October 3, 1950, Armed Forces Hour, OPI Records; Rosten to Director of Public Information, September 28, 1950, Armed Forces Hour, OPI Records.

31. Alex MacNeil, *Total Television: A Complete Guide to Programming from 1948 to the Present*, 2nd ed. (New York: Penguin Books, 1984), 77; Raymond L. Carroll, "Factual Television in America: An Analysis of Network Television Documentary Programs, 1948–1975," unpublished Ph.D. dissertation, University of Wisconsin-Madison, 1978, 100, and "Government Issue: The Army's 'Big Picture' is almost as widely seen as the Army itself," *TV Guide*, March 16, 1957, 22–23; Radio-Television Handbook, AFFE/PIO, May 1953, Radio and Television Miscellaneous Materials, Box 6, Rosengren Papers.

32. Jack Gould, "Programs in Review," *New York Times*, January 13, 1952, II, 11:2; quoted in MacDonald, *Television and the Red Menace*, 117.

33. "Congressmen Hit any Film Curb," *New York Times*, January 9, 1954, 2:1; Jack Gould, "'Atrocities in Korea' Finally Shown," *New York Times*, February 8, 1954, 30:7.

34. "Time, Inc. Buys 'Crusade in Europe' Film Series for Video Showings," *New York Times*, April 7, 1949, 58:6. See numerous requests for interviews and footage, and see records of phone calls from Allen Dibble of the March of Time, Pictorial Branch Chronological File, May–December 1949, Box 661, ASD Records.

35. Fred Hif, "Television in Review," *New York Times*, May 8, 1949, II, 9:6. See the analysis of Eisenhower's use of television in Sig Mickelson, *From Whistle Stop to Sound Bite: Four Decades of Politics and Television* (New York, Praeger, 1989); Steve M. Barkin, "Eisenhower's Television Planning Board: An Unwritten Chapter in the History of Political Broadcasting," *Journal of Broadcasting* 27:4 (Fall 1983), 319–31, and Craig Allen, *Eisenhower and the Mass Media: Peace, Prosperity, and Prime-Time TV* (Chapel Hill: University of North Carolina Press, 1993); Jack Gould, "Television in Review," *New York Times*, May 15, 1949, II, 9:1; *New York Times*, May 5, 1950, 23:3.

36. Horton to Dibble, June 20, 1949, Pictorial Branch Chronological File, Box 661, ASD Records; Memo for Record #127, July 14, 1949, Pictorial Branch Chronological File, Box 661, ASD Records. See, for instance, Memo for Record #38, July 6, 1949, Pictorial Branch Chronological File, Box 661, ASD Records; "Pacific," *New York Times*, November 4, 1951, II, 11:1.

37. Memo for Record #14, August 2, 1949, Pictorial Branch Chronological File, Box 661, ASD Records; Yovin to Smith, June 23, 1949, record #177, Pictorial Branch Chronological File, Box 661, ASD Records.

38. Vance Kepley, Jr., "The Origins of NBC's Project XX in Compilation Documentaries," *Journalism Quarterly* 61 (Spring 1984), 20–26.

39. McCormick to Roberts, August 16, 1950 and Roberts to McCormick, August 30, 1950, Dillon folder, OSD Records.

40. Memorandum for NBC from Henry Salomon, Jr., July 31, 1950, OPI Records.

41. Robert W. Sarnoff, "Proposed Television History of the U.S. Navy in World War II," Victory at Sea, Box 277, Taylor Papers; *Broadcasting*, January 19, 1953, 54; A. William Bluem, *Documentary in American Television: Form, Function, Method* (New York: Hastings House, 1965), 146. Bluem named Salomon's accomplishment to have been moving beyond journalistic or chronological development to provide artistic and thematic unity. "The true theme of 'Victory at Sea' was an expression of a dominant emotional statement about men and nations at war. . . . More than 20 years after Pearl Harbor, Henry Salomon's noble vision of humanity is as inspiring as ever." A later generation found the same thematic unity to be self-righteous and moralistic, promoting anachronistic and naive concepts of American democracy and actions. In 1973, Peter Rollins decried the series' dedication to militarism and American superiority. Opposition to the war in Vietnam had transposed the American triumph in World War II. Peter C. Rollins, "'Vic-

tory at Sea': Cold War Epic," *Journal of Popular Culture* VI:3 (Spring 1973), 463–82.

42. Salomon to Sarnoff, April 9, 1951, Victory at Sea (U.S. Navy Project), Box 277, Taylor Papers.

43. Ibid.

44. Confidential Office Communication, Wolff to Mickelson and Gitlin, March 15, 1955, CBS Files 290, Murrow Papers.

45. "The Wild Blue Yonder," *Time*, November 12, 1956; Mickelson to Murrow, January 25, 1957, CBS Files 281, Murrow Papers; Confidential Office Communication, Wolff to Mickelson and Gitlin, March 15, 1955, CBS Files 290, Murrow Papers.

46. MacDonald, *Television and the Red Menace*, 118.

47. Mickelson to Murrow, January 25, 1957, CBS Files 281, Murrow Papers; Author's transcript, "Air Power: The New Doctrine," 1957, Library of Congress Motion Picture, Film and Television Division.

48. "The Times of Our Lives," *TV Guide*, November 30, 1957, 20; "As We See It," *TV Guide*, August 2, 1960, 3. See also Bob Stahl, "Hot Film," *TV Guide* March 28, 1959, 5–7; and *TV Guide*, March 1, 1958, 27.

49. Bluem, *Documentary in American Television*, 168.

50. Clayton R. Koppes and Gregory D. Black, *Hollywood Goes to War: How Politics, Profits, and Propaganda Shaped World War II Movies* (Berkeley: University of California Press, 1987); Memorandum for the Chief of Naval Operations, CCS 385 (6-4-46), Section 16, JCS Records; Memorandum for the Chairman, Joint Chiefs of Staff, July 5, 1956, CCS 385 (6-4-46), Section 24, JCS Records. My thanks to Chris Simpson for these documents.

51. Salomon to Sarnoff, December 14, 1951, and Sarnoff to Salomon, December 18, 1951, Victory at Sea, Box 277, Taylor Papers.

52. Schooley to Gammons, November 9, 1954, October 1–December 31, 1954 (2), Box 1, Schooley Papers; Schooley to The Chief of Information, Department of the Army, June 24, 1955, April 1–June 30, 1955 (1), Box 1, Schooley Papers; Knight to Director, Office of Public Information, Department of Defense, October 1–December 31, 1954 (2), Box 1, Schooley Papers.

53. "Description of 'On Guard' Units . . . " (undated), Document M-3280, Part XVIII, Cold War Military Recruiting Films; David Culbert, ed., *Film and Propaganda in America: A Documentary History* (New York: Greenwood Press, 1990), Vol. 5 [microfiche supplement]; Alex McNeil, *Total Television: A Complete Guide to Programming from 1948 to the Present*, 2nd ed. (New York: Penguin, 1984), 480.

54. "High Adventure on the High Seas," *TV Guide*, November 26, 1955, 8; J. P. Shanley, "TV: M/Sgt. Phil Silvers," *New York Times*, September 21, 1955; "Navy Log," *TV Guide*, October 29, 1955, 21.

55. "High Adventure on the High Seas," *TV Guide*, November 26, 1955, 8–9.

56. MacDonald, *Television and the Red Menace*, 119.

57. "Duty, Honor, Country," *TV Guide*, December 8, 1956, 4–6; McNeil, *Total Television*, 706.

58. MacDonald, *Television and the Red Menace*, 118; "The Cartoon That Came to Life," *TV Guide*, January 3, 1959, 20–22.

59. "Opening the Door On Some Secrets," *TV Guide*, December 27, 1958, 23.

60. "As an Astronaut, He's Way Out," *TV Guide*, August 2, 1960, 11; Murray Schumach, "Going Far Out on Television," *New York Times*, November 15, 1959, II, 12:1.

Chapter Seven: The Most Vigorous Anticommunist Campaign

1. For example, Daniel C. Hallin, *The "Uncensored War": The Media and Vietnam* (New York: Oxford, 1986), 121. Television news is widely reckoned to have come of age in 1963 for a combination of three reasons: an often-cited Roper poll that revealed for the first time more people said they got their news from television than from any other source; NBC and CBS's expansion of the nightly news broadcasts to thirty minutes from fifteen; and the well-praised round-the-clock coverage of the Kennedy assassination and funeral; Daniel C. Hallin, "The American News Media: A Critical Theory Perspective," in John Forester, ed., *Critical Theory and Public Life* (Cambridge: MIT Press, 1985), 121, reprinted in Hallin, *We Keep America on Top of the World: Television and the Public Sphere* (London: Routledge, 1994), 25.

2. Richard H. Rovere, *Senator Joe McCarthy* (New York: Harper and Row, 1959), 168.

3. Douglass Cater, *The Fourth Branch of Government* (Boston: Houghton Mifflin, 1959), 106, 69; the *Times* quote is from January 14, 1954, cited in David Caute, *The Great Fear* (New York: Simon and Schuster, 1978), 449.

4. James Aronson, *The Press and the Cold War* (Indianapolis: Bobbs-Merrill, 1970), 24; Michael Schudson, *Discovering the News: A Social History of American Newspapers* (New York: Basic Books, 1978), 169.

5. Edwin R. Bayley, *Joe McCarthy and the Press* (New York: Pantheon, 1981), 215.

6. The Hearst press included New York's *Journal-American* and *Daily Mirror*, the *Los Angeles Examiner*, and the *San Francisco Examiner*. The Patterson-McCormick papers included the *New York Daily News*, the *Chicago Tribune*, and the *Washington Times-Herald*.

7. McCarthy's targets at the state department shared Bayley's view of news diversity. A memo forecasting reactions to an upcoming McCarthy speech distinguishes between the hostile, "impartial," and friendly press, with only the word "impartial" in quotation marks. This suggests that public affairs officials shared Rovere and Cater's view that prestigious papers' minimal objectivity served McCarthy. Unsigned, undated (probably 1951), Department of State memo entitled "McCarthy." Folder W, Alphabetical Correspondence Files Box 3, Barrett Papers.

8. *America at Mid-Century*, January 13, 1951, Box 310, McCall Papers.

9. *America at Mid-Century*, January 20, 1951, Box 310, McCall Papers.

10. Jack Gould, "Mr. Paley Speaks: CBS Chairman Decries TV Timidity and Urges Medium to Earn Prestige," *New York Times*, May 30, 1954.

11. Bruce H. Westley and Malcolm S. MacLean, Jr., "An Objectivity Study of Three CBS News Broadcasters," November 28, 1955, Policy: 1955 Objectiv-

ity Study, Box 1, Mickelson Papers. Mickelson next wanted to follow up to see if the few trespasses erred consistently one way or another, and how this reflected on the network's capacity for balance. Mickelson to Stanton, December 6, 1955, Policy: 1955 Objectivity Study, Box 1, Mickelson Papers.

12. Nielsen Ratings, Boxes 22–24, State Historical Society of Wisconsin Archive.

13. Thomas B. Morgan, "The Program That Likes It Hot (Part One)," *TV Guide*, July 1, 1961, 19.

14. *Meet the Press*, December 23, 1951, author's transcript.

15. Erik Barnouw, *The Sponsor: Notes on a Modern Potentate* (New York: Oxford University Press, 1978), 130; Ray Scherer, "The News in Washington," in Ray Eldon Hiebert, ed., *The Press in Washington* (New York: Dodd Mead and Co., 1966), 98; Morgan, "Part One," 18.

16. See Chapter Eight in Nancy E. Bernhard, "Ready, Willing, Able: Network Television News and the Federal Government, 1948–1960," unpublished Ph.D. dissertation, University of Pennsylvania, 1991; and William C. Adams and Paul H. Ferber, "Television Interview Shows: The Politics of Visibility," *Journal of Broadcasting* 21:2 (Spring 1977), 141–49; Irving R. Levine, "'Thirty Minutes on That Show Can Age You 10 Years,'" *TV Guide*, February 17, 1973, 7; Morgan, "Part One," 18.

17. Edward Barrett to The Secretary (Acheson), July 9, 1951, The Secretary, 1951, Box 6, Barrett Papers; on staying away from controversy, see minutes of the Public Relations Working Group, February 1, 1951, Russell Papers.

18. Oral history interview, Lawrence Spivak, 1976, Louis G. Cowan Broadcasting Collection, William E. Wiener Oral History Library, New York Public Library.

19. William C. Adams and Paul H. Ferber, "Television Interview Shows: The Politics of Visibility," *Journal of Broadcasting* 21:2 (Spring 1977), 141; I. F. Stone, "Me and Marxism: Invitation – to a Dog-Fight," *New York Daily Compass*, November 14, 1949, 5, cited in Robert C. Cottrell, *Izzy: A Biography of I. F. Stone* (New Brunswick: Rutgers University Press, 1992), 156–59.

20. Tom Wicker reported Kennedy's quip during an informal talk at the Joan Shorenstein Barone Center for Press and Politics, John F. Kennedy School of Government, Harvard University, March 22, 1993; Childs quoted in Morgan, "Part One," 18.

21. Arthur Krock, "A TV Dream That Will Never Come True," *New York Times*, February 26, 1957, 28:5; Mindy Nix, "The meet the press game," in Gaye Tuchman, ed., *The TV Establishment* (Englewood Cliffs: Prentice Hall, 1974), 71.

22. Alvin Gouldner, "The Sociologist as Partisan," *American Sociologist 3* (1968), 114. See also Peter Novick, *That Noble Dream: The "Objectivity Question" and the American Historical Profession* (Cambridge: Cambridge University Press, 1988), 303.

23. Spivak oral history.

24. See Chapter 13, "Relativist Democratic Theory and Postwar America" in Edward A. Purcell, Jr., *The Crisis of Democratic Theory: Scientific Naturalism and the Problem of Value* (Lexington: University of Kentucky Press, 1973).

25. Michael Parenti, *Inventing Reality: The Politics of the Mass Media* (New York: St. Martin's, 1986), 122; Caute, *The Great Fear*, 447 and 449.

26. March 19, 1950; July 2, 1950; June 3, 1951; January 25, 1953; July 19, 1953; December 13, 1953; October 3, 1954.

27. Aronson, *The Press and the Cold War*, 75–76.

28. Robert Griffith, *The Politics of Fear: Joseph R. McCarthy and the Senate*, 2nd ed. (Amherst: University of Massachusetts Press, 1987), 100.

29. See particularly Thomas G. Paterson, *Meeting the Communist Threat* (New York: Oxford University Press, 1988), 4–15; and Thomas Hill Schaub, *American Fiction in the Cold War* (Madison: Univeristy of Wisconsin Press, 1991), 4–22. Peter Novick documents this trend among historians in *That Noble Dream: The "Objectivity Question" and the American Historical Profession* (Cambridge: Cambridge University Press, 1988), 303; Paterson, *Meeting the Communist Threat*, 6; Hannah Arendt, *Totalitarianism* (Part Three of *The Origins of Totalitarianism*) (New York: Harcourt Brace Jovanovich, 1968 [1951]), 156 and passim. See also Richard Pells, *The Liberal Mind in a Conservative Age: American Intellectuals in the 1940s and 1950s* (New York: Harper and Row, 1985), 93–94; Novick, *That Noble Dream*, 282.

30. Edward S. Herman and Noam Chomsky, *Manufacturing Consent: The Political Economy of the Mass Media* (New York, Pantheon, 1988), 30.

31. Paterson, *Meeting the Communist Threat*, 15.

32. Schaub, *American Fiction in the Cold War*, 5 and 7; quoted in Novick, *That Noble Dream*, 346.

33. Paley, "The Road to Responsibility," speech to the National Association of Radio and Television Broadcasters, May 25, 1954, CBS News Policy, 1954, Box 1, Mickelson Papers.

34. Paley, "The Road to Responsibility." This quote is lifted verbatim, except for the corporate "we" vs. the chairman's "I," from a written answer to *Newsweek* magazine's question to the network, "What should be the ground rules for fairness?" in the wake of the Murrow-McCarthy broadcast two months earlier. Paley to *Newsweek*, March 17, 1954, CBS News Policy, 1955–58, Box 1, Mickelson Papers.

35. Rovere, *Senator Joseph McCarthy*, 166.

36. Aronson, *The Press and the Cold War*, 73.

37. Michael Curtin, "The Discourse of 'Scientific Anticommunism' in the 'Golden Age' of Television Documentary," *Cinema Journal* 32:1 (Fall 1992), 3–25; and *Redeeming the Wasteland: Television Documentary and Cold War Politics* (New Brunswick: Rutgers University Press, 1995).

38. Such calls have been coming for more than a decade. See Robert A. Hackett, "Decline of a Paradigm? Bias and Objectivity in News Media Studies," *Critical Studies in Mass Communication* 1:3 (September 1984), 229–59.

Conclusion: Selling America

1. Quoted in Bernstein, "The CIA and the Media," *Rolling Stone* October 20, 1977, 57.

2. Sanford J. Ungar, "The Case of the Inconvenient Correspondent," *Columbia Journalism Review* (November/December 1990), 58.

3. Kati Marton, *The Polk Conspiracy: Murder and Cover-up in the Case of CBS News Correspondent George Polk* (New York: Farrar, Straus, Giroux, 1990), 162.

4. Marton, *The Polk Conspiracy*, 164.

5. Lindley quoted in Bernstein, "The CIA and the Media," 63; Interim Report of the Committee to Inquire into the Murder of George Polk, Committee to Investigate the Polk Murder, 1948–53, Box 101, Miller Papers; *The George Polk Case* (Report of the Overseas Writers of the Special Committee to Inquire into the Murder at Salonika, Greece, May 16, 1948, of Columbia Broadcasting System Correspondent George Polk), May 21, 1951, 1.

6. Marton, *The Polk Conspiracy*, 203.

7. Ibid.

8. Marton, *The Polk Conspiracy*, 194.

9. Ibid.

10. Edmund Keeley, *The Salonika Bay Murder: Cold War Politics and the Polk Affair* (Princeton: Princeton University Press, 1989), 360.

11. Marton, *The Polk Conspiracy*, 251.

12. *The George Polk Case*, 9, 11. CBS Report Number Four on the Murder of George Polk, April 27, 1949, reprinted in *The George Polk Case*, 58.

13. Morgan to Lippmann, March 17, (1949), Committee to Investigate the Polk Murder, 1948–53, Box 101, Miller Papers; Keeley, *The Salonika Bay Murder*, 81.

14. Quoted in Keeley, *The Salonika Bay Murder*, 325 and 328.

15. Daniel Schorr, *Clearing the Air* (New York: Berkeley Books, 1978), 277.

16. Bernstein, "The CIA and the Media," 66; House Permanent Select Committee on Intelligence, Subcommittee on Oversight, "The CIA and the Media" (Washington, D.C.: Government Printing Office, 1979), 315; Daniel Schorr, "The CIA Cloud over the Press," *New York Times*, July 20, 1976, 31:2; Stuart H. Loory, "The CIA's use of the press: a 'mighty Wurlitzer,'" *Columbia Journalism Review* (September/October 1974), 12.

17. House Permanent Select Committee, "CIA and the Media," 335; A. M. Sperber, *Murrow: His Life and Times* (New York: Freundlich, 1986). 635; Hugh Morrow, former *Saturday Evening Post* correspondent, quoted in Bernstein, "The CIA and the Media," 58.

18. House Permanent Select Committee, "The CIA and the Media," 320–21.

19. The three journalist-agents were Sam Jaffee of CBS and ABC, and Frank Kearns and Austin Goodrich of CBS. A number of *New York Times* articles at the time of the Congressional investigations into the intelligence services brought these to public attention. See John M. Crewdson, "Pose as Journalists Laid to 11 in CIA," *New York Times*, January 23, 1976, 1:3–8:3; John M. Crewdson, "TV Newsman Spied on Russians at U.N.," *New York Times*, January 22, 1976, 1:3–36:3; John M. Crewdson, "Senators Won't Seek Newsmen's Names at C.I.A.," *New York Times*, February 18, 1976, 24:4; John M. Crewdson, "An Ex-CBS Writer is Linked to C.I.A.," *New York Times*, February 11, 1976, 24:1; Daniel Schorr, "The CIA Cloud over the Press," *New York Times*, July 20, 1976, 31:2; William Safire, "Bill Paley's Big Secret," *New York Times*, March 1, 1976, 23:2; "CIA Data Asked by

Times and CBS," *New York Times*, February 10, 1976; "Times Request Rejected By CIA," *New York Times*, February 13, 1976, 9:1; "Times and CBS Deny Backing CIA Refusal to Name Reporters," *New York Times*, February 11, 1976, 24:2; Nicholas M. Horrock, "C.I.A. to Stop Enlisting Agents from the Press and the Church," *New York Times*, February 12, 1976, 1:8; "C.I.A. Statement," *New York Times*, February 12, 1976, 13:8; David E. Rosenbaum, "C.I.A. Will Keep More Than 25 Journalist-Agents," *New York Times*, April 27, 1976, 26:4; Taylor Branch, "The Trial of the CIA," *New York Times*, September 12, 1976, VI:35ff.; Schorr, *Clearing the Air*, 203–6 and 275–81; Lewis J. Paper, *Empire: William S. Paley and the Making of CBS* (New York: St. Martin's Press, 1978); on debriefing, see Bernstein, "The CIA and the Media," 59.

20. "The Kangaroo Court," *Time*, July 16, 1951, 54; "Bob Barclay's Beat," *Newsweek*, August 6, 1951, 47.

21. Bernstein, "The CIA and the Media," 59, 64; Paley quoted in Schorr, *Clearing the Air*, 278; Paper, *Empire*, 304.

22. Paper, *Empire*, 304; and Schorr, *Clearing the Air*, 278–79; Bernstein, "The CIA and the Media," 62.

23. Sperber, *Murrow*, 635; quoted in Leonard Mosley, *Dulles: A Biography of Eleanor, Allen and John Foster Dulles and Their Family Network* (New York: Dial Press, 1978), 457.

24. Jeffrey B. Abramson, F. Christopher Arterton, and Gary R. Orren, *The Electronic Commonwealth: The Impact of New Media Technologies on Democratic Politics* (New York: Basic Books, 1988), passim.

BIBLIOGRAPHY

Books and Monographs

Abramson, Jeffrey B., F. Christopher Arterton, and Gary R. Orren. *The Electronic Commonwealth: The Impact of New Media Technologies on Democratic Politics.* New York: Basic Books, 1988.

Acheson, Dean. *Present at the Creation: My Years in the State Department.* New York: Norton, 1969.

Arendt, Hannah. *The Origins of Totalitarianism.* New York: Harcourt Brace Jovanovich, 1951.

Aronson, James. *The Press and the Cold War.* Indianapolis: Bobbs-Merrill, 1970.

Barnouw, Erik. *The Sponsor: Notes on a Modern Potentate.* New York: Oxford University Press, 1978.

Tube of Plenty: The Evolution of American Television, rev. ed. New York: Oxford University Press, 1982.

Baughman, James L. *Television's Guardians: The FCC and the Politics of Programming, 1958–1967.* Knoxville: The University of Tennessee Press, 1985.

Bayley, Edwin R. *Joe McCarthy and the Press.* New York: Pantheon, 1981.

Blanchard, Margaret. *Exporting the First Amendment: The Press-Government Crusade of 1945–1952.* New York: Longman, 1985.

Blondheim, Menahem. *News Over the Wires: The Telegraph and the Flow of Public Information in America, 1844–1892.* Cambridge: Harvard University Press, 1994.

Bluem, A. William. *Documentary in American Television: Form, Function, Method.* New York: Hastings House, 1965.

Boddy, William. *Fifties Television: The Industry and Its Critics.* Urbana: University of Illinois Press, 1990.

Brands, H. W., Jr. *Cold Warriors: Eisenhower's Generation and American Foreign Policy.* New York: Columbia University Press, 1988.

Brooks, Tim, and Earle Marsh. *The Complete Directory to Prime Time TV Shows, 1946–Present,* 3rd ed. New York: Ballantine Books, 1985.

Campbell, Richard. *60 Minutes and the News: A Mythology for Middle America.* Urbana: University of Illinois Press, 1991.

Cater, Douglass. *The Fourth Branch of Government.* Boston: Houghton Mifflin, 1959.

Caute, David. *The Great Fear: The Anti-communist Purge Under Truman and Eisenhower.* New York: Simon and Schuster, 1978.

Cogley, John. *Report on Blacklisting II: Radio and Television.* New York: The Fund for the Republic, Inc., 1956.

Cohen, Bernard C. *The Public's Impact on Foreign Policy.* Boston: Little Brown and Company, 1973.

Cook, Blanche Wiesen. *The Declassified Eisenhower: A Startling Reappraisal of the Eisenhower Presidency.* New York: Penguin, 1984.

Coontz, Stephanie. *The Way We Never Were: American Families and the Nostalgia Trap.* New York: Basic Books, 1992.

Cottrell, Robert C. *Izzy: A Biography of I. F. Stone.* New Brunswick: Rutgers University Press, 1992.

Curtin, Michael. *Redeeming the Wasteland: Television Documentary and Cold War Politics.* New Brunswick, NJ: Rutgers University Press, 1995.

Davis, Elmer, and Byron Price. *War Information and Censorship.* Washington, D.C.: American Council on Public Affairs, 1943.

Deibel, Terry L., and John Lewis Gaddis, eds. *Containment: Concept and Policy,* Vol. 1. Washington, D.C.: National Defense University Press, 1986.

Foley, Karen Sue. *The Political Blacklist in the Broadcasting Industry: The Decade of the 1950s.* New York: Arno Press, 1979.

Fones-Wolf, Elizabeth. *Selling Free Enterprise: The Business Assault on Labor and Liberalism, 1945–60.* Urbana: University of Illinois Press, 1995.

Forester, John, ed. *Critical Theory and Public Life.* Cambridge: MIT Press, 1985.

Fox, Frank W. *Madison Avenue Goes to War: The Strange Career of American Advertising, 1941–45.* Provo: Brigham Young University Charles E. Merrill Monograph Series in the Humanities and Social Sciences 4:1, June 1985.

Fraser, Steve, and Gary Gerstle, eds. *The Rise and Fall of the New Deal Order, 1930–1980.* Princeton: Princeton University Press, 1989.

Gaddis, John Lewis. *The United States and the End of the Cold War: Implications, Reconsiderations, Provocations.* New York: Oxford University Press, 1992.

Gary, Brett. *Nervous Liberals: Scholars, Lawyers, and the War on Propaganda, 1919–1948.* New York: Columbia University Press, 1999.

Gates, Gary Paul. *Air Time: The Inside Story of CBS News.* New York: Harper and Row, 1978.

Geelhoed, E. Bruce. *Charles E. Wilson and Controversy at the Pentagon, 1953 to 1957.* Detroit: Wayne State Press, 1979.

Griffith, Robert. *The Politics of Fear: Joseph R. McCarthy and the Senate,* 2nd ed. Amherst: University of Massachusetts Press, 1987.

Hallin, Daniel. *The "Uncensored War": The Media and Vietnam.* New York: Oxford University Press, 1986.

We Keep America on Top of the World: Television Journalism and the Public Sphere. London: Routledge, 1994.

Henderson, John W. *The United States Information Agency.* New York: Praeger, 1969.

Herman, Edward S., and Noam Chomsky. *Manufacturing Consent: The Political Economy of the Mass Media.* New York, Pantheon, 1988.

Hiebert, Ray Eldon, ed. *The Press in Washington.* New York: Dodd Mead and Co., 1966.

Hiebert, Ray Eldon, and Carlton E. Spitzer, eds. *The Voice of Government.* New York: John E. Wiley and Sons, 1968.

Hixson, Walter. *Parting the Curtain: Propaganda, Culture, and the Cold War, 1945–1961.* New York: St. Martin's Press, 1997.

Hyman, Sydney. *The Lives of William Benton.* Chicago: University of Chicago Press, 1969.

Johnson, Loch K. *America's Secret Power: The CIA in a Democratic Society.* New York: Oxford University Press, 1989.

Kaufman, Burton I. *The Korean War: Challenges in Crisis, Credibility, and Command.* New York: Knopf, 1986.

Keeley, Edmund. *The Salonika Bay Murder: Cold War Politics and the Polk Affair.* Princeton: Princeton University Press, 1989.

Kennan, George. "The Sources of Soviet Conduct," reprinted in *American Diplomacy.* Chicago: University of Chicago Press, 1984.

Kirby, Edward M., and Jack W. Harris. *Star-Spangled Radio.* Chicago: Ziff-Davis, 1948.

Koppes, Clayton R., and Gregory D. Black. *Hollywood Goes to War: How Politics, Profits, and Propaganda Shaped World War II Movies.* Berkeley: University of California Press, 1987.

Larson, Deborah Welch. *Origins of Containment: A Psychological Explanation.* Princeton: Princeton University Press, 1985.

Lears, Jackson. *Fables of Abundance: A Cultural History of Advertising in America.* New York: Basic Books, 1994.

Lerner, Daniel, ed. *Propaganda in War and Crisis.* New York: George W. Stewart, 1951.

Long, Stewart Lewis. *The Development of the Network Television Oligopoly.* New York: Arno Press, 1979.

MacDonald, J. Fred. *Television and the Red Menace.* New York: Praeger, 1985.

MacNeil, Alex. *Total Television: A Complete Guide to Programming from 1948 to the Present,* 2nd ed. New York: Penguin Books, 1984.

Marchetti, Victor, and John D. Marks. *The CIA and the Cult of Intelligence.* New York: Alfred A. Knopf, 1974.

Markel, Lester, ed. *Public Opinion and Foreign Policy.* New York: Harper and Row for the Council on Foreign Relations, 1949.

Marton, Kati. *The Polk Conspiracy: Murder and Cover-up in the Case of CBS News Correspondent George Polk.* New York: Farrar, Straus, Giroux, 1990.

May, Lary, ed. *Recasting America: Culture and Politics in the Age of Cold War.* Chicago: University of Chicago Press, 1989.

McChesney, Robert W. *Telecommunications, Mass Media, and Democracy: The Battle for the Control of U.S. Broadcasting, 1928–1935.* New York: Oxford University Press, 1993.

McQuaid, Kim. *Big Business and Presidential Power: From FDR to Reagan.* New York: William Morrow, 1982.

Uneasy Partners: Big Business in American Politics, 1945–1990. Baltimore: Johns Hopkins University Press, 1994.

Metz, Robert. *CBS: Reflections in a Bloodshot Eye.* Chicago: Playboy Press Books, 1975.

Mickelson, Sig. *America's Other Voice: The Story of Radio Free Europe and Radio Liberty.* New York: Praeger, 1983.
From Whistle Stop to Sound Bite: Four Decades of Politics and Television. New York: Praeger, 1989.

Mosley, Leonard. *Dulles: A Biography of Eleanor, Allen and John Foster Dulles and Their Family Network.* New York: Dial Press, 1978.

Mott, Frank Luther. *American Journalism: A History, 1690–1960,* 3rd ed. New York: Macmillan, 1962.

Novick, Peter. *That Noble Dream: The "Objectivity Question" and the American Historical Profession.* Cambridge: Cambridge University Press, 1988.

O'Connor, John, ed. *American History/American Television.* New York: Ungar Books, 1983.

Paper, Lewis J. *Empire: William S. Paley and the Making of CBS.* New York: St. Martin's Press, 1978.

Parenti, Michael. *Inventing Reality: The Politics of the Mass Media.* New York: St. Martin's, 1986.

Paterson, Thomas G. *Meeting the Communist Threat.* New York: Oxford University Press, 1988.

Pells, Richard. *The Liberal Mind in a Conservative Age: American Intellectuals in the 1940s and 1950s.* New York: Harper and Row, 1985.

Persico, Joseph. *Edward R. Murrow: An American Original.* New York: McGraw-Hill, 1988.

Pirsein, Robert William. *The Voice of America: A History of the International Broadcasting Activities of the United States Government, 1940–1962.* New York: Arno Press, 1979.

Purcell, Edward A., Jr. *The Crisis of Democratic Theory: Scientific Naturalism and the Problem of Value.* Lexington: University of Kentucky Press, 1973.

Ritchie, Michael. *Please Stand By: A Prehistory of Television.* Woodstock, NY: Overlook Press, 1994.

Rovere, Richard. *Senator Joe McCarthy.* New York: Harper and Row, 1959.

Sanders, Jerry. *Peddlers of Crisis: The Committee on the Present Danger and the Politics of Containment.* Boston: South End Press, 1983.

Schaub, Thomas Hill. *American Fiction in the Cold War.* Madison: University of Wisconsin Press, 1991.

Schiller, Dan. *Objectivity and the News: The Public and the Rise of Commercial Journalism.* Philadelphia: University of Pennsylvania Press, 1981.

Schlesinger, Arthur M., Jr. *The Cycles of American History.* Boston: Houghton Mifflin, 1986.

Schorr, Daniel. *Clearing the Air.* New York: Berkeley Books, 1978.

Schudson, Michael. *Discovering the News: A Social History of American Newspapers.* New York: Basic Books, 1978.

Simpson, Christopher. *Blowback: The First Account of America's Recruitment of Nazis, and Its Disastrous Effect on Our Foreign and Domestic Policy.* New York: Macmillan, 1988.

Science of Coercion: Communication Research and Psychological Warfare, 1945–60. New York: Oxford University Press, 1994.

Slater, Robert. *This . . . Is CBS: A Chronicle of 60 Years.* Englewood Cliffs, N.J.: Prentice-Hall, 1988.

Smith, Sally Bedell. *In All His Glory: The Life of William S. Paley, the Legendary Tycoon and His Brilliant Circle.* New York: Simon and Schuster, 1990.

Smulyan, Susan. *Selling Radio: The Commercialization of American Broadcasting, 1920–1934.* Washington, D.C.: Smithsonian Institution Press, 1994.

Sperber, A. M. *Murrow: His Life and Times.* New York: Freundlich Books, 1986.

Spigel, Lynn. *Make Room for TV: Television and the Family Ideal in Postwar America.* Chicago: University of Chicago Press, 1992.

Steel, Ronald. *Walter Lippmann and the American Century.* New York: Vintage, 1980.

Steinberg, Cobbett. *TV Facts.* New York: Facts on File, 1985.

Suid, Lawrence H. ed., and David Culbert, editor-in-chief. *Film and Propaganda in America: A Documentary History, Volume 4, 1945 and After,* and Volume 5, microform supplement. New York: Greenwood Press, 1990.

Talese, Gay. *The Kingdom and the Power.* Garden City: Doubleday, 1978.

Thompson, Loren B., ed. *Defense Beat: The Dilemmas of Defense Coverage.* New York: Macmillan, 1991.

Tuchman, Gaye, ed. *The TV Establishment.* Englewood Cliffs: Prentice Hall, 1974.

Voss, Frederick S. *Reporting the War: The Journalistic Coverage of World War II.* Washington, D.C.: Smithsonian Institution Press, 1994.

Whitfield, Stephen J. *The Culture of the Cold War.* Baltimore: Johns Hopkins University Press, 1991.

Winkler, Allen M. *The Politics of Propaganda: The Office of War Information, 1942–45.* New Haven: Yale University Press, 1978.

Wolfe, Alan. *The Rise and Fall of the Soviet Threat: Domestic Sources of the Cold War Consensus.* Boston: South End Press, 1984.

Yergin, Daniel. *Shattered Peace: The Origins of the Cold War and the National Security State.* Boston: Houghton Mifflin, 1978.

Articles

Adams, William C., and Paul H. Ferber. "Television Interview Shows: The Politics of Visibility," *Journal of Broadcasting* 21:2 (Spring 1977), 141–49.

Barkin, Steven M. "Eisenhower's Television Planning Board: An Unwritten Chapter in the History of Political Broadcasting," *Journal of Broadcasting* 27:4 (Fall 1983), 319–31.

Baughman, James L. "The Promise of American Television," *Prospects* 11 (1986), Vol. 2, 119–134.

Bernstein, Carl. "The CIA and the Media," *Rolling Stone* (October 20, 1977), 55–67.

Beville, Hugh M., Jr. "The Challenge of the New Media: Television, FM and Facsimile," *Journalism Quarterly* 25:1 (March 1948), 3–11.

Cassirer, Henry R. "Television News: A Challenge to Imaginative Journalists," *Journalism Quarterly* 26:3 (September 1949), 277–80.

Cook, Blanche Wiesen. "First Comes the Lie: C. D. Jackson and Political Warfare," *Radical History Review* 31 (1984), 42–70.

Curtin, Michael. "The Discourse of 'Scientific Anticommunism' in the 'Golden Age' of Television Documentary," *Cinema Journal* 32:1 (Fall 1992), 3–25.

The George Polk Case [Report of the Overseas Writers of the Special Committee to Inquire into the Murder at Salonika, Greece, May 16, 1948, of Columbia Broadcasting System Correspondent George Polk], May 21, 1951, privately published report.

Gouldner, Alvin. "The Sociologist as Partisan," *American Sociologist 3* (1968), 105–20.

Griffith, Robert. "The Selling of America: The Advertising Council and American Politics, 1942–1960," *Business History Review* (Autumn 1983), 388–412.

Hackett, Robert A. "Decline of a Paradigm? Bias and Objectivity in News Media Studies," *Critical Studies in Mass Communication* 1:3 (September 1984), 229–59.

Kepley, Vance, Jr. "The Origins of NBC's Project XX in Compilation Documentaries," *Journalism Quarterly* 61 (Spring 1984), 20–26.

Lears, Jackson. "The Concept of Cultural Hegemony: Problems and Possibilities," *American Historical Review* 90:3 (June 1985), 567–93.

"Making Fun of Popular Culture," *American Historical Review* 97:2 (December 1992), 1417–26.

Levine, Lawrence. "The Folklore of Industrial Society: Popular Culture and Its Audiences," *American Historical Review* 97:2 (December 1992), 1369–99.

Loory, Stuart H. "The CIA's use of the press: a 'mighty Wurlitzer,'" *Columbia Journalism Review* (September/October 1974), 9–17.

Lucas, W. Scott. "Campaigns of Truth: The American Psychological Offensive Against the Soviet Union, 1947–54," forthcoming.

Mackey, David R. "The Development of the National Association of Broadcasters," *Journal of Broadcasting* 1 (Fall 1957).

McChesney, Robert W. "Off Limits: An Inquiry into the Lack of Debate over the Ownership, Structure, and Control of the Mass Media in U.S. Political Life," *Communication* (1992), Vol. 13, 1–19.

Pimlott, J. A. R. "Public Service Advertising: The Advertising Council," *Public Opinion Quarterly* 12:2 (Summer 1948), 209–19.

Repplier, Theodore S. "Advertising Dons Long Pants," *Public Opinion Quarterly* (Fall 1945), 269–78.

Rollins, Peter C. "'Victory at Sea': Cold War Epic," *Journal of Popular Culture* VI:3 (Spring 1973), 463–82.

Rosenthal, A. M. "TV Antics Can Kill the Press Conference," *International Press Institute Report* (October 1953), 4.

Schiller, Dan. "An Historical Approach to Objectivity and Professionalism in American News Reporting," *Journal of Communication* 29 (August 1979), 46–57.

Smith, Desmond. "TV news did not just happen – it had to invent itself." *Smithsonian* 20:3 (June 1989), 74–90.

Ungar, Sanford J. "The Case of the Inconvenient Correspondent," *Columbia Journalism Review* (November/December 1990), 58–59.

Varney, Harold Lord. "How TV Molds Your Mind," *The American Mercury* (April 1954), 51–58.

Vlanton, Elias. "A Murder and Its Meaning," *The Nation* (January 28, 1991), 95.

Wala, Michael. "Selling the Marshall Plan at Home: The Committee for the Marshall Plan to Aid European Recovery," *Diplomatic History* 10:3 (Summer 1986), 247–65.

Weinberg, Sydney. "The Writers' Quarrel in the Office of War Information," *Journal of American History* 55:1 (June 1968), 73–89.

Trade Journals, Magazines, Newspapers

Broadcasting and Telecasting
Editor and Publisher
The New Republic
Newsweek
The New York Times
Time
TV Guide
U.S. News and World Report
Variety
The Washington Post

Government Publications

Digest of General Bills with Index, 82nd Congress, 1st session (Washington, D.C.: Library of Congress Legislative Reference Section, 1951).

Foreign Relations of the United States, 1950, Vol. 1 (Washington, D.C.: Government Printing Office, 1966).

House Permanent Select Committee on Intelligence, Subcommittee on Oversight, "The CIA and the Media" (Washington, D.C.: Government Printing Office, 1979).

Public Papers of the Presidents: Harry S Truman, 1950 (Washington, D.C.: Government Printing Office, 1965).

Manuscript Collections

Assistant Secretary of Defense Records, News Division, National Archives, Washington, D.C.

Assistant Secretary of State for Public Affairs Records, 1945–50, National Archives, Washington, D.C.

Assistant Secretary of State for Public Affairs Records, 1945–1950, National Archives II, College Park, MD.

Assistant Secretary of State for Public Affairs Records, 1947–50, National Archives, Washington, D.C.

Edward W. Barrett Files, National Archives, Washington, D.C.

William F. Brooks Papers, National Broadcasting Company Records, State Historical Society of Wisconsin Archive, Madison, WI.

Central Decimal File, General Records of the Department of State, National Archives, Washington, D.C.

ECA Office of Information, Office of the Director, Records of U.S. Foreign Assistance Agencies, National Archives II, College Park, MD.

Dwight D. Eisenhower Records as President, Dwight D. Eisenhower Library, Abilene, KS.

Charles W. Jackson Papers, Harry S Truman Library, Independence, MO.

C. D. [Charles Douglas] Jackson Papers, Dwight D. Eisenhower Library, Abilene, KS.

Joint Chiefs of Staff Records, National Archives, Washington, D.C.

Francis C. McCall Papers, National Broadcasting Company Records, State Historical Society of Wisconsin Archive, Madison, WI.

Carl W. McCardle Papers, Dwight D. Eisenhower Library, Abilene, KS.

Sigfried Mickelson Papers, State Historical Society of Wisconsin Archive, Madison, WI.

Justin Miller Papers, National Association of Broadcasters Records, State Historical Society of Wisconsin Archive, Madison, WI.

Edward R. Murrow Papers, Fletcher School of Diplomacy, Tufts University, Medford, MA.

National Association of Broadcasters Library, Washington, D.C.

Office of Public Information Files, Department of Defense, 1950, National Archives, Washington, D.C.

Public Affairs Records, 1949–53, Office of the Secretary of Defense, Department of Defense, Arlington, VA.

Spencer R. Quick Papers, Harry S Truman Library, Independence, MO.

William E. Robinson Papers, Harry S Truman Library, Independence, MO.

Roswell P. Rosengren Papers, Harry S Truman Library, Independence, MO.

Francis H. Russell Papers, National Archives, Washington, D.C.

Howland H. Sargeant Papers, Harry S Truman Library, Independence, MO.

Herschel Schooley Papers, Dwight D. Eisenhower Library, Abilene, KS.

Fred A. Seaton Papers, Harry S Truman Library, Independence, MO.

Eric Sevareid Papers, Library of Congress, Washington, D.C.

Lawrence Spivak Papers, Library of Congress, Washington, D.C.

Davidson Taylor Papers, National Broadcasting Company Records, State Historical Society of Wisconsin Archive, Madison, WI.

Harry S Truman Papers as President, Harry S Truman Library, Independence, MO.

Abbott W. Washburn Papers, Dwight D. Eisenhower Library, Abilene, KS.

Dissertations

Blanchard, Margaret. "Americans First, Newspapermen Second?: The Conflict Between Patriotism and Freedom of the Press During the Cold War, 1946–1952," Ph.D. dissertation, University of North Carolina, 1981.

Carroll, Raymond L. "Factual Television in America: An Analysis of Network Television Documentary Programs, 1948–1975," Ph.D. dissertation, University of Wisconsin-Madison, 1978.

Chittick, William O. "The Domestic Information Activities of the Department of State," Ph.D. dissertation, The Johns Hopkins University, 1964.

Stewart, Robert Hammel. "The Development of Network Television Program Types to January 1953," Ph.D. dissertation, Ohio State University, 1954.

Swartz, James E. "The Professionalization of Pentagon Public Affairs: The Evolution of a Role in United States Government, 1947–1967," Ph.D. dissertation, University of Iowa, 1985.

Oral Histories

Edward W. Barrett, Harry S Truman Library.
William Benton, Columbia University.
Gordon Gray, Harry S Truman Library.
Noel Macy, Harry S Truman Library.
Leonard Reinsch, Harry S Truman Library.
Howland W. Sargeant, Dwight D. Eisenhower Library.
Lawrence Spivak, Louis G. Cowan Broadcasting Collection, William E. Wiener Oral History Library, New York Public Library.
George Tames, Harry S Truman Library.

Personal Interviews and Correspondence

Robert Saudek, 1989.
Dr. John Steelman, 1989.

Films and Kinescopes

Air Power. Library of Congress, Washington, D.C.
American Forum of the Air. Library of Congress, Washington, D.C.
Battle Report. National Archives, Washington, D.C.
The Big Issue. Library of Congress, Washington, D.C.
The Big Picture. UCLA Film and Television Archive, Los Angeles.
Camel News Caravan. Museum of Broadcasting, New York, and Museum of Broadcasting, Chicago.
CBS News with Douglas Edwards. Museum of Broadcasting, New York, and Museum of Broadcasting, Chicago.
Crusade in Europe. Library of Congress, Washington, D.C.

Crusade in the Pacific. UCLA Film and Television Archive, Los Angeles.

Diplomatic Pouch. National Archives, Washington, D.C.

Face the Nation. Museum of Broadcasting, Chicago, and Library of Congress, Washington, D.C.

Meet the Press. Library of Congress, Washington, D.C.

Navy Log. Library of Congress, Washington, D.C.

Newsweek Views the News. UCLA Film and Television Archive, Los Angeles.

Nightmare in Red. National Archives, Washington, D.C.

People's Platform. Museum of Broadcasting, New York.

See It Now. Library of Congress, Washington, D.C.; Museum of Broadcasting, New York City; UCLA Film and Television Archive, Los Angeles.

Today with Mrs. Roosevelt. Museum of Broadcasting, Chicago.

Twentieth Century. Library of Congress, Washington, D.C.

U.N. in Action. Museum of Broadcasting, Chicago.

Victory at Sea. UCLA Film and Television Archive, Los Angeles.

The Walter Winchell Show. Museum of Broadcasting, New York, and Museum of Broadcasting, Chicago.

West Point Story. Library of Congress, Washington, D.C.

Youth Wants to Know. Library of Congress, Washington, D.C.

INDEX

LaVergne, TN USA
30 December 2009

168474LV00004B/31/A